£81.75 - Jan 2000

HOUSEHOLDS, WORK AND ECONOMIC CHANGE:
A COMPARATIVE INSTITUTIONAL PERSPECTIVE

RECENT ECONOMIC THOUGHT SERIES

Editors:

Warren J. Samuels
Michigan State University
East Lansing, Michigan, USA

William Darity, Jr.
University of North Carolina
Chapel Hill, North Carolina, USA

Other books in the series:

Magnusson, Lars: MERCANTILIST ECONOMICS
Garston, Neil: BUREAUCRACY: THREE PARADIGMS
Friedman, James W.: PROBLEMS OF COORDINATION IN
  ECONOMIC ACTIVITY
Magnusson, Lars: EVOLUTIONARY AND NEO-SCHUMPETERIAN
  APPROACHES TO ECONOMICS
Reisman, D.: ECONOMIC THOUGHT AND POLITICAL THEORY
Burley, P. and Foster, J.: ECONOMICS AND THERMODYNAMICS:
  NEW PERSPECTIVES ON ECONOMIC ANALYSIS
Brennan, H.G. and Waterman, A.C.: ECONOMICS AND RELIGION:
  ARE THEY DISTINCT?
Klein, Philip A.: THE ROLE OF ECONOMIC THEORY
Semmler, Willi.: BUSINESS CYCLES: THEORY AND EMPIRICS
Little, Daniel: ON THE RELIABILITY OF ECONOMIC MODELS:
  ESSAYS IN THE PHILOSOPHY OF ECONOMICS
Weimer, David L.: INSTITUTIONAL DESIGN
Davis, John B.: THE STATE OF THE INTERPRETATION OF KEYNES
Wells, Paul: POST-KEYNESIAN ECONOMIC THEORY
Hoover, Kevin D.: MACROECONOMETRICS:
  DEVELOPMENTS, TENSIONS AND PROSPECTS
Kendrick, John W.: THE NEW SYSTEMS OF NATURAL ACCOUNTS
Groenewegen, John: TRANSACTION COST ECONOMICS AND BEYOND
King, J.E.: AN ALTERNATIVE MACROECONOMIC THEORY
Schofield, Norman: COLLECTIVE DECISION-MAKING: SOCIAL CHOICE
  AND POLITICAL ECONOMY
Menchik, Paul L.: HOUSEHOLD AND FAMILY ECONOMICS
Gupta, Kanhaya L.: EXPERIENCES WITH FINANCIAL LIBERALIZATION
Cohen, Avi J., Hagemann, Harald, and Smithin, John:
  MONEY FINANCIAL INSTITUTIONS AND MACROECONOMICS
Mason, P.L. and Williams, R.M.:
  RACE, MARKETS, AND SOCIAL OUTCOMES
Gupta, Satya Dev: THE POLITICAL ECONOMY OF GLOBALIZATION
Fisher, R.C.: INTERGOVERNMENTAL FISCAL RELATIONS

HOUSEHOLDS, WORK AND ECONOMIC CHANGE: A COMPARATIVE INSTITUTIONAL PERSPECTIVE

edited by

Jane Wheelock
University of Newcastle
upon Tyne, UK

Åge Mariussen
Nordland Research Institute
Bodø, NORWAY

Kluwer Academic Publishers
Boston/Dordrecht/London

Distributors for North America:
Kluwer Academic Publishers
101 Philip Drive
Assinippi Park
Norwell, Massachusetts 02061 USA

Distributors for all other countries:
Kluwer Academic Publishers Group
Distribution Centre
Post Office Box 322
3300 AH Dordrecht, THE NETHERLANDS

Library of Congress Cataloging-in-Publication Data
Households, work and economic change : a comparative institutional
　perspective / edited by Jane Wheelock, Åge Mariussen.
　　　p.　cm. -- (Recent economic thought series ; 57)
　Includes bibliographical references and index.
　ISBN 0-7923-9930-7 (alk. paper)
　1. Work and family--Great Britain--Congresses.　2. Work and
family--Norway--Congresses.　3. Households--Great Britain-
-Congresses.　4. Households--Norway--Congresses.　5. Great Britain-
-Economic conditions--1993- --Congresses.　6. Norway--Economic
conditions--1945- --Congresses.　I. Wheelock, Jane, 1944-　　．
II. Mariussen, Åge.　III. Series.
HD4904.25.H68　1997
306.3'6'0941--dc21　　　　　　　　　　　　　　　　　　　　　97-16300
　　　　　　　　　　　　　　　　　　　　　　　　　　　　　　　　CIP

Copyright © 1997 by Kluwer Academic Publishers

All rights reserved. No part of this publication may be reproduced, stored in a retrieval system or transmitted in any form or by any means, mechanical, photo-copying, recording, or otherwise, without the prior written permission of the publisher, Kluwer Academic Publishers, 101 Philip Drive, Assinippi Park, Norwell, Massachusetts 02061.

Printed on acid-free paper.

Printed in the United States of America

CONTENTS

List of contributors	xiii
FOREWORD	xv
Economic and social change	xv
Readers' guide	xviii
Acknowledgements	xxi
INTRODUCTION: Institutional transformation	1
Åge Mariussen and Jane Wheelock	
Household, work and gender in transformation	1
Games and habits	2
The institutional approach and embedding change	4
Households, work and economic change	8

PART I THE SIGNIFICANCE OF THE HOUSEHOLD IN ITS MACRO CONTEXT

Chapter 1 Perspectives on the household in a changing economy	13
Åge Mariussen and Jane Wheelock	
Overview	13
Economics and sociology: divorce and remarriage?	17
Approaches to deregulation and economic change: where is the household?	24
Recognising and locating the household: seeing the whole economy	27
Changing livelihoods and meanings: global and local	30
The remarriage: replacing the old order of the male breadwinner?	34
Chapter 2 Behind the lace curtains	37
Elizabeth Oughton, Jane Wheelock and Agnete Wiborg	
States, markets and households	37
Identifying the household	41
Household flourishing	44
Changing meanings and values	46
Working towards the future	49
Conclusions	52

Chapter 3 Social security, employment and the household 53
Michael Hill

Introduction: institutional stresses 53
Social insurance as a basis for income maintenance 55
Social assistance and means tests: equality with efficiency? 57
Institutional inconsistencies 58
Income maintenance systems in practice: who gains and who loses? 59
Households, gender divisions and the 'group' model 61
Conclusions 62

PART II ECONOMIC RESTRUCTURING, LABOUR MARKET CHANGE AND THE HOUSEHOLD 65
Åge Mariussen and Ian Stone

Chapter 4 British market-led restructuring: a case study of Wearside 71
Ian Stone

Introduction 71
Economic and policy context 72
    Wearside: background
    Local regeneration policies
Deindustrialisation and labour market shock 75
    Shipbuilding and marine engineering
    UK and overseas owned branch plants
    Indigenous firms
    Coalmining
    Services
Labour market adjustment to economic restructuring 79
    Numbers in employment
    Population change
    Economically active population
    Unemployment
Conclusions 83

Chapter 5 Corporatist restructuring: a Scandinavian case study 85
Åge Mariussen

Flashback: constructing corporatism 86
Corporatist restructuring 91
Structural changes 95

Corporatist and market-led restructuring compared 99
Åge Mariussen and Ian Stone

PART III CHANGING LIVES AND LIVELIHOODS

SECTION A: Household responses to industrial change and unemployment — 103
Jane Wheelock

Chapter 6 The family and the social division of labour during industrial restructuring — 107
Allan Sande

Local historical and cultural contexts	108
The effects of industrial restructuring on everyday life	109
Gender identity and the division of labour	110
Continuity and change in gender divisions	111

Chapter 7 Gender responses to male unemployment; or, is Andy Capp dead? — 113
Jane Wheelock

Introduction	113
Classifying differences	114
No easy option	117
Dignity in the face of change	118

Chapter 8 Reflecting flexibility: from the security of regular employment to coping with casual work — 121
Asbjørn Karlsen

The changing local economy — 121
Flexible firms, flexible households, reflexive workers? — 122
Work and household experiences for temporary workers — 123
    John (35), a steelworker seeking a new career
    Henry (39), a joinery worker using skills in the informal economy
    Heidi (32), a welder coping with casual work in different segments of the labour market
    Martin (40), a carpenter tied to his workplace and hard hit by new manpower policies
Household adaptations — 128
Reflecting flexibility — 130

SECTION B: Changes in family and household based production — 133
Neil Ward and Agnete Wiborg

Chapter 9 'Nationalisation' of rural households? New teams for old tasks in agricultural households   137
Agnete Wiborg

Introduction   137
The local setting   138
Farm work: from household work to one man's work   139
Housework: from women's work to household work   143
Changes in tasks and teams   145

Chapter 10 Economic restructuring, environmental consciousness and farm family succession in Britain   147
Neil Ward and Philip Lowe

Introduction   147
Succession and family farming   148
Succession and the environmental consciousness in agriculture   151
Conclusions   156

Chapter 11 Survival and flexibility in the urban small business household   157
Jane Wheelock

Local economic development and small business households   157
A model of flexibility   158
The costs and benefits of flexibility for the small business household   162
Conclusions: surviving economic change   163

SECTION C: Shifting youth transitions and identities   167
Robert Hollands

Chapter 12 From shipyards to nightclubs: the restructuring of young 'Geordie' work, home and consumption identities   173
Robert Hollands

Introduction   173
Young adults and the meaning of post-industrial work   174
Home sweet home? Negotiating work and consumption   177
From shipyards to nightclubs: youth cultural identification in the post-industrial city   181
Conclusion   184

Chapter 13 Marginalised young men and successful young women: young people entering adulthood   187
Tone Magnussen

Introduction 187
Young men choosing a traditional working career 189
Young women making modern choices 191
The struggles of young men versus the success of young women 192

CONCLUSIONS Changing economies, changing households 195
Jane Wheelock and Åge Mariussen

Summing up 195
Institutional comparisons: empirical analysis 197
Theoretical implications 201
Policy implications 204

Bibliography 207

Index 231

ILLUSTRATIONS

Figures

1.1	Institutional change as a theme in economics and sociology	15
1.2	The household in the total economy	28
2.1	The household in the production, reproduction and consumption cloverleaf	39
10.1	Characteristics of the two extreme groups of farmers, 'sceptics' and 'radicals'	155
11.1	Flexibility in the family economic unit	161

Tables

II.1	Changing employment structure in Wearside and Mo i Rana, selected years	67
II.2	Employment change comparisons, Wearside/Great Britain and Mo i Rana/Norway, selected years	68
II.3	Major industrial sectors, Wearside and Mo i Rana, selected years	69
II.4	Employment in Wearside and Mo i Rana: gender and part-time/full-time breakdown, selected years	70
7.1	The degree of change in the organisation of household work	116
10.1	Economic status categories and family succession	150
12.1	Economic position of young adults (16-29) in Newcastle	176
12.2	Marriage rates by age and sex in Newcastle	178

LIST OF CONTRIBUTORS

Michael Hill, Professor of Social Policy, University of Newcastle upon Tyne, UK
Robert Hollands, Lecturer, Department of Social Policy, University of Newcastle upon Tyne, UK
Asbjørn Karlsen, Research Associate, Nordland Research Institute, Bodø, Norway
Philip Lowe, Duke of Northumberland Professor of Rural Economy, and Director, Centre for Rural Research, University of Newcastle upon Tyne, UK
Tone Magnussen, Research Associate, Nordland Research Institute, Bodø, Norway
Åge Mariussen, Senior Research Associate, Nordland Research Institute, Bodø, Norway
Elizabeth Oughton, Lecturer, Department of Geography, University of Durham, UK
Allan Sande, Lecturer, Nordland University College, and formerly researcher at Nordland Research Institute, Bodø, Norway
Ian Stone, Reader in Economics and Director, Northern Economic Research Unit, University of Northumbria at Newcastle, UK
Neil Ward, Lecturer, Department of Geography, and formerly researcher at the Centre for Rural Economy, University of Newcastle upon Tyne, UK
Jane Wheelock, Reader in Social Policy, University of Newcastle upon Tyne, UK
Agnete Wiborg, Lecturer, Nordland University College and formerly Research Associate, Nordland Research Institute, Bodø, Norway

FOREWORD

The household is often regarded as irrelevant to economic development and change. This book argues that contemporary economic and political change make household level behaviour increasingly of significance for the economy. The book investigates interrelations between household and economic change, through a comparison between Britain and a Scandinavian country, Norway. The conclusions which emerge from these investigations are relevant to policy makers both in social democratic Scandinavia and more neo-liberal countries such as Britain. This means that the analysis is also relevant to a public concerned with a more general discussion: where is economic and social change taking our increasingly turbulent and divided societies?

The comparative approach taken in the book is amenable to the application of institutional theory, which is here used to analyse work. Institutional theory is interdisciplinary. We think that the result is interesting to students of economics, political science, sociology and geography, as well as to research and policy specialists from these disciplines. This varying readership may find different parts of the book of particular interest. A readers' guide is provided below.

Economic and social change

Northern Europe, like other Western countries, is implementing policies of economic restructuring. These policies are necessary, so it is claimed, to cope with increased competition from the new industrial tigers of South East Asia and other newly industrialised nations of the Third World. State owned industry is privatised; state interventions, subsidies, monopolies, laws and other regulations limiting the market are abolished. The labour market becomes more flexible, and so do firms and the public sector, because flexibility is perceived as the way to increased competitiveness.

According to a recent essay by Ralph Dahrendorf (*The Responsive Community*, Summer 1995), the costs of succeeding in this race for flexibility are inequality and loss of social cohesion. As Dahrendorf sees it, social cohesion is a precondition for democracy. People living in Northern Europe share a history of political stability guaranteed by democratic traditions, post-Second World War growth and a welfare state which has guaranteed a certain level of equality and social security. Do we have to give up welfare, stability and democracy to become more competitive? Surely, other answers must be found.

Other answers are indeed being sought. In the European Union, social integration is on the agenda. Policies to promote social integration or cohesion can be seen as counter-policies to handle the unintended side-effects of growing flexibility. There are important variations between different national policies of restructuring. At one time the national, state level absorbed global economic turbulence. This was achieved with Keynesian policies of national regulation and government redistribution to industries in trouble. Any remaining ill effects were cushioned by welfare state guarantees. This route is now rejected in a number of countries; but the rejection happens in different ways and occurs at different speeds. This book is based on a comparison between a Scandinavian country, Norway, and Britain. The discussion arising from this comparison, however, has a more general relevance.

In a number of respects, Britain and Norway present two extreme solutions to the Dahrendorf dilemma at the level of national policy. The UK began a policy of market-led restructuring, making the labour market more flexible from the early 1970s, whereas Norway delayed this process until the late 1980s. Even then, in Norway market forces were far from completely let loose. On the contrary, the market was to be balanced with corporatist restructuring efforts, under the slogan 'restructuring in safety' *(omstilling i trygghet)*, where national and local actors cooperate to reach new solutions. Today, several Scandinavian countries implement more market-led, Anglo-American solutions, while public opinion in Britain seems increasingly to favour a more Scandinavian, social democratic approach to economic and social policy.

So, British experiences are certainly relevant to discussions on restructuring policies in Scandinavia, while Scandinavian ways of solving the problem are not irrelevant to the contemporary debate in the UK. The flexible market solutions of Britain and the corporatist solutions of Norway represent two extremes of the continuum of the restructuring dilemma. This dilemma is of central concern for a number of European countries, such as Sweden and Finland, where failing government income and growing foreign debts are now leading to rapid policy drives in the UK direction: towards deregulation, growing flexibility, and to removing welfare cushions.

The national is not the only relevant level, however. In a world of state level deregulation and regional industrial fragmentation, economic and political change are handled by people who cooperate locally in their efforts to live dignified and flourishing lives. Local cooperation may take place at a regional level. Regions may sometimes organise efficient and competitive answers to global challenges. However, some of these cooperative efforts go on at the most basic level of social cohesion and organisation: at the level of the household. Restructuring and deregulation transform the household into an increasingly important part of the economy, as household members are forced into rethinking their ways of making a living.

Different regions have differing experiences of deregulation and increased labour flexibility. If we are to analyse this phenomenon, it is valuable to identify cases where the most 'advanced' experiences are found. The editorial project was fortunate in being able to draw on empirical work undertaken in two such localities. Northern Norway and North East England share a history of industrial development with resource based industries at the core of their local economies. These industries have encountered the waves of the global market, where resource based production is threatened by fall'ing prices. These peripheral, former resource based regions represent examples which illustrate an extreme case of what is going on elsewhere. These regions deserve attention, for they provide lessons for others.

Despite differences in the balance of power in national policies, and resulting differences in national level solutions between Britain and Scandinavia, there is noticeable similarity in the way people relate to change in their daily lives, in organising and reorganising their households, in these two parts of Northern Europe. Comparisons give us opportunities to learn something. That lesson has implications for discussions of the widespread dilemma posed by economic restructuring.

The in-depth household studies we draw upon for this book have largely been undertaken in two regions with long standing experience of deep economic change. The Anglo-Norwegian team met for two extended seminars, which were followed up with smaller meetings. The locations where we met provided - often poignant - illustrations of what we were studying.

Our first meeting was held on the banks of the River Tyne in Newcastle. In terms of European industrial history, these banks represent important nodes in a regional production system where coalmining, shipbuilding and shipping used to be central elements. This regional industrial system is now gone. The large shipyards, once central to the British shipbuilding industry, are closed. The well-known Armstrong engineering works are much reduced. De-industrialisation initiated a process which has radically altered North-East economy and society alike. The banks of the Tyne have been turned into post-modern locations for offices and conference hotels - in one of which we met - in a region where new inward investment is attracted by a flexible labour market, promoted and supported by local development agencies. The change from mining and shipbuilding into flexible services also affects youth culture, in a way which is central to our discussion of economic and social change in the household. In the evening, we found ourselves surrounded by young people, who are following the shifting centre of gravity from the old town centre to the redeveloped waterside. They are out on the town where their fathers and forebears once worked. Riverside transformations of industrially based working environments into leisure- and service-driven facilities are common throughout de-industrialising Britain.

Our second meeting was held in Sulitjelma in northern Norway. Sulitjelma is located in a mountainous area, where rich copper ore was discovered in the middle of the 19th century. By the turn of the century, this had become the second largest industrial site in Norway, exploited by a British owned company. The mines were closed by the Norwegian government in 1991. The deep tunnels from which the ore was extracted are now filled with water. Former miners show tourists round those sections which can easily be maintained as an industrial museum. Our hotel had recently been extended, based on funding provided by the Norwegian government, in an effort to solve the problems generated by the decision to close mines which were not market competitive. On the weekend we met, the traditional miners' parade was being held. Those who have left the community return for it, wearing traditional holiday clothing. We found a parade which had once been dominated by the industrial workforce, made up of public sector employees, and led by post office workers. There are numbers of other industrial and rural societies which have experienced similar restructuring in Norway.

The group of researchers responsible for this book come from institutions which are located in regions with a number of local similarities: largely from the University of Newcastle upon Tyne, in North-East England, and the Nordland Research Institute in Bodø, north of Norway's Arctic Circle. These institutions have long been making in-depth studies of economic change and restructuring, and the experiences associated with it. As researchers, we came together sharing a concern for the increasing contradictions between policies of economic development and the human needs of those who live in the regions we study. In this book, we present an analysis of these experiences: studies of the reorganisation of household and work needed to cope with economic change.

The members of the group are Professors Michael Hill and Philip Lowe, Dr Jane Wheelock (Reader in Social Policy), Dr Robert Hollands and Dr Neil Ward of the University of Newcastle upon Tyne; Dr Elizabeth Oughton of the Department of Geography at Durham University; and Dr Ian Stone (Reader in Economics) of the University of Northumbria; Research Associates Asbjørn Karlsen, Tone Magnussen, Agnete Wiborg, Allan Sande; and Senior Research Associate Åge Mariussen, of Nordland Research Institute, Bodø.

The book was written as a collective effort to draw together a selection of empirical projects which had been undertaken separately, yet which were based on common conceptual and methodological foundations. All the authors were engaged in the entire project, through the editorial seminars. Jane Wheelock and Åge Marjussen were the coordinators. We would like to thank the Norwegian Social Science Research Council who were generous enough to fund the editorial collective through their AREG programme on work and regional development. This programme was organised by the Norwegian Research Council, partly financed by the Ministries of Industry and Municipal Affairs.

Readers' guide

How do households, and the people who live in them, sustain themselves in the face of change? This is the question we work with, and we argue that they do so by finding new ways to organise work. Observations and analysis of how people find new ways of organising work are presented, discussed and compared. The editorial collection shows households where breadwinners have been made redundant; where young adults are unemployed; or where women have taken on new labour market roles; and households dependent on farming, self-employment or small business activities. The case studies drawn together here show how the internal dynamics of the household economy are linked with processes that arise from economic restructuring. They examine and compare responses of household coping strategies to growing flexibility in labour markets, and the interrelations between small firms and the household. They look at the ways in which this can lead to exclusion and differentiation in urban as well as rural settings.

The evidence presented questions market-based understandings of economic behaviour and change, by looking at the creation of meanings, identities and values at the level of the household. It develops a new understanding of the relation between the household and the formal economy. In economic and political science, household and family are not considered an important focus. Even in rural sociology, the household has been a marginal unit for study. The family has certainly been a focus for studies of family relations and emotions by psychologists and family sociologists. But these studies do not relate the organisation of tasks inside the household to political and economic processes outside it.

To open this box, we have to use institutional theory, to see how distinctions between public and private, society and household, market and non-market, work and family life, are constructed and reconstructed. The ways these constructions are made in the social sciences and by lay actors in their households are different, but interrelated. The orthodox economic approach to the study of households is inadequate, based as it is on the presupposition of individuals who simply maximise their own narrowly economic well-being. From an institutional perspective, we focus on how actors create and recreate stability and order, through reflexive conflicts, involving negotiation and reinterpretation of the institutions within which work is organised. These institutional transformations are initiated in the big games of the global economy and by national policy processes, but the conflicts are fought out, and solutions found, at the level of the household.

This book tries to rectify the way in which the household has been ignored. In doing so, it rediscovers relationships between sociology and economics. It builds an interdisciplinary understanding of how households are embedded and re-embedded in local and national economies undergoing rapid change. An holistic understanding of work allows us to understand social reproduction and regulation, including power relations based on gender and generation. At the level of the household, gender identity is a central issue, both at the practical level, in the definition of tasks and duties, and at the symbolic level. Institutional transformation also means changing gender definitions.

It is in the Introduction that the relevance of an institutionalist approach to the household and economic change is put forward, drawing on sociological, economic and political science perspectives. The Introduction is important for researchers and others who wish to engage with our underlying analytical approach, and for students from any discipline who want to understand more about the institutionalist perspective on theories of social, economic or cultural change. For students in particular, it might make sense to return to the Introduction after reading the more policy- and empirically-based parts of the book. We hope that readers who skip the Introduction to start with, will find their curiosity sufficiently aroused to read it at a later stage.

Following the Introduction, the book is divided into three main parts. In Part I, the significance of the household in its macro context is discussed in three chapters. It presents the context for the case studies to be presented in Part III. The institutional perspective is particularly developed in Chapters 1 and 2. In Chapter 1, by Jane Wheelock and Åge Mariussen, the household is seen from the outside: from the point of view of different disciplinary perspectives, economic restructuring and the relation between the formal, and the informal, or complementary economy.

In Chapter 2, Elizabeth Oughton, Jane Wheelock and Agnete Wiborg discuss the household as seen from the inside, from *Behind the lace curtains*. Students and researchers interested in how institutional theory can be applied to relationships between the household and the formal economy, will want to read these chapters right away. They pose questions which are picked up on empirically in Part III, and in the concluding chapter. Those more interested in the empirical chapters will find themselves returning to Part I later, in order to deepen and contextualise their understanding of what they have read.

In Chapter 3, the institutional context is further underlined, as the major differences in social policy are discussed by Michael Hill. Here, Professor Hill draws contrasts in social policy which set the scene for the subsequent discussion of Part II, also picked up upon in the concluding chapter. This chapter opens the agenda on the social consequences of economic restructuring. People interested in social policy questions may start by reading Chapter 3 and then go on to Chapters 4 and 5 in Part II, and to the concluding chapter.

In Part II, economic restructuring policies in Britain and Norway are compared by Ian Stone and Åge Mariussen, through a discussion of the interrelation between national level policy, local industrial development and local labour markets in two chapters (4 and 5) which are linked by a brief introduction and a comparative conclusion. Here, differences between market-led and corporate restructuring are discussed, based on two empirical examples: Wearside in North-East England and Mo in Northern Norway. People interested in economic restructuring policy may start here, and proceed through the subsequent sections of Part III to the Conclusions.

In Sections A, B and C of Part III, empirical case studies of households are presented and compared. In IIIA, household responses to industrial change and unemployment are discussed in three chapters, by Jane Wheelock, Allan Sande and Asbjørn Karlsen. In IIIB, changes in family and household based production are discussed by Neil Ward, Philip Lowe, Agnete Wiborg and Jane Wheelock. In this section, both urban and rural household based production are analysed, looking at farming households and at urban small business households. In IIIC, Robert Hollands and Tone Magnussen discuss the interconnections between economic restructuring, youth identities and householding. Readers who wish to know what is going on at an empirical level, should read Part III in its entirety.

Each of the three subsections of the third part have an introduction by the authors setting the analytical scene for the ensuing empirical chapters. In the Conclusions the empirical analysis of Part III is summed up. The questions raised in the Introduction, and in the chapters of Parts I and II are answered here. So are the policy conclusions.

We hope that with these suggestions you can enjoy reading this book as much as we enjoyed writing it.

ACKNOWLEDGMENTS

There are many people we need to thank for their part in this book. Without the financial support of funding bodies in Britain and Norway the empirical studies which provide the basis for this book would not have been possible. The Equal Opportunities Commission financed the research on which Chapter 7 is based; the Economic and Social Research Council that for Chapters 10, 11 and 12. The Norwegian Research Council's AREG Programme supported the research for Chapters 6, 8, 9 and 13. It was also the generous support of the Norwegian Research Council which enabled the collaborative work of bringing the book together to take place.

All of us who have written chapters for this book would like to thank the many Norwegian and English men and women who gave so generously of their time and effort when they were interviewed. Their cooperation has been essential to this project.

We would also like to express our gratitude to Dorothy McLoughlin for her devoted preparation of the manuscript, and to Anna Flowers for copy editing and proof reading. Writing and preparing the book has been a collective effort, which has made our job as editors all the more enjoyable. We hope that readers do not spot any errors; if you do, they remain the responsibility of the editors.

Last but by no means least, this book about the household could not have been written without the support our families have given us.

Thank you all!

INTRODUCTION

INSTITUTIONAL TRANSFORMATION

Åge Mariussen and Jane Wheelock

Households, work and gender in transformation

What are the interrelations between households and economic change? This question can only be answered by looking at the way work is organised. So what about work organisation in households? A household is a small group of people, often, but not always, a family, who cooperate to solve tasks, so as to sustain the basic material, social and emotional needs of the group. Households control resources, and depend on income from different sources. Household incomes may come in a variety of forms, such as money, goods or services.

The household is flexible. Tasks are handled by teams. People in households respond to economic change by establishing new teams to handle old tasks, and by changing the tasks they take upon themselves. New tasks are accepted, old tasks may be rejected or lost. Flexibility is certainly an overused term. Broadly, flexibility has to do with organisation of work. Changing work organisation is often accompanied by changes in the rules and habits which are directly referred to - or implied - when work is organised and reorganised. These explicit or implicit rules of the game are called institutions.

Contemporary debates on institutional theory pick up on the relation between social institutions and the economy. Granovetter's perspective on how the economy is embedded in social institutions (Granovetter, 1985, 1992 - drawing on Polanyi, 1946) makes an important contribution here, as does the debate on reflexive modernisation (Beck, Giddens and Lash, 1994). These debates derive from older themes in economics, sociology and political theory.

Thus, institutional theories of modernisation were central for classical sociologists, like Weber, Parsons and Smelser (for further details see Chapter 1). Parsons and Smelser discuss the relation between society and economy as a relation between integration and adaptation (Parsons and Smelser, 1956, Holton and Turner, 1986, Smelser, 1995). The dilemma discussed by Dahrendorf - already referred to in the Foreword - is the dilemma posed by an increasing tension between the need that western economies have to adapt to new global economic conditions on one hand,

and the necessity for societal integration on the other.

Throughout this book, contributing authors argue that this tension between adaptation and integration is intimately related with a theme that feminist economics has contributed to our understanding: namely gender (Waller and Jennings, 1991). The crux of our argument is that economic change puts pressure on the institutions of gender. Attempts to follow the old rules of men's and women's work under contemporary conditions leads to tensions and disintegration. The old games change, but only slowly. Empirical investigation of the interrelations between households, work and economic change requires analysis in terms of gender as one form of institutional transformation.

In order to study institutions as they are created and transformed, the appropriate method is not to cover a few variables in a large number of cases, randomly drawn from some larger universe, but rather to analyse interconnections between several variables through time, in a limited number of cases. In this book, we present the outcome of available empirical material relevant to such a method. The material derives from recent British and Norwegian studies based on different methodologies, but primarily drawn from qualitative case studies. As with any qualitative material, the number of cases is limited, and they cannot be seen as statistically representative. The material is drawn from particular locations and some chapters analyse developments at the level of the location. However, this is not primarily a geographical analysis of locations or regions. Our concern is with processes where actors and institutions make the connections between household, work and economic change. The focus is on individuals interacting in a household context. It is comparison between cases that enables us to develop a more general theory about these processes, with a number of variables interconnected through time. The central concern in this method, then, is not the number of cases, but rather the scope of their variation. Let us now go on to clarify this scope.

Games and habits

Work is generally looked at as the actions of individuals participating in the labour market or in labour market institutions. In this book, it is not the individual, but the individual in his or her household context, who provides the key to understanding work and work institutions. The links conventionally made in economics between the macro- and the micro-level are seen in terms of relationships between individuals and a static model of the macro-economy. But how individuals behave is moulded by the household they live in. One of the things we all start to learn as children in the household, is how to work. Usually, we learn what work is, and how to work, from our mother and father.

One of the basic 'rules of the game' we engage in has to do with the way work is classified. A number of activities, both in the formal economy and in the complementary, household economy, may be classified as work, some are not. Work is a word with different meanings and definitions. People work in the formal economy, as employees, as private entrepreneurs, public servants or managers; people work in the informal, black economy or in the equally informal, green neighbourhood economy, where they may help each other or exchange services between relatives, neighbours or family members. People are also working in their homes, in the various tasks of householding, bringing up their children, preparing meals and so on.

To work is to do something which others classify as work. To classify is to give meaning and to make moral evaluations. As Wadel points out (Durkheim, 1968; Wadel, 1983), to classify an activity as work is to give the actor and her activity respect, dignity and inclusion. To work is to be morally included. To organise work, then, is a basic way of organising social cohesion and integration, of including. Often, classifying work is also to define the activity as appropriate for a man or a woman, to give a gender to the activity: it is women's work to sew, unless you happen to be a sailor; it is men's work to drive the tractor. Allocating a gender to work is often taken for granted. We do lots of things without reflecting upon them, because we take practices, routines and procedures for granted, without discussion. What is taken for granted is not reflected upon, and therefore not changed. It is just done in practice. Taking practice for granted is a powerful mechanism shaping institutions - and tradition.

One of the central theoretical issues in contemporary debates among sociologists is to ask how the 'taken for grantedness' of tradition is to be understood. In the so-called 'Neo-Kantian controversy', two positions are defined. To Anthony Giddens, social structure is a skilled accomplishment of actors, who are in a position to withdraw and reflect. Institutions are open to reinterpretation and transformation through reflexion. Contemporary change imposes new kinds of uncertainties on actors, uncertainties which lead to increased reflexivity and to an institutional transformation which is called modernisation.

To Pierre Bourdieu (Bourdieu, 1992), on the other hand, social structures are a result of a 'logic of practice', which is beyond actors' reflexive capacity. A central concept is 'habitus'. People are formed by work and other practical experiences, and this creates abilities, skills, reflexes, tastes, norms (doxa), emotions and classifications. This formation of the person takes place without words; it is the outcome of practical experience.

When the taken-for-granted is challenged, the values of the old world (doxa) are defended, by clinging to orthodoxy. However, what is defended, may actually no longer be taken-for-granted. The defence may reinterpret old values, or maintain them by other means. Orthodoxy often means that the very institution being defended is transformed, or even destroyed. Following on from Bourdieu, Lash uses the concept 'reflexivity loosers' to describe actors caught in a process of institutional transformation where they relate to change through a defence of tradition (orthodoxy), yet without being able to adapt to the new big games around them (Lash, 1994).

The challenges to the small games people play - and sometimes control - in their everyday lives, are generated in big games, which are usually beyond their control. 'Rules of big games' may lay down principles regulating control over resources, such as capacity to allocate money and power to command people. Institutions have to do with both 'micro-level' activities, such as what is going on in households, and 'macro-level' activities, such as government decisions, or decisions and actions taken by international actors in the various big games of our increasingly globalised economy. Norms may be protected by law, by the police, by legislation regulating property rights, as well as by other mechanisms of control and allocation of resources and authority.

Processes of macro-level institutionalisation are at the level of the state, or at international levels. The degree of reflexive coordination between micro- and macro-change is low. The outcomes of the attempts of actors in the small games to adjust to changing big games are, therefore, indeterminate. It is quite possible to have results which are unintended and undesired by everyone. Deregulation is a fashionable type of macro-level institutional change which seems to embrace the spirit of the times in this final decade of the millenium. These macro-level institutional transformations generate new 'rules of the big games' of industrial development, with a variety of industrial restructuring processes. Changing rules take the games in new directions, sometimes drawing in new players, as they generate industrial and labour market change.

Actors at the level of the household must adapt to this deep swell of change, generated in global and national economies, and resulting in ever greater flexibility and deregulation. However, in adapting, local actors have to interpret what is going on and relate to it. A variety of solutions may be found in the 'small games' at the level of the household. Existing institutional principles for the organisation of work get reinterpreted, or rejected and replaced with others.

Actors involved in this process confront the Neo-Kantian controversy, not as a theoretical controversy, but as a practical problem. Do they find new solutions through reflection, or do they stick to, and defend the old ways of doing things?

Often, micro-change at the level of the household and macro-change at the global or national level are considered separately. In this book, we try to point out their interrelations. There are connections between big and small games. The rules of the various games we participate in may conflict, imposing contradictory and inconsistent demands on us. Economic restructuring and changing forms of flexibility generate new demands, and sometimes new inconsistencies and structural tensions between different sets of rules, and different institutional principles.

In the end, however, we all have to cope to fulfil our human needs. The household is at the end of the chain of events generated by economic change. Contradictions and dilemmas created by the changing rules of the big games of global and national economic and political change are handled and mirrored at the micro-level of the household, in the way people cooperate to fulfil their human needs, trying to live dignified and flourishing lives.

Contemporary processes of economic change, deregulation and policies for increasing economic flexibility, turn household-level activites into an increasingly important part of the whole economy. This book proposes an institutional approach, where the impact of macro-economic change can be studied at a micro level.

The institutional approach and embedding change

Within economics, institutional theory pays attention to the political dimensions of economic behaviour, to values, culture and the role of the state. It has only been a strong tradition in the United States, developed from the work of Veblen (1912). Mainstream economics does not confront these issues directly. Often, such factors are included in terms of the assumptions made before the model is built. This is the approach that the Chicago based school of the New Household Economics takes. Alternatively, in a form of economic disciplinary imperialism, political and social behaviour, as well as economic behaviour, are interpreted as actions of rational economic maximisers. Institutional economics in contrast, introduces power into economics through the understanding of institutions as power structures. In sociology, the institutional approach has meant something rather different, as we will show in Chapter 1.

A synthesis of economic and sociological understandings of what makes up an institutional approach then, provides us with a useful set of tools for analysing empirically the impact of economic change on work and the household. At an empirical level, what we are looking at is the construction and reconstruction of institutions. Institutions are on the one hand power structures, where power is not simply seen in Marxist class-power terms, nor is it wished away, as in orthodox economics. Institutions on the other hand are concerned with the formation of values through habits; institutions embed meanings and values through practice and routines (Hodgson 1988)

How do values and power structures change with liberalisation, with the extension of markets through deregulation, and what difference do varying forms of economic and social regulation make? New ways of regulating give rise to institutional conflicts: between individual- and market-based values, and social values of solidarity and reciprocity. Under the impact of economic change, the household as a set of stabilised institutional structures undergoes transformation. Household members renegotiate the household as an institution either - as we have seen - by moving within established rules of the game, or by instigating changes in the rules themselves.

Institutional conflict at a variety of levels fuels this process, as household members face problems of how to maintain or re-establish order in the face of macro-level changes. When behaviour involves practical solutions to these problems, the household is making organisational changes to the tasks and teams undertaking different forms of paid and unpaid work inside and beyond the household. This means negotiations - and reinterpretations of the meaning of work. These negotiations and reinterpretations will also be taking place in the light of changes in the relative significance of individualised market values and reciprocal values of social and household interdependence. At the micro-level, people may respond to economic change by making value compromises with those they live with in households. In the context of economic change, they may experience challenges to their established sets of values - as for instance when women are drawn into employment, or as young males experience unprecedented rates of unemployment for example.

By adopting a perspective which looks at the household as an institution it is possible to show that what Stanfield (1986) drawing on Polanyi (1946) calls 'substantive institutional analysis' has much to contribute to an economics of the household. Such an approach uses a method grounded in concrete empirical awareness to allow human experience to speak for itself. Conventional economic theory sees psychology as the basic grounding for economic behaviour, and this is the case for the New Household Economics of Gary Becker and his followers. In contrast, for institutionalists, it is the cultural context that establishes the behaviours and norms that are encouraged or allowed in the process of satisfying material wants. (Waller and Jennings, 1991)

So, why is an institutionalist approach able to provide special insights? How far has the institutionalist analysis of the household actually progressed, and what still remains to be done? (See Wheelock, 1994; Wheelock and Oughton, 1996).

The methodology of institutionalism lends itself, firstly, because it looks at power and at power relations. It therefore moves away from the atomistic individualism which ignores the household as a family unit whose overall structure, including that of gender and age, is crucially important.

Secondly, the focus on cultural processes and the social construction of knowledge encourages questions about the nature of rational choice when people form and maintain households together. It is therefore possible to look at how the institutions of the family household and of the labour market interact with each other, asking what choices households make about their work strategies and how members divide their time between paid work in the formal economy and unpaid work in the complementary economy.

Thirdly, institutionalists examine the processes of evolutionary change. Such an approach encourages analysis of how the relation between the household and the economy evolves over time. For the individual household, movement through the life cycle of marriage, birth of children, and their eventual leaving home, introduces a dynamic element into family work strategies and household behaviour. But structural economic changes, such as rising female participation in the labour market or increased male unemployment, can also influence the behaviour of different household members. In other words, processes both endogenous and exogenous to the household contribute to the dynamic character of economic behaviour. These form crucial causal links between the complementary and the formal economy which are mediated by changing household work strategies.

The sustainability of the household relies not only on current strategies, but on inter-generational long-term family projects. The division of labour within the household according to age, gender and kinship relations may be expected to substantially affect these projects. There must therefore be a concern, not only with how the household maintains its livelihood in the here and now, but how it reproduces itself and its activities for the future.

As Waller and Jennings (1991) point out, there are two further advantages to substantive analysis, though neither of them have necessarily been achieved in practice. One is to address the importance of the links between market and non-market activities, which it is difficult for formalist economic accounts to include. The second is that gender roles can be unpacked, for 'reification of the market in formalist economics constitutes the acceptance of our current prioritisation of gender roles as appropriate and natural' (Waller and Jennings, 1991; 490). This approach then, examines the 'economic character' of the household, arguing that economic motivation must be examined in a household, rather than an individual context. The economic character of the household can be built up from a study of the ways in which judgements about values are made.

Comparative research on the household, based on a substantive institutional approach can thus be put into effect with a number of specific research objectives.

The first objective provides a material basis for subsequent interpretation of behaviour. It identifies and compares household strategies for the organisation and planning of resource use and exploitation within and beyond the household. Comparative research can include the inter-generational transfer of resources, the application of market and non-market labour, temporal aspects of consumption, and gender. Investigations of the commonalities and differences in the diffusely felt experience of livelihood can thus be undertaken.

Secondly, it is important to examine the way in which intra-household relations, gender, conjugal and kinship status affect and are affected by the economic activity of the household. This contributes to a theoretical model of household economic behaviour that is sensitive to the embedded nature of economic behaviour within a social, cultural and political context. Such a model needs to be responsive to the gender of the individual, their position within age, or alternative hierarchical, structures of the household; and their specific contribution both actual and potential within the formal and the complementary economy. An understanding of the process of decision making, whether explicit or implicit, is vital.

Thirdly, one needs to gain understanding of the process of the economic socialisation of individuals within households. This involves examination of the development of economic values and beliefs within the household: the way in which these have been inherited or adapted from the previous generation, and the form in which they are passed on to children. It also means asking how people within households build their economic understanding of a changing economic context.

Lastly, what are the processes for sustaining and reproducing the household? Past behaviour, present strategies and plans for the future illuminate the decision making process, where differing weight is given to individuals within the household. Responses to risk and uncertainty in terms of inter-generational transfers in the form of inheritance, dowry, gifts and provision for old age are important, as is the tension between individual acquisition and long-term reproduction. Ray Abrams humanises the language of economics by talking of how people's memories and ambitions colour their economic behaviour[1].

For these reasons, substantive institutional analysis shows that the household is a key institution in the process of evolutionary change. Such a method of analysis is quite different from the mainstream approach to economics as a science of choice (Becker, 1965, Mincer, 1962). Stanfield follows Polanyi (1946) in his substantive approach, which, as Waller and Jennings see it, means analysing 'the economy as an instituted process of interaction serving the satisfaction of material wants' (Waller and Jennings, 1991; 488). Economic behaviour is therefore treated as a cultural process where behaviour is learned. The value standard of conventional economics takes a 'more is better' approach, thereby promoting an econocentric culture (Stanfield, 1982; 77). A substantive view of the economic process argues that 'the economy is the instituted process or culturally patterned arrangements by which a given human group provisions itself as a going concern' (Stanfield, 1982; 71). Polanyi saw market society as one in which the economy is disembedded from society. 'The need is to examine the relation of lives to livelihood and subordinate the economy to the lives it properly should serve...precisely to re-embed the economy in society' (Stanfield, 1982, 73).

Households, work and economic change

This issue of re-embedding the economy in society highlights one of the fundamental questions of sociology, the 'problem of order'. Put simply, how is everything interconnected, so that society functions as a whole? This was one of the questions that troubled the classical sociologists, like Durkheim and Parsons. It has not on the whole troubled economists, for Adam Smith asserted that the pursuit of individual self-interest in the market brought about social harmony, and economists have never seen any need for empirical verification of their founder's presuppositions. It has remained a battleground for sociology ever since, particularly in the critical debate on the structural functionalist approach suggested by Parsons (Giddens, 1981). In Parsonian sociology, it was assumed that the household contributed to the economy through socialising people into work roles in the formal economy.

In some of the critical interpretations of Parsonian functionalism, order is created by some kind of automatic coherence. Drawing on biological analogies, households may be automatically embedded in the changing economy, because different institutions all contribute to the same overriding goal, in a process of normative integration. Yet our contemporary world does not seem to strike any observer - whether social science academic or policy maker - as particularly stable or morally integrated. This is the point of view of Dahrendorf, to whom we referred in the preface. The 'construction of order' then, is far removed from any kind of biological-type spontaneous process; normative cohesion and social integration are by no means the automatic end-point.

What Dahrendorf describes looks rather like a process where social integration is undermined by the attempts of western national economies to adapt to the new global economic environment. This relation between economic change and social integration should be seen as a field for empirical investigation. Processes involving different solutions to contradicting institutional principles, and the varying attempts of actors to reflect and adapt, need empirical examination. This is provided in Part III. The limitations of reflexion, and of the 'reflexivity loser' option at a micro-level should be acknowledged as an empirical possibility. 'Order' should not be seen as a single, clearly defined structural solution, but rather as different options, where stability is created. Order can be studied through a focus on how people handle economic change at the level of the household. A variety of outcomes of this interrelationship between big and small games are to be anticipated.

We expect to find some households adapting to change, in ways which make it possible to sustain human needs in the face of economic turbulence. These adaptations in the small games may be important for human dignity and welfare, and they may also prevent social disintegration. However, they may not necessarily be of any significance for the prosperity of formal economy. This type of outcome is investigated empirically in Part III, Section A, in terms of how households respond to industrial change and unemployment. In other cases, we expect to find linkages between household and production which make production strategies feasible. Such enabling solutions to the changing rules of big games are possible where households form the basis for production for the market. These sorts of changes in the little games are investigated in Part III Section B.

The relation between adapting and enabling should be seen as analytical. It is possible that households which adapt to restructuring policies, are also making these policies possible, in which case adaption has an element of enabling. We must then ask how institutional transformations which result in such positive relations between household and economic change are created. What are the preconditions for the kind of order that can be created by embedding economy and household? We return to these issues in the Conclusions.

However, we can also posit less hopeful outcomes. Economic change may in fact generate institutional disjunctions between the household and the economy. This is particularly relevant as far as the long-term processes of gender identity formation and socialisation are concerned. These longer-term processes are highlighted in the ways that the next generation who are on the verge of forming their households behave. The delayed transition to independent householding for young people is discussed in Section C. The Conclusions indicate that there may be substantial problems of order in the relationships between big and small games, and we put forward some policy proposals for bringing them into line with each other.

Notes

1. Personal communication, Krakow, June, 1995.

PART I

THE SIGNIFICANCE OF THE HOUSEHOLD IN ITS MACRO-CONTEXT

CHAPTER 1

PERSPECTIVES ON THE HOUSEHOLD IN A CHANGING ECONOMY

Åge Mariussen and Jane Wheelock

Overview

This book opens up the relation between the household and economic change as a field of empirical research which links micro- and macro-phenomena. Why has this field largely been neglected to date? The neglect, we argue, derives from the division of intellectual labour between different theoretical disciplines. The orthodox perspective dominating sociology and economics sees the interrelation between households and a changing economy as generally uninteresting from a practical or empirical point of view, and moreover, as unimportant for theory. We argue that such a perspective is the outcome of the way in which the boundaries between economics and sociology were established from the late nineteenth century. The present chapter tells a story of the divorce and potential remarriage of economics and sociology. We show that there have been a number of remarriage brokers who have attempted over the years to bring the divorced couple back together again as they try to understand their joint progeny, the household.

Locating the household in the disciplinary debates on the borders between sociology and economics is the starting point from which this chapter identifies the interface between household and economy. By the end of the chapter we show that whether economists and sociologists wish to get back into bed with each other or not the household, as their joint offspring, is a key institution in theorising and understanding economic change and development. Once we take this understanding on board, gender becomes integrated into the analysis. It is no longer possible to get away with adding gender on as an afterthought to other theoretical constructions, as has been so prevalent in more recent debates in sociology and economics. The way in which gender is incorporated as a fundamental factor in any household level of analysis is then further explored when we go *Behind the lace curtains* in the next chapter.

Divorces are generally complex and messy events, and the disciplinary divorce we describe here is no exception. To simplify the story we focus on key thinkers and arguments in each of the disciplines: where the development of institutional or organisational analysis provides insight into links between the micro-phenomena of the household and the macro-phenomena of economic change. (These are represented in Figure 1.1). The first section follows a variety of attempts at remarriage which start from a micro-perspective on how institutions are differentiated from each other during modernisation, as markets develop and the organisation of firms changes. The ensuing conflicts between institutional principles, including those of gender, are modelled in very different ways by Weber, Parsons, Karl Polanyi, Williamson and economic sociologists such as Granovetter. The second section starts from a macro-perspective which examines how the institutional organisation of the economy has changed towards post-Fordism since the demise of the long post-war boom. The debate on macro-economic regulation has largely ignored the role of the household in changes in the organisation of production and consumption. The following section indicates how micro-household and macro-economic change issues can be integrated in a view of the whole economy based on the complementary nature of formal (paid) and informal (unpaid) economic activity. The penultimate section integrates the micro-local, and the macro-global economies, by asking how changing livelihoods affect household lives. One way of achieving this is to analyse the interaction between production and consumption and the formation of a household moral economy.

Theories of modernisation regularly argue that the economy is progressively being disembedded from society. The economy, in other words, now belongs to a separate institutional sphere, one in which the economic rationality of utility maximisation dominates. This sphere is the modern, formal and measurable economy. The measurable economy can be studied as a closed system, in isolation from society, using the assumptions and analytical tools of neo-classical economics. The ethics, power and cognitive structures of formal economic organisations separate work in formal organisations from the households of employees. Modernisation, in other words, involves a process of institutional differentiation. The family of the employee is regarded as irrelevant to her formalised position in the organisation. Formalised work in modern organisations takes place in buildings which are physically separated from the households of employees, their homes. Working hours are regulated, and are separate from the time spent in the household. Welfare state arrangements regulate the world which falls outside the benefits from formal organisations and takes overall care of household needs. These two spaces are dominated by different values, attitudes and psychologies, through distinctions developed in a process of cultural transformation called 'modernisation'. Market performance becomes a given for economists, while it is a cultural outcome of modernisation for sociologists.

This line of thought is often used to define and defend the disciplinary borders between sociology and economics. In each discipline, the attention, rewards and interests of its experts are directed towards the central disciplinary questions. Anything near the border gets ignored because it is distant from the main field of interest. The interrelation between household and economy, as an example of the 'in-between', is uninteresting. This in-between case connects to a set of more or less subconscious assumptions, which tend to do the thinking through sets of analogies

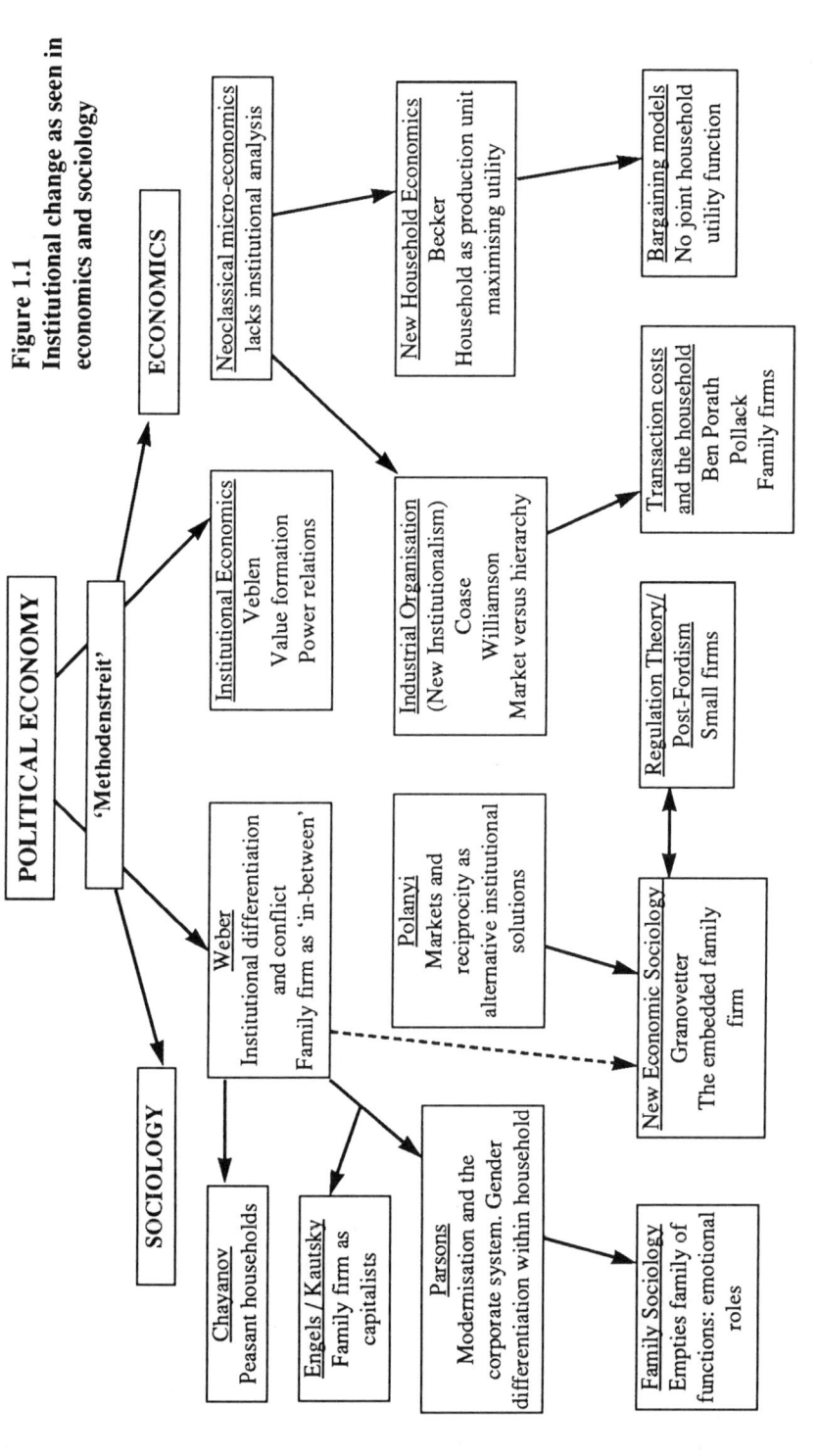

**Figure 1.1
Institutional change as seen in economics and sociology**

(Douglas, 1986). The dichotomy between household and economy is often associated with a series of contrasting equivalents, which work like this:

Household   :   firm
Traditional   :   modern
Private   :   public
Mother   :   father

With these analogies in mind, the word 'household' is connected to spheres which traditionally, a decent economist does not venture into. For assumptions about economic maximising, scarcity and choice, are fundamental to the neo-classical models of post-*Methodenstreit* economics, and institutional issues are left aside. The New Household Economics approach initiated by Gary Becker (1965) made a radical departure from that tradition (see Figure 1.1). It incorporated the assumption that utility maximisation guides relations inside the household as well as outside, recognising that individuals do not just make choices between market work and leisure, but also work in the home. Time then becomes included as a scarce resource with competing uses. (For further details see Wheelock and Oughton, 1996). This move towards a remarriage of economics and sociology remains one-sided however. The Chicago based school used its assumptions of utility maximisation to set more sociological explanations to one side, leaving sociologists to labour with the emotional life of the family, and the organisational problems of an increasingly differentiated welfare state.

The modern is often established as a contrast to the past and the primitive. The past is studied by historians, while social anthropologists focus on primitive societies. In traditional society, people are driven by norms, superstitions, emotions and traditions. They organise in small communities which are thought to be tightly integrated. They produce in households or in small family firms. Empirical facts which do not correspond to the model of modern institutional differentiation, such as the persistence of household based production, or of family firms in modern economies, are either forgotten, overlooked, or labelled as a thing of the past which is due to disappear (but see for example, Mayer, 1975; Bechhofer and Elliott, 1981;1986). Such phenomena can therefore be disregarded by anyone interested in modern society or economy.

Today, these paradigmatic definitions are breaking down. Over the last two decades, the empirical realities of economic restructuring and changes in the forms that flexibility takes have opened the door between economics and politics, as economists have attempted to develop institutional and regulation theory to explain what is going on. Politics is remarried to an economics where the 'flexible economy' is a central empirical concern, as further discussed in the second section of the chapter. Among the early classical political economists, there was no distinction between sociology and economics, nor between society and economy. Economics was assumed to be embedded in society. Today, this tradition is being revived, through the new economic sociology.

In addition to these theoretical developments, research has begun in the field between household and economy. While orthodox economics has remained concerned with the measurable, formalised economy, the informal economy has been recognised and investigated by development economists amongst others. In the third section of this chapter, 'the whole economy' - where formal and the informal are seen together - is discussed. Seeing the whole economy further implies that both production and consumption must be considered. Another hole in the wall dividing disciplines derives from the analysis of regional space. Households are localised in space, as are firms and other institutions of the formalised economy. It is geography that has focused on this spatial link, as described in the final section of the chapter.

Economics and sociology: divorce and remarriage?

To the classical political economists of the nineteenth century, societal institutions such as the household, were a part of the economy, and the economy in turn was a part of society. Politics were seen as integral to this relationship, and economics was 'political economy'. In our intellectual history, it was the late nineteenth century German *Methodenstreit* movement arguing over the philosophy of methods that separated economics - as a discipline occupied with the measurable, formal aspects of economic life - and other social sciences, such as sociology, where society was the object. The founding of modern neo-classical economics in the final quarter of the last century, focusing on what was measurable, took this distinction as one of its paradigmatic assumptions.

An early attempt at a remarriage between economics and sociology which throws light on the relationship between household and economy comes from Max Weber (see Figure 1.1). The relation between households and the rest of the economy is central to Weber's economic theory. His point of departure was the concept use value, itself a crucial concept for the classical school of political economists. Resources utilised in householding are available in the household as use values. Sometimes we relate to use values directly with things we use to fulfil the needs of our households. On these occasions, we are engaged in what Weber called 'calculations in kind'. We calculate in kind when we select from different ingredients to prepare a meal for the members of the household, and when we decide what is to be done - and who must do what - for the meal to be prepared. This is done to fulfil human needs. Such needs are often determined by emotional, traditional or normative preferences; for instance, our views of what makes a proper Sunday family lunch.

Calculations in kind are oriented towards the satisfaction of wants (Weber, 1947; 202 ff.). They are calculations which are not informed by price comparisons, for there are no markets in a household: no price information as a basis for comparison. The rationale for choice is different when there is no price information. He used the phrase *Haushalten* to refer to this calculus in kind, where needs are budgeted against available resources to optimise a normatively defined goal.

According to Weber, the fulfilment of human needs - as these are defined by the values of household members - is the institutional context within which work is organised in the household. However, most households depend on use values obtained through markets, often bought by income from participation in the labour market, but also by other means, such as state transfers, property ownership, gifts or inheritance. Thus, the household gains most of its use values because it possesses the universal means of getting them: money. It may therefore be tempting to use money calculations as if they gave a real measure of human needs. Weber insists that calculation in terms of money is a 'formal' type of rationality, as opposed to the 'substantive' rationality we engage in when we try to find out how our needs may best be fulfilled.

The formal character of money calculus is laid bare when calculation of the means, money, leads to action which is contrary to the end, fulfilment of human needs. This happens if an actor sacrifices the end in order to maximise the means. Self-sacrifice for the sake of accumulation of money was central in Weber's work on the Protestant ethic and the spirit of capitalism (Weber, 1930). The mind of the accumulating Protestant is filled with a calling, which compels him or her to accumulate money. In order to optimise the means, money, she may sacrifice her human needs. This self-denial is possible and understandable with a new definition of time. Thanks to the Protestant's calling, her eyes are directed towards the future rewards of asceticism. Short-term self-denial is justified by the anticipation of long-term benefit, where the spirit of capitalism comes from within the person.

To Weber, institutional differentiation between household and firm (Weber, 1947; ff.) depends on two things. First is the specification of the particular type of work which goes on outside the household. This specification is based on the interaction between actors' own definitions of occupations, and their definition by the labour market, *Erwerben*. Secondly, there is submission of that occupational work to an organisation outside the household. This submission to an institutional context outwith the household is not without problems, however. Inside an industrial organisation, Weber argues that it is not the Protestant calling which compels people to submit, but the hierarchy of the firm. Within the firm, the parallel to Protestant asceticism is the oppression of the interests of the worker by a bureaucratised management devoted to capital accumulation.

Weber is one of the founders of modernisation theory. The theory of bureaucracy as the dominant form of modern organisation, is one of his masterpieces. In a close reading of Weber however, one discovers both normative and theoretical ambiguity in the project of modernisation itself. His dichotomies, including those of *Haushalten* and *Erwerben*, are discussed as contingent outcomes of a process which is open and full of contradictions (Mommsen, 1989). Weber discusses these dichotomies as abstract categories, not as labels attached to specified historical periods. This level of abstraction is central to his theory. The dilemmas posed by these dichotomies remain relevant today.

To Weber then, money calculus and capital accumulation is just one of several institutions which occupational work, *Erwerben*, can be submitted to. A major part of Weber's discussion of industrial organisation is based on the hybrid forms of this dilemma. Between the extremes, he found different organisational forms, such as the family firm. In a family firm, work may be submitted to the same values as that of household work. Alternatively, the household may be submitted to the values of capital accounting. The family firm owned by a craftsperson is a further alternative.

The craftsperson is not a morally detached money owner, he (or she) is a master of an art - and she submits her *Erwerben* to fulfilling the standards of her craft. In Weber's perspective, then, we find a wide array of possible middle forms between the human needs of *Haushalten* at one end of the scale, and of capital accounting at the other. There are also very different organisational solutions, as the firm may be more or less integrated with or separated from the household, with a greater or lesser clash between institutionally based values.

Weber's discussion of the intermediate forms between *Haushalten* and *Erwerben* was echoed amongst German socialists in the Second International, where there were discussions over the family firm (Shanin, 1990). Some socialists - Engels and Kautsky being the most prominent - claimed that the small family firm was the starting point for capitalist accumulation. In the young Soviet Union, an agricultural economist, Chayanov, argued that Russian peasants were not accumulating capital. When peasant families had satisfied their needs, they stopped working, something they would not have done had they wanted to accumulate capital. The peasant economy was a non-capitalist alternative to capitalist accumulation. But Stalin supported the view of Kautsky and Engels. This was a misfortune both for Chayanov - who disappeared - and for the Russian peasants, who were collectivised. The hybrid forms of *Haushalten* and *Erwerben* were thus also central amongst Marxists when they developed the practical political consequences flowing from the institutional ambiguity of the hybrids that had been Weber's theoretical concern (see Figure 1.1).

Talcott Parsons wrote as a child of the times when economics and sociology had become distinct disciplines (see Figure 1.1). In picking up on Weber's theme of institutional differentiation, Parsons dispensed with many of Weber's ambiguities and dichotomies. This had implications for the way in which Parsons conceptualised the household economy relationship. Parsons was more positive towards modernity, at the same time as having a more unidimensional perspective on modernisation than Weber (Holton and Turner, 1986; Alexander, 1982). It was Parsons who translated Weber's books on economic theory into English. In his foreword to the English translation of Weber's *Wirtschaft und Gesellschaft*, Parsons only discusses the problem of the formal rationality of money in relation to the national level, however. Here, argues Parsons, the limitations of the formal rationality of money calculus are visible, because markets cannot provide for all needs. He goes on to discuss the possibility of a state level *Haushalten*, in terms of the modern social institutions of the welfare state. For Parsons, the dichotomy between *Haushalten* and *Erwerben* is supplemented with a third element, the redistributive state.

His sole reference to Weber's discussion of family firms - and the institutional contradictions of these firms - is as the 'classical individualistic capitalism of the nineteenth century'. This, Parsons claims, disappears with the 'corporate system of recent times' (Parsons, in Weber, 1947; 42). The corporate system of recent, modern times is *Erwerben* submitted to capital accounting and modern bureaucracy, while hybrid 'individualistic capitalism', including the family firm, belongs to the past. *Haushalten* too is dealt with as a thing of the past. This standpoint was later confirmed in Parsons' and Smelser's 1956 book *Economy and Society*, where family capitalism, and the significance of the family for economic organisation, is analysed purely as a nineteenth century phenomenon.

Parsons took Weber's institutional analysis of modernisation further, highlighting the progressive development of institutional differentiation. With institutional differentiation, various tasks which at one time had been taken care of inside the household, are handed over to other institutions. The economic institutions separated from the family are subjected to money calculus. The economy as a separate sphere is thus constructed historically as well as theoretically. Rational economic man is the result of cultural development. This confirms that the modern economy is populated by actors subjected to the formal rationality of money calculus, justifying the assumptions of maximising economic actors made by neo-classical economics. With modernity, a rationality achieved through institutional differentiation dominates. The institutional ambiguity so central to Weber has gone. It is only when rational actors go home that they suddenly become emotional, basing their relations on romantic love and biologically defined parental roles. (In economics, the New Household Economics also eliminates institutional ambiguity by assuming that the household maximises utility in the same way as any other economic institution.)

How then can order and integration between the economic and the social fields under this unidimensional modernity be achieved? It is in the book he wrote with Smelser, *Economy and Society* (1956) that Parsons undertook an analysis of the inter-relations between the economy and politics and the institutions promoting integration and stability, such as the household (Parsons and Smelser, 1956; Smelser and Swedberg, 1994). To Parsons, the central functional task for the economy was adaptation of the social system to its environment. The question for politics was goal attainment. Adaptation and goal attainment were differentiated from institutions providing for integration and pattern maintenance, such as the family. Perhaps Parsons and Smelser are then arguing that the economy can be looked at in isolation from the household? Not so.

Economy and Society discusses households in relation to both consumption and socialisation. First, the household is the income unit, receiving income from the economy. Parsons and Smelser therefore explicitly regard the household as central to any discussion of social stratification. However, the household also contributes to the economy through socialisation into occupational roles. This is done in two ways, both of which came from the value commitment of the man to his role as a 'good provider' for the needs and prestige of the household. The good provider is also socialised into a dedicated employee (Holton and Turner, 1986; 59-61). This transforms the Weberian conflict between *Haushalten* and *Erwerben* into harmony. In the modern world, where the man is the breadwinner, and the family depends on his income and status, the socialisation of men into the values of *Erwerben* becomes consistent with the needs of *Haushalten*.

But this consistency between *Haushalten* and *Erwerben* depends on a specific gender definition: the breadwinning man and the domestic housewife. In the years following the publication of Parsons and Smelser's book in 1956, such gender definitions were to be questioned, both in theory and practice. The notion of consistency between employee and firm is also at variance with much of the later literature on industrial relations, where the loyalty of the employee to the firm is questioned, following on from Braverman's classic text on *Labour and Monopoly Capital* (1974).

This question of strain between different institutional principles is central to the critique of Parsons. Parsons' emphasis on normative consensus leads to neglect of what Giddens calls disjunction, and conflict of institutional principles (Giddens, 1979; 1981). Disjunction or consensus is a hypothesis which can be tested empirically. The order which results from compromises between institutional principles is not given, but is rather an open, empirical question. In a world which is normatively disintegrated, actors construct new solutions.

What emerges as valuable from Parsons' and Smelser's analysis, is their insistence on the significance of the interrelations between institutions. In a modern, institutionally differentiated society, the interface between household and economy is centred round stratification and socialisation. This interface is, however, contingent upon specific gender definitions. Thus, the interrelation between changing gender definitions and institutional disjunction between household and economy is put on the agenda. Parsons and Smelser failed to recognise this contingency themselves, however, and so stand accused of favouring the order of the male breadwinner. The same is true of New Household Economists, where changing gender values are incorporated in an exogenously determined set of household values (the utility function), and so are not subject to investigation or question (see Wheelock and Oughton, 1996).

Meanwhile, the theory of institutional differentiation also found expression within the discipline of sociology itself, which was divided into different, specialised sub-disciplines. One of these sub-disciplines is family sociology (see Figure 1.1). Family sociologists regard the modern family as emptied of functions, and focus on the emotional aspects of family life, such as the emotional relations between gender and generations. Two Norwegian family sociologists, Holter and Aarseth, summarise the attitude of family sociology towards the economy of household as follows:

> In our culture, romantic love is the basis for the formation of households, and a main condition for the sustainability of the household. Houses may burn down and families may die, but the internal basis of family breakdown is absence of love.
> (Holter and Aarseth, 1993; 122, translated by Å.M.)

Analysis of the interrelations between household and economy is not of central concern to family sociologists. This derives from their use of family and household as synonyms. In anthropology, this is not the case. Anthropologists use family to describe social relations connected with kinship and marriage, while household describes activities related to dwelling, labour and economy. The division between tasks and teams is useful here (Rudie, 1969/70; Grønhaug, 1974; Löfgren, 1974; Yanagisako, 1979). In forming teams to handle tasks, the household also relates to other households, public services and communities. In the anthropological literature, the household is a flexible unit. It is not locked into a single set of task and team solutions, such as the male breadwinner-domestic housewife combination.

In anthropological theory, the relation between family reciprocity and market is discussed by Polanyi (1946). Polanyi introduced the idea of an interrelation between three modes of resource transfer: exchange, which takes place in the market; reciprocity, which refers to norms which define obligations; and redistribution of resources, carried out by some central authority (see Figure 1.1). Like Weber, Polanyi was concerned with the historical development of the market institution. For Polanyi, market and reciprocity are alternative institutional solutions, which can be combined in different ways.

This link between family reciprocity and economic restructuring surfaces in a different way in organisational theory. How can we understand firms as organisations? Coase led the way in encouraging economists to look at the firm as an economic institution, but approached this question from a different direction than Weber (Coase, 1937). While Weber was concerned with the dividing line between household and firm, Coase focused on the distinction between firm and market (see Figure 1.1). Coase, and his most prominent student, Williamson (1975; 1987) wanted to answer the question of why external markets with price mechanisms co-exist with the internal heirarchy of decision making in firms - 'the visible hand of management' as Chandler (1977) so graphically puts it. Williamson's answer is that firms are institutions which provide short cuts, or substitutes, for information in a way that makes the outcomes of individual decision making in markets more predictable, more stable. This is explained in terms of 'transaction costs'. A major example of the transaction costs that markets impose on those who use them, is the difficulties of regulating ongoing market relationships by means of contracts. For complete long-term contracts which cover all contingencies are costly to write. The transaction costs arising from drawing up and enforcing market contracts can be overcome by using governance structures internal to the firm instead.

Organisational economists therefore supplement fundamental economic concerns with individual choice with questions about *institutional* choice. For those who have been called 'new institutional' economists, the problem of institutional choice concerns whether activities should be mediated by markets, or carried out within firms, or indeed within households or governments. Opportunistic behaviour in the market - from wide boys, cowboy operators, criminal elements etc. - is limited through the operation of management hierarchies within firms and other institutions. The identity of economic agents becomes fundamental to many types of economic interactions. In the household, identity predominates, though it is also important in the market (Ben-Porath, 1980). It is the identity of your milkman as a trustworthy individual (or not!) that makes doing business with him and relying on him to deliver milk to your door possible, reducing risk. The advantages of the household derive from its ability to integrate activities with pre-existing, ongoing, significant personal relationships. The small number of economists who have recognised the significance of transactions costs to an analysis of the household, see the household as a governance structure (see Figure 1.1). In contrast, the neo-classical New Household Economics ignores the internal organisation and structure of families and households (Pollak, 1985) .

The theme of opportunism finally provoked a sociological response. The economically rational opportunist can be socialised when his or her actions are submitted to a societal institution. This door was opened by Granovetter's view that economic transactions are 'embedded' (Granovetter 1985; 1992) (see Figure 1.1). One of the empirical phenomena which Granovetter used to illustrate this was the Weberian in-between organisation, the family firm. Not only was the firm able to prevent opportunism, but so was the family. The concept of embedding showed how transactions take place in the context of societal institutions, such as families, socialising actors into trustworthy economic actors, and in that way providing protection against opportunism. This protection is given by norms, embedding, and thereby regulating, transactions.

Granovetter utilised theories from social anthropology in this analysis, in particular the Polanyian concept of reciprocity. The contribution a person makes in a reciprocal relation is that he or she will honour some kind of norm. A reciprocal relation is entered into on the presumption that at some stage the norm will provide certain rights in return. Perhaps rather oddly, Granovetter did not refer to Parsons' and Smelser's discussion of this point, nor did he refer to Weber's classic discussion. Instead, he imported a concept from the theory from social anthropology into sociological theory. Granovetter provides a route for linking micro- and macro-issues, for the family once more becomes a central institution in understanding economic development, particularly through the study of family firms and small firm development. In Granovetter's family firms, it is family reciprocity that is used to organise economic activity.

This rekindling of interest in family firms has led to important investigations of the phenomenon in several parts of the world (Granovetter, 1992). It has reopened one of the paths which Weber discussed as an intermediate form, between *Erwerben* and *Haushalten*. Parsons' claim just after the Second World War that individualistic capitalism was an exclusively nineteenth century phenomenon has being brought back into question in the 1990s. Even though Granovetter makes no reference to Weber, he reopens the Weberian question of the submission of firms to a set of values which can be different from those of capital accumulation.

'New economic sociology', as it has been called, thus reopens the path closed off by *Economy and Society*. However, there is still some way to go before the path is cleared. In *The Handbook of Economic Sociology*, edited by Smelser and Swedberg (1994), a whole part discusses 'intersections of the economy', yet there is no chapter on either the household or the family there. Paradoxically, in the chapter on 'Gender and the Economy', Milkman and Townsley point out how gender research is ghettoised and not integrated in economic sociology:

> It is insufficient to simply acknowledge the presence of women or of gender inequality in economic institutions and processes. The ways in which those institutions and processes constantly reproduce gender relations, and are reproduced by them, must be analysed and theorised as well.
> (Milkman and Townsley, in Smelser and Swedberg, 1994; 614).

An important statement! It is surely surprising then that, in a book edited by Smelser and Swedberg in the mid-nineties, a theme which was central to Parsons and Smelser back in 1956 - the interrelation between gender socialisation in the household and economic change - is not tackled. This is all the more surprising because the new perspectives on economic change which we spell out in the next section make the relations between gender, household and the economy into a vital and promising field of investigation (Ellingsaether, 1995)[1]. Our aim in this book is to develop and build upon the tools of institutional analysis that Weber first used to draw sociology and economics back together. Let us continue the story of how the remarriage of economics and sociology can be effected.

Approaches to deregulation and economic change: where is the household?

In this section we follow those who start from a macro-perspective on the economic organisation of production and consumption in industry, services and agriculture. We draw together some of the theoretical and empirical literature which points towards the need for a set of micro-foundations for such a macro-perspective, based in an understanding of the household.

Economic change has led to analyses which reject simple models of modernisation and growth. Ideas of regulatory regimes, incorporating political dimensions, were reintroduced to explain the economic crises which surfaced in the 1970s. Aglietta (Aglietta, 1979) argued that post-war prosperity had been based on a system of monopolistic regulation, where large-scale enterprise relied on a process of capital intensive accumulation for its profits. This involved raising the productivity of labour by applying Taylorist principles of scientific management. There was also emphasis on mass production of goods for which economies of scale were possible, often known as Fordism. Mass production led to a sustained rise in the productivity of labour, with a consequent renewal of the opportunities for investment. Within such a framework it is possible to argue that by the early seventies the regime of intensive accumulation had come to an end, and that capital responded with a set of post-Fordist techniques to control the labour process. The end of this regime of intensive accumulation was both a cause, and a reflection, of the destruction of the post-war international economic order based on US hegemony (Aglietta, *op.cit*), of which the oil crisis of 1973 was but one indicator (Armstrong, Glyn and Harrison, 1991).

Subsequent to regulation theory, theories of flexibilisation, post-Fordism, flexible specialisation, and other sources of entrepreneurship and innovation, were put forward. Guides to 'possibilities of prosperity' - to quote a subtitle from 1984 - were in high demand. The concepts of Fordism and post-Fordism refer to different regimes of accumulation, where different markets, defined through regulations, establish dominating strategies of production. Post-Fordism refers to deregulation and privatisation, and attenuation of the welfare state. There is also increasing differentiation in consumption patterns, and hence in markets too. This differentiation of markets necessitates new production strategies: increasing flexibility in production, flattening of industrial hierarchies and increasing emphasis on small firm strategies.

Such strategies are directed towards niche production where networks of craft based, innovative small firms replace the old giants of the Fordist area. Industrial districts (Brusco, 1982; Piore and Sabel, 1984) are regional production systems where producers adapt to the new markets through new and constantly changing niche products. The flexibly specialised firms of these networks enjoy the advantages of regional competition - and cooperation with similar firms.

Italy was seen as one country leading in the process of increasing production flexibility. During the 1970s, modern, industrial Italy witnessed a breakdown of large scale, modern industrial organisation, and a resurgence of the artisani craft based firm, often organised on a family basis. Artisani are an in-between form. The first Italian analysis of the phenomenon of industrial districts, thick with artisani, dates back to 1979 (Bagnasco, 1981). In English, the phenomenon was discussed by Brusco in 1982 (Brusco, 1982), and picked up on by Piore and Sabel in their 1984 book, which had the ambitious title of *The Second Industrial Divide* (Piore and Sabel, 1984). Economies of flexible specialisation, where craft based small firms organised cooperative production systems, were out-competing the old dinosaurs of industrial organisation, large-scale corporations. The competitive edge of flexibly specialised firms was based on a Schumpeterian logic of innovation, where it was claimed that cooperative, flexibly specialised small firms were able to adapt to niche markets. Unlike the Chayanovian peasants of pre-revolutionary Russia - and indeed of southern Italy - the innovative, northern Italian artisani were both clearly dynamic, and undoubtedly capitalist. Artisani households were submitted to the needs of the firm, and not the other way around.

If we go inside the flexibly specialised firms of Sabel and Piore, we find actors who are enjoying the advantages which Weber found in craft based industry, with strong elements of *Haushalten* incorporating a unity between control and knowledge. To Sabel and Piore, the craftsperson regains control, because his or her networks with other craftspeople are beyond the control of the owners of capital, based as they are on the innovative capacity of these networks. In an economy where market differentiation reduces the importance of advantages of scale and of standardised products, the capacity to innovate niche products becomes the name of the game. In such an economy, knowledge regains control. Ownership becomes uninteresting, because industrial development depends simply on the dynamics of networks of skilled people. Sabel and Piore rediscovered one of the Weberian dilemmas of the formal character of money calculus, the dilemma of the separation of knowledge from control. The hero of their theory is the skilled, specialised craftsperson who wrenches control from the hierarchy of submission to money owners. The craftsperson does this through the capacity to be flexible, a capacity which depends upon this blurred specification.

In the heated debate that followed, the claim for a new general theory of development was rejected. It became apparent that industrial districts were not to be found everywhere (Asheim, 1993; Amin and Thrift, 1994a,b; Zeitlin, 1994). In later contributions (Glimstedt, 1993; Sabel and Zeitlin, n.d.), Sabel modified the 1984 thesis to argue that craft based, innovative flexible specialisation may be an important alternative strategy, but that it relies upon certain institutional conditions which may not always be present. So, whilst the generality of flexible specialisation is highly debatable, institutional theory remains of growing importance among economists. One important reason for this interest is the character of contemporary processes of economic restructuring. Empirical reality is opening up a number of questions which cannot be readily answered within the framework of the old disciplinary assumptions (Smelser, 1995).

It is interesting to realise that the household preconditions for flexible specialisation were not considered by Sabel and Piore. In contrast, the connection between regulation, production and household is central in the debate on Fordism and post-Fordism among rural sociologists. Here, the point of departure is the national and international regulation of food markets. National level deregulation, the development of more liberal global food trade through the General Agreement on Trade and Tariffs (GATT) and regional international food markets (such as the European Union market defined by the Common Agricultural Policy) for example, open up a productivist line of development. The international food trade, dominated by a large-scale Fordist food industry, is seen as pushing hybrid family farms and firms aside. This means that the relation between family farming and capital accumulation is a central theme for policy (e.g. Redclift and Whatmore, 1990; Whatmore, Lowe and Marsden, 1991).

Post-Fordist tendencies connected with niche food markets, as well as post-productivist strategies based on new ways of diversifying production (for example, through tourism, ecological niche products, variation in land use, micro-markets) create a framework of variety. Norwegian food policy, with its national food market (Almås, 1990), forms a laboratory where *Haushalten*, and the capacity to integrate small-scale farming with other jobs in a household economy, assumes a central position. Norwegian farming is based on the farm household's capacity to combine various sources of income from different industries - and from the public sector (Brox, 1966, 1986; Seierstad, 1985).

The debate over a transition between Fordism and post-Fordism is also concerned with consumption. Intensive accumulation in the post-war period went along with a transformation of the conditions of existence of the wage earning class. Mass consumption of standardised goods was maintained by a Keynesian welfare policy, where strong unions cooperated with large scale industry. The consumers of these standardised goods are households, enjoying high levels of employment, social security and rising wage levels.

There are several views of the effect of the changing patterns of consumption on the household economy. The first looks at the growth of mass consumption and the 'commodification' (an awkward term, which implies the extension of the purchase of commodities on the market) this entails. Such a view sees the progressive displacement of the family as a unit of production and its increasing importance as a unit of consumption. Women entering the labour market have a significant effect on demand because they boost family incomes and purchase labour-saving consumer durables.

Gershuny (1978), in contrast, argues that the growth of the service economy, which seems to be part and parcel of changing consumption patterns, is more accurately the expansion of a self-service economy. Households purchase consumer durables and undertake the service function of, say, washing, at home using a washing machine, instead of going out to a launderette. Such an argument runs counter to the commodification argument. Gershuny's model of socio-technical innovation - the use of capital goods in the household, rather than the purchase of their services in the market - is useful in that it links the household to the process of accumulation, though Gershuny himself does not examine gender implications of his model.

Deregulation impacts not only on industrial structure, organisation and innovative dynamics, but also on consumption. These economic changes, both in rural and urban areas, have a deep impact on, and in many cases also depend upon, how flexibly the household can organise itself. The ways of organising the new flexible economy are not, as Parsons and Smelser thought back in 1956, reducible to some remnant of the nineteenth century which can be overlooked or forgotten. It nevertheless remains the case that in most of the post-Fordist literature, there is little or no interest in the significance of the household for the processes which it describes and analyses. The household is more explicitly addressed by people concerned with the informal economy and consumption, to whom we now turn for guidance on how to integrate micro- and macro-perspectives.

Recognising and locating the household: seeing the whole economy

Most models of economic change concern themselves with the formal economy, in a context which makes only minor modifications to maximising economic man as the fundamental actor. The household becomes identified purely as a site for consumption, and attention focuses on exchange relations in the market, rather than reciprocal or cooperative relations in household based networks. The view that the household is no longer concerned with production is buttressed by national income statistics which make no attempt to measure the domestic and caring work that goes on in households. Yet this work maintains the current and future workforce, and is essential to the production of human capital (Folbre, 1994; O'Hara, 1995). The statisticians are therefore hiding the important production role of women within the household, since it is predominantly women who undertake these forms of work (Waring, 1989).

In this book, we argue that an holistic approach which incorporates the household, and a consequently broader view of economic motivation will provide a more fruitful analysis. This section shows how the household as an institution plays an essential role if we are to gain a view of the whole economy - including hybrid or in-between organisations - and its changing activities. This view needs to incorporate the informal, or complementary economy, as well as the formal economy, where Ray Pahl's study of household behaviour in *Divisions of Labour* on the Isle of Sheppy in southern England was an influential starting point (Pahl, 1984).

It is particularly by examining the economic character of the household, and developing an understanding of its moral economy, that we can investigate the borders between the formal and the complementary. Such an examination asks how

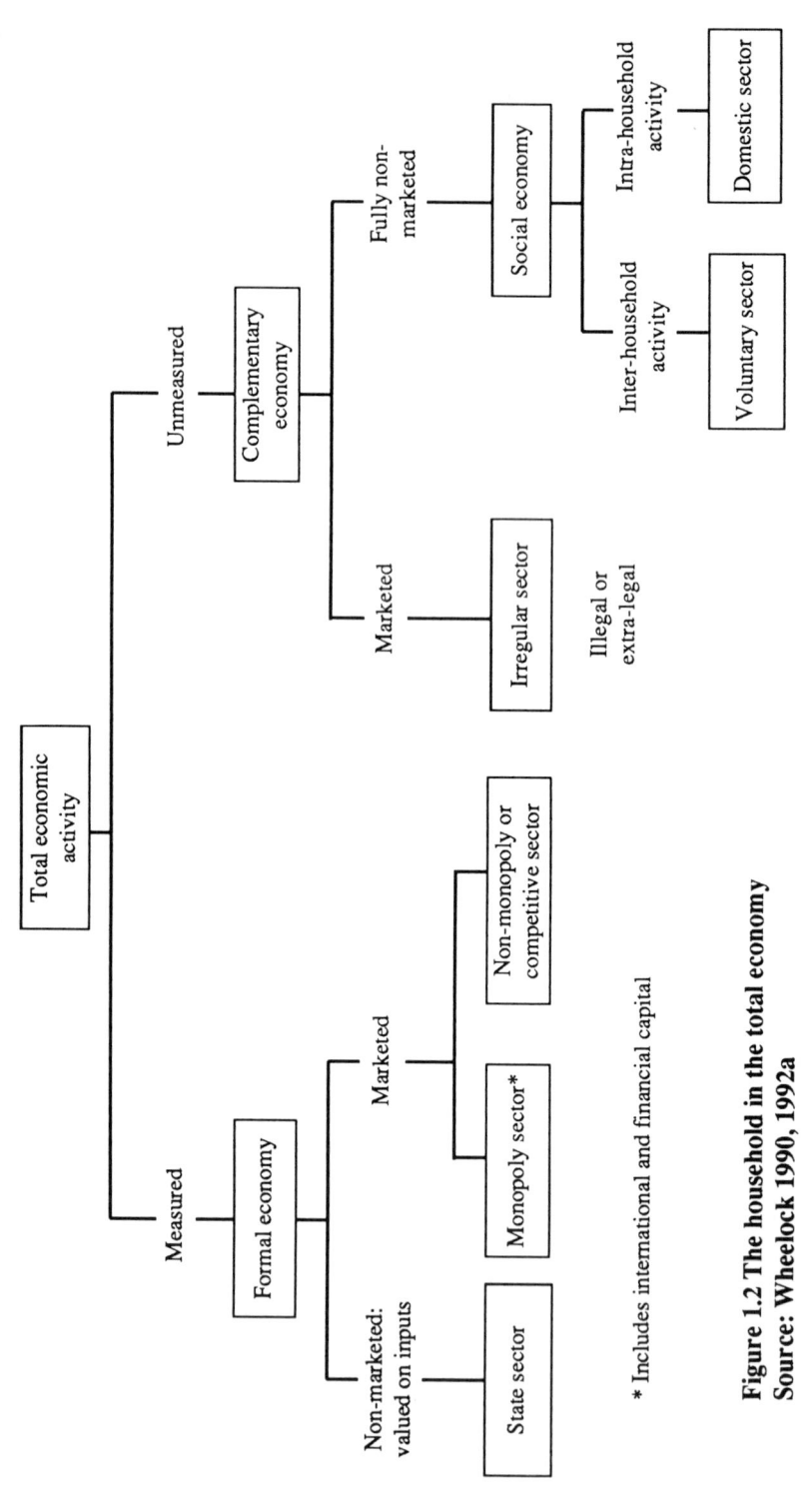

Figure 1.2 The household in the total economy
Source: Wheelock 1990, 1992a

the household both reflects the institutional values of society, and creates its own institutional values, through consumption and production activies. It provides the link between how individual households sustain themselves, and the maintenance or growth of the macro-economy. It is of critical importance in understanding the process of economic change and development. The household lies at the heart of the transformation of institutional structures relating to the reproduction of labour power, the family. It is a vital link between the reproduction and accumulation of capital, as well as for the ways people define and redefine gender roles.

How can the complementary relationship between formal and informal be understood? Broadly speaking, the division between the formal and the complementary economy follows the line between measured and unmeasured economic activity. Formal economic activity is recorded in the national income accounts (Smith, 1986). But just as the formal economy has two sectors, one private and marketed and the other a non-marketed state sector, so too does the complementary economy (see Figure 1.2). These are the marketed irregular sector and the non-marketed social economy. The output of the social economy is not sold on the market, and its labour is unpaid. The institutions of the social economy are self-generated informal ones, which operate independently of regular economic institutions. There are essentially two sorts of institutional relations in the social economy: intra-household relations and inter-household ones.

Within the household sector, work for self-consumption for the family unit takes place. As Mingione (1985) and others (e.g. Pahl, 1984) have suggested, household work can be broken down into domestic work, consisting of housework and caring; and extra self-consumption. Extra self-consumption can be distinguished by the fact that although these goods and services could be purchased on the market, the work is actually done within the household on an unpaid basis. In the voluntary sector, work is also unpaid, but this time it is undertaken between households. It can consist of what Bulmer (1986) aptly calls 'neighbouring', or of self-help or voluntary work. Extra self-consumption may also be transferred from the individual household and undertaken on an inter-household basis. In addition, the child care and other caring functions of domestic work may be partly transferred to the voluntary sector on an unpaid basis. Households are flexible organisations where various tasks may be given to different teams.

Whilst it may not always be easy to draw the boundaries between the voluntary and the irregular sectors, a feature of the latter is that its output is marketed. What distinguishes it from the formal economy is its institutional framework as either illegal or extra-legal. The boundaries of the irregular economy are flexible over time, because they are defined by changing social attitudes as codified in changes in the law. The irregular sector of the complementary marketed economy together with the self-employed sector of the formal marketed economy make up a petty competitive sector, where the small scale of the activities distinguishes it from monopoly and non-monopoly sectors.

The complementary sector is neither parasitic nor residual. It operates in the interstices of formal institutions, not as an alternative society but as a complementary economic activity to the formal. So, for example, while the state and the private sector within the formal economy may have taken on some aspects of the production and reproduction of labour power (such as education, training, pension provision and health), the household sector still retains much of its responsibility here. The boundary between the formal economy and the household sector is established in how production decisions within the household are made. The household thus enacts a set of activities which are complementary to the formal, money economy.

Household work strategies provide the interface between the formal and the informal economies. The household, as the unit of reproduction, must apply its working activities to earning and to directly supplying goods and services through self-consumption. The individuals within a household negotiate or otherwise decide a balance between work for income and for self-consumption. These decisions are made in the light of social and economic changes brought about by economic restructuring, which may alter the gender divisions of labour within the household. (For further details see Wheelock, 1992a.) But what of the empirical reality of the impact of economic change - whether global or local - on households? It is to this different interpretation of the relationship between the micro and the macro, as that between the local and the global, that we finally turn.

Changing livelihoods and meanings: global and local

To Weber, *Haushalten* and *Erweben* were ideal types, theoretical constructions intended to throw light on a mixed and changing reality. In Parson's interpretation, modernisation - conceived as a one-way route to institutional differentiation which empties the household of functions - became a paradigmatic dogma, leaving key empirical phenomena in darkness. Thus for Parsons, the gender division of labour in the household was taken as given. But any post-war west European ideal of a male breadwinner supporting his children and a non-working wife is far from the reality of today. Indeed, Mingione (1991) suggests that a single wage being enough to support a household has been the historical exception.

Edwards *et al.* (1985) propose three historical phases in livelihood patterns since the Industrial Revolution. The earliest phase saw proletarianisation, and the indiscriminate employment of women and children. There was however, persistence of productive household systems (based on agricultural, craft or putting-out activities for example) with family wage systems. Hard times may bring shifts from the latter to the former. Smith and Wallerstein (1992) show evidence for this in their historical studies of changing householding patterns.

The second, homogenisation phase involved the abolition of child labour, a decrease in the employment of women, and the creation of domestic work within working-class households. The male breadwinner was adopted as a trade union ideal, with wage demands based on claims for a family wage. The third, segmentation phase, sees a marked return to the employment of married women, as well as the growth of a structural surplus population and a return to informal ways of working. This phase is partly conditioned by the availability of the services of a welfare state to lighten women's domestic load, and the contradictions arising from sexual discrimination, where women are paid less than men.

Combinations of economic and demographic change thus encourage a growing heterogeneity of livelihood strategies. The patterns of reproduction for individual households become prone to difficulties of survival at particular stages of the family life cycle. These include when the husband-father is the only one earning a sufficient wage whilst there are children in the household. This may become more marked when teenage children find difficulty in getting jobs, but are caught up in conspicuous consumption. Households with long-term unemployed adult children will also face problems. If the husband-father is unemployed when there are dependent children, wives are unlikely to be unable to earn 'breadwinner' levels of wages in replacement. Households of lone mothers face low female wages and inadequate welfare provisions. Elderly households may be affected by declining welfare provisions.

Indeed, it would seem that the links between employment patterns and patterns of social reproduction have been destabilised throughout the developed world, and that they are now moving to Third World patterns. Evidence suggests that both the western European family wage system combined with secondary wages and welfare state provisioning, and the eastern European and socialist system of low wages, high employment and basic welfare are giving way to persistently low wages combined with informal sources of livelihood (see Mingione, 1991).

But how do changing livelihoods affect lives? Economists have tended, for the sake of analytical convenience, to make hard distinctions between production and consumption, and more recently, this approach has also been adopted by sociologists studying consumption. Part of the reason for this arises from the failure to look inside the household. Changing sources of household livelihoods indicate that in the real world production and consumption are closely interconnected, where unpaid activities in particular bridge any hard and fast distinction between the two. For consumption involves work. This production facet is easily ignored because the work of consumption is hidden within the household, performed as it is on an unpaid basis, largely by women.

We have already seen that those taking part in the Fordism-post-Fordism debate are aware of the macro-links between changing structures of production and consumption, and of qualitative changes in consumption patterns. Economists since the *Methodenstreit* have only rarely paid attention to the interconnections between production and consumption at the micro-level. What is more, it is only quantitative changes in overall levels of consumption that have interested them, not qualitative changes. J.M. Keynes (1936) opened up the study of macro-economics by focusing attention on consumption in households, and quantifying their propensity to consume or save the income they received. A whole generation of policy makers became concerned with how well oiled the wheels of buying were (Fine and Leopold, 1993), and the household was simply a black box where consumption activities were located. Galbraith was a maverick economic voice when he talked of the affluent society, and of women as a crypto-servant class managing consumption (Galbraith, 1975).

The production role of households disappeared almost without trace until Gary Becker opened the black box with his New Household Economics, by pointing out that the household was more than a unit of production because it also produced human capital, bringing up children and nurturing adults (Becker, 1965). Becker, however, was heavily criticised by socialist feminists for not dealing with power and authority within the household and therefore being unable to deal with gender. During the 1970s some of those involved in the Marxist inspired domestic labour debate argued that the 'production for use' (unpaid domestic and caring consumption or work) that went on inside the household was as exploitative as the 'production for exchange' going on in the labour market. Whilst men performed surplus labour in the workplace and were therefore exploited by capitalists, women performed surplus labour in the home exploited by their menfolk. (For a full exploration of these issues see Close and Collins, 1985.)

In sociology, simplistic economistic views of ways of life based on production were being overthrown in favour of a post-modern approach. The analysis of consumption came to the fore as part of a wider debate on post-modernity, with a movement from a focus on production work roles to identity. Consumption is then not so much based on any already existing set of needs; it is an active engagement in creating and maintaining a sense of identity. Beck (1992), coming as he does from a background of family and industrial sociology, poses the contradictions between life and work under what he calls 'reflexive modernity' in a stark light. This most recent phase of socio-economic development sets people free from the certainties and modes of living of the industrial epoch, giving people the opportunity to actively (and 'reflexively') shape their lives. This has its down side. Competition and mobility are needed for production, with labour markets requiring that individuals 'get on their bikes'. This contradicts household and neighbourhood reliance on sacrifice and collective values. The market turns people into self-providers, while work within the household means dependence. The ultimate market society requires everyone to be free, and so it must be a childless society, argues Beck.

As with other analyses of post-modernism, Beck sees reflexive modernity as a capitalism without classes, though one in which there are inequalities. This redefines inequalities as individually determined. Folbre (1994) is not so naive. With Beck, she accepts that economic change makes gender (and race) discrimination increasingly illogical. However, any strategy that seeks equal rights for women, also encourages women to develop masculine preferences. She argues that if class and race inequalities are not tackled, child care and teaching will only be undertaken by men and women from disadvantaged strata, acting as domestic servants in public and private institutions.

The idea of the household as a 'moral economy' (Thompson, 1971) highlights the importance of the interactions between consumption and production. The moral economy of the household derives on the one hand from its nature as a social, cultural and economic unit actively engaged in the consumption of objects and the creation of meaning (Silverstone and Hirsch, 1992). The function of consumption is to make sense for people by presenting a set of meanings that are coherent and intentional, creating a world of values. But the household does not consume in a vacuum. Its moral economy is also based on a set of social relations which establishes mutual obligations to help members to survive.

Household work strategies promote welfare and social mobility within the

Perspectives on the household in a changing economy   33

household, while income strategies distribute benefits between household members. Changing technology also plays a role in forming household values, which may in turn affect work and income strategies. Through its moral economy the household links the production, consumption and distribution activities of its members. This moral economy is based upon a value system which both draws upon, and affects society's wider value system. However, norms and values are not utilities which can be easily replaced as times change. It is because the neo-classical New Household Economics is not concerned to question the origins of utility, taking norms and values as given, that the model of the household that it puts forward is not very useful when it comes to analysing the effects of economic change (Wheelock and Oughton, 1996).

Norms and values may be specific to localities. Household and work are closely connected by space. Usually, work takes place near employees' homes, at a distance which makes it possible to travel there and back in a day. These time-space paths of people commuting back and forth create patterns and localities, which tend to be relatively stable over time. In these localities, we find different types of household-work interconnections, where household adaptations and workplace characteristics are closely integrated. The themes of stratification and socialisation discussed by Parsons and Smelser are observable here, as characteristics of a space which is segmented by the specific household-work interrelations of the locality. Among geographers, industrial sociologists and urban sociologists, the significance of these interrelations to the development of localities or communities with specialised work cultures and labour markets is a long-standing area of study. Among rural sociologists, the relation between different agricultural or agro-industrial specialisation and organisational structures in agriculture and households are recognised as important. The notion of 'community', where society and space are interconnected, is central in sociology, though also disputed.

Recently, the literature on 'modernity' has led to increased interest in the global-local dimension in identity construction, resulting from increased worldwide communication. The Weberian German Protestant and Granovetter's Italian artisani were local phenomena, protected against each other by the once safe walls of physical distance. In an age of global electronic communication, increased migration and cheap air travel, physical distance loses importance. The rural-urban distinction is questioned: are not rural areas in fact integrated in urban space? Another area where local space is discussed, is in relation to the national level. As pointed out by Porter (Porter, 1992) and others, national regulations, national infrastructure development programs and national policies in general, may be important in shaping industrial and innovation networks. Space is shaped by national regulations and policies, through which specific interlocking combinations of household and production are constructed. One example of this is the case of the nationalised Norwegian agriculture, considered in Chapter 9.

The contemporary anthropological and sociological literature on modernisation is concerned with the effects of increased self reflection (reflexivity) and - thereby - increased fluidity in identity construction and reconstruction (Giddens, 1990; 1991; 1994b). Local identity is no longer protected by the lines of defence of tradition as tacit and shared - but unspoken. We live in an increasingly globalised culture. The notion of stable local interrelations between household and economy can thus be brought into question. The order of community is disputed.

What then is left of these interconnections? In the introduction, we used the allegory of rules of small and big games to introduce the theme of institutional analysis. Are the small local games breaking up as a result of the big games of global culture? Indeed, there is no doubt that small games are breaking down all the time. However, we would like to think that Giddens is right in insisting on the significance of face-to-face discourse as a basis for interpreting institutional transformation. We do not just assimilate the icons transmitted to us through TV, video, internet and all the other electronic media, we also interpret these signs in face-to-face discussions. These discussions take place in the household, and in other local places. What we should be looking for in times of economic and cultural change, then, is not only the dissolution of local culture, but also its reconstruction.

The remarriage: replacing the old order of the male breadwinner?

To Weber, the distinction between *Haushalten* and *Erwerben* was never a one-dimensional classification of historical periods. It was rather a dilemma, with different and contingent results. The household was capable of organising work in a different way from that of the modern, formal organisation. To Parsons, however, the household was differentiated from the modern organisation, as far as the organisation of work was concerned. The family or household had stopped organising production by the end of the nineteenth century. The remaining interchanges between household and economy were:

- wages, which, as an input to the household, were connected with stratification
- motivation of the male breadwinner, as a dedicated employee with a responsibility to his household
- socialisation of boys into the role of male breadwinners/dedicated employees

It was through these interchanges that household and economy made different contributions to the same, objective, order. This order was mediated and strengthened by locality, where specified interconnections of socio-economic strata and socialisation were 'locked up' in local cultures.

The old order, as described in theories of 'simple modernisation', is lost. This means that economic change cannot simply be studied as a pure 'macro' phenomenon. In order to understand economic change, we must understand what is happening at the micro-level, where people, as indicated above, relate to household and work in new ways, to recreate some kind of new order. In the attempts that people make, however, gender becomes central. Thus we need to investigate the significance of gender to contemporary economic change.

- Changing stratification. People - and households - moving up and

down the social ladder, as, for example, some are fired, others retire or yet others gain from the change.
- Changing gender roles, as men's and women's position in the labour market, and on the domestic scene, alters.
- Changing life plans which challenge identities, as habits of socialisation in the household are rendered invalid. Children cannot be socialised into a labour market with gender identities which are no longer available.
- Changing the organisation of work, as the labour market becomes more flexible and the informal economy more important. The household comes back on stage to organise production, either through delivering flexible labour, or by organising production within the household itself.
- Changing culture, as local culture breaks down and is reinterpreted through global symbols, culture often takes new directions.

This link between micro and macro cannot be made if analysis remains locked within single disciplines. The interrelations between household and economy must be reconstructed along institutionalist lines.

Notes

1. Ellingsaether makes a strong case against what she calls the 'dualistic paradigm' of gender research, where the female world is conceived as different from the masculine one. 'The theoretical premise of a shared female life world has resulted in a theoretical understanding of women as an invariant gender category' (Ellingsaether, 1995, 48). Instead, Ellingsaether argues for 'a better comprehension of the dynamic change of gender categories' (ibid. 359). We very much agree, and take such an approach as given. This book takes the proper object of study as gender categories (and practices), in the context of which female and male lifeworlds should be seen.

CHAPTER 2

BEHIND THE LACE CURTAINS[1]

Elizabeth Oughton, Jane Wheelock and Agnete Wiborg

States, markets and households

In this chapter we seek to develop an economics of the household. We aim to do this through first identifying the social, political and economic contexts of the household and secondly by examining the household itself as an institution. From an institutional perspective it is possible to imagine the economic, social and political environments as related and mutually affecting contexts which are associated with a common knowledge and understanding of behaviour. Such institutional patterns of behaviour are not necessarily formalised, for example as encompassed by legislation, but may often be encoded in common practice. Each environment is subject to change, though change may take place at a different pace in each of them. As a regulatory power the state influences the relative significance of these different environments and the nature and pace of change within them.

What we are witnessing at the present time is very rapid change in the economic environment. In contrast with rational choice models of economic behaviour where economic actors make instantaneous responses to changing circumstances, institutionalists emphasise the way in which institutions create and reinforce habits of action and thought. As Hodgson (1994) points out, this does not mean that institutions are immutable, but it is important 'to see socio-economic development as periods of institutional continuity punctuated by periods of crisis and more rapid development' (p 26). What interests us in this book is to understand the complex interaction between stasis and change, for purposive behaviour in the household will be guided by habits of thought as well as by rational calculations.

In Chapter 1 we argued that economic restructuring initiates processes of change at the household level. The household itself is an institution in that it is a way of organising relations between people to provision and support their day-to-day existence. The recognition of who constitutes the household will also be culturally specific. Households survive on the basis of inputs from each of three circuits:

purchased goods and services from the market circuit, services and goods from the state circuit and unpriced goods and services from the domestic circuit, usually produced within the household itself. Each circuit also requires inputs of labour from the household, but each individual may provide different sorts and amounts of labour input to the three circuits. These issues can be represented in a production, reproduction and consumption cloverleaf as in Figure 2.1. The diagram puts the household and the individuals in it at the centre of the three production circuits that are essential for the functioning of any economy: market production, non-market production and state production.

One of the issues that the diagram highlights is that it may be more important to try to understand how domestic commodity production has been transformed by the extension of market relations, rather than how it has survived commoditisation. The process of production is not then just seen in terms of capital accumulation but broadened to include the processes of consumption and livelihood, where production and reproduction are integrated (Whatmore, 1991). This means that personal relations and meanings must be included too, which is precisely what the empirical studies in Part III aim to demonstrate. Gender and generation are key factors affecting status and personal relations. Both are affected by the dynamics of the external environments, but equally interpretations of gender and generation roles are endogenously developed.

Representing economic activity in this cloverleaf form highlights the fact that economic agents within the household are wearing a number of different hats in turn, and that for the household to survive and prosper, all three circuits are necessary. It is possible that production activities can shift between one circuit and another. Despite these possibilities for substitution, it remains important that the circuits are complementary to each other; all three are required to provide for the consumption needs of the household. In Northern Europe people have come to expect support from the state circuit and over time in the household lifecycle the state may contribute to consumption in different ways, whether through the provision of education, old age pensions or other forms of consumption support. The changing role of the state as provider of livelihood insurance and an income safety net is explored in Chapter 3 through a comparison of British and Norwegian policies.

The cloverleaf reminds us that people, and the human capital they incorporate, cannot be produced either by markets or the state. 'Successful economic development is not a simple function of competitive markets, but the product of a balance between individual and collective incentives in both production and social reproduction'. (Folbre, 1994; 88). Indeed the household has a vital role to play in maintaining and reproducing human capital for this and the next generation. The kind of social democracy found in both Britain and Norway distributes the cost of social reproduction by providing support for education, family allowances, health care and so on. Nevertheless, the costs of children to individual parents far outweigh the economic benefits, in part because younger workers - also parents - are taxed to support the old (Folbre, 1994).

The diagram also provides a reminder that the motivations for the behaviour of individuals active in each circuit may differ. In the market circuit, economic agents

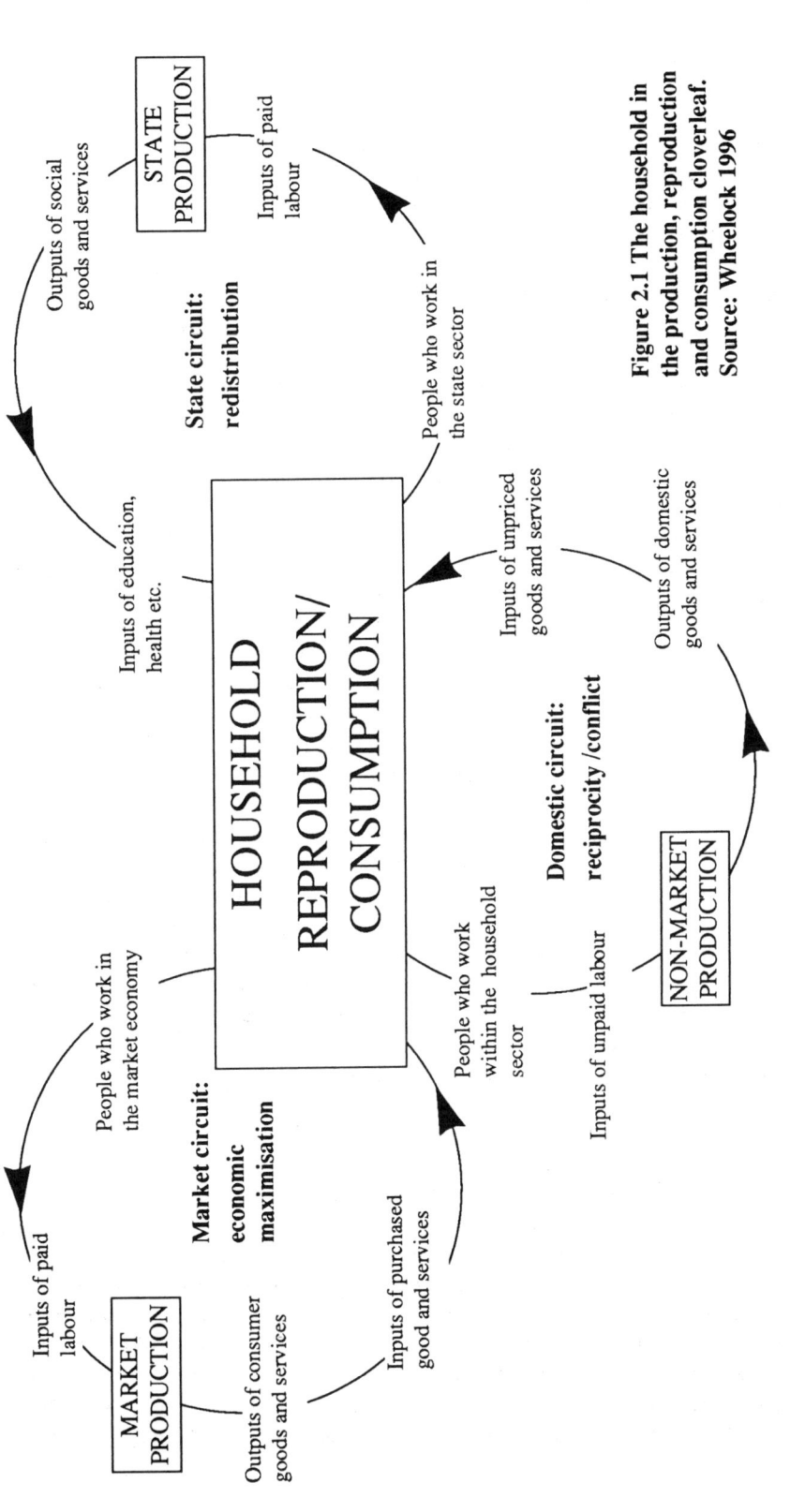

Figure 2.1 The household in the production, reproduction and consumption cloverleaf.
Source: Wheelock 1996

behave, in the main, to maximise their economic benefits. This is in line with the predominant stream of thought in economics which follows Adam Smith in seeing the 'propensity to truck, barter and exchange' as a basic economic motivation. Here, the conflicting interests of self-seeking individuals are harmonised through the market mechanism. In the domestic circuit, where economic agents are living together in households, actions are likely to be based on some form of cooperation. Economic anthropologists call this reciprocity, where the obligation to give, receive and return is a mode of integrating the inherent opposition between the self and the other. Such reciprocity will be tempered by power relations. Finally, in the state circuit, the motivation is that public services and goods should be redistributed between households and individuals in line with need.

The interrelations between the individual values of the market and the associative or collective values of the national and local state, trade unions etc. have long been recognised. They are incorporated in arguments about the desirability of promoting choice or coercion, efficiency or exploitation, through relatively greater emphasis on state or market circuits as the most appropriate institutions through which to orchestrate growth and development. That the forces regulating economic and social change and development cannot be understood in economic terms alone was recognised by Polanyi (1946) amongst others. Folbre takes this further when she points out that the cooperative values of the household sector - predominantly female values of love, rescue of life, nurturing and so on - are also regulations of society at large (Folbre, 1994), and not simply of the household. Networks of reciprocity limit market tensions, but they also absorb them in a way that is not done by associative regulatory systems (Mingione, 1991).

Shifts from one circuit of the cloverleaf to another have important implications for the structure of an economy and for its institutional foundations, and it is worth being aware of changes in the relative weight of different sectors if we are to fully understand economic behaviour. For there is not only the possibility of macro-economic shifts between circuits. Individuals within households may participate in more than one circuit and may also move between circuits. Indeed, changes in the economic structure may in turn influence what individuals do. For example, when men become unemployed, they may take on more domestic and child care responsibilities, relieving their employed wives of some of these tasks (see Chapter 7).

We have now reached a point where we need to look at some of the issues raised so far in more detail. The literature provides a whole variety of theoretical and operational definitions of the household. We discuss some of the issues surrounding the identification and definition of the household in next section of this chapter. Because this book is concerned with the influence of economic change on households, what we need for our purposes is a dynamic definition. Actors reorganise their daily lives to be able to cope with new conditions, and structural and institutional conditions are imposed upon them from the outside. What do we mean when we say that actors reorganise household activities as a result of economic restructuring? The question of household change must be seen at two levels. First there is the level of the actors, who are trying to cope in changing conditions, and this is discussed in the third section. Such adaptations are often seen in terms of household work strategies. The deeper waves of institutional transformation, where power relations and definitions of gender are transformed, are examined in the fourth section. In the penultimate section we look particularly at the factors influencing the ways in which households anticipate and accommodate the future.

Identifying the household

The household is the locus for a number of sets of relations: family, conjugal and economic. The processes that affect people's lives most directly - work and consumption - take place at the household level. The household is the place where decisions about these processes are taken, in turn affecting people's lives and livelihoods. From the theoretical point of view an understanding of the extent to which, and the way in which, 'some resources are managed and claimed collectively, if not equitably' (Evans, 1991) must take place at this level. From the point of view of the policy maker, the household may also be important for defining structural parameters, access to resources and socio-economic position. However, the use of the household as the focus for the analysis of economic behaviour is not without its difficulties. We need to be able to identify and define the household theoretically and to operationalise the concept in practice. In this section of the chapter we outline a working definition that will underpin the empirical studies reported in the second part of this book.

In Chapter 1 a distinction between household and family was made: the household is described in terms of activity, while the family is based on a social relationship. Studies of family relations do not relate the organisation of tasks within the household to political and economic processes outside the household. The household is based on function. Such an approach is supported in anthropological studies in which household is distinguished from family (Keesing, 1976; Yanagisako, 1979; Gullestad, 1985). 'Household' is related to aspects of family life to do with economy, work and dwelling, while 'family' concerns the kinship and marriage relations which bind people together. The household deals with activities, while family has to do with social relations. Fortes' definition of household still has some validity when he writes that: 'the domestic group is essentially a householding and housekeeping unit organised to provide the material and cultural resources needed to maintain and bring up its members'(in Goody, 1958; 8). Both family and household can be considered as flexible social units which can be adapted to changing ideological and economic conditions (Löfgren 1974).

Harris (1981) has pointed out that household has been read frequently as a synonym for nuclear family, which is assumed to be a very widespread institution. However, even within Britain, where the popular belief is still that the nuclear family is the main basis of the household, more recent official approaches have tried to broaden the concept. The 1991 UK census defines a household as a single person living alone or, a group *who may or may not be related* living, or staying temporarily at the same address, with common housekeeping. This definition captures for us the issue that the members of the household do not necessarily have to be related, but it does not encompass the broader economic relationships which may be established with a person living outside the household. The Norwegian ideal too equates household with nuclear family. However, social practice in Norway - as in Britain - shows that this particular household composition is only one possibility amongst many. The consequences of divorce and separation, where children may share their time between parents who may or may not stay single, indicate some of the possibilities.

Roberts (1991) proposes a definition of the household which is clearly based upon function, the household being 'the basic unit of society in which the activities of production, reproduction, consumption and the socialisation of children take place'. Most importantly, from our perspective, this definition does not require that members of the household be co-resident, nor do they need to be related through kinship or marriage. A second definition, based upon the functional activities of the household and of particular use in the analysis of policy effects is Messer's: '...that group of people, their relationships and activities, who acknowledge a common authority in domestic matters, a "budget unit", or "a group who have a common fund of material and human resources and rules for practices and exchange within it."' (1983 quoted in Messer, 1990).

It is by these criteria of activity and function that we wish to identify and define the household. We are looking for the basic social unit of the society, a unit whose boundary is formed by common agreement on the management of its resources, both the management of resource inflows into the household, and their use and distribution. This conceptual definition of the household can be used anywhere at any time. In practice though it will produce households of very different types depending specifically on place, culture and history. By different types we mean that membership of the household may be characterised by individuals with very different relationships, kin or non-kin, depending upon the specific context. Thus the definition of the household creates a boundary, a recognisable and accepted border to the household as a social unit. We would nevertheless agree with Wallerstein and Smith when they argue that we should not presume a single, globally recognised, boundary defining the structure of the household, but that '...the bounding of households is itself an historical process which not only can but must be analysed, as it is probably the key process in the functioning of house holding and is what integrates this structure into the larger network of structures that constitute the capitalist world-economy.' (1990, 14)

The concept of the boundary can be pursued a little further in helping us to understand the nature of the household. The boundary produces not just a definition and shape to the household but, to continue with the analogy, the characteristics of the boundary also affect the household and the nature of its relationships with the external world. An understanding of these characteristics helps us to define the household as economic agent, and assess the household's response to economic change. For example, is the boundary rigid or flexible? Does it accommodate new members, whether kin or not, easily? How binding are the ties to members leaving the household to set up new households of their own? Similarly, we can ask how porous is the boundary with respect to the behaviour of household members? That is, to what extent does behaviour appropriate to the economic processes and activities within the household permeate the environment outside the household, and vice versa? All of these questions are relevant to the circuits described in the cloverleaf model (Figure 2.1) in that they affect not only the activities and their processes in the different circuits, but also the relationships between them. The relevance of our concern with the nature of the boundary is clear from looking at early economic models of household behaviour. The rigid and opaque shell of the black box hid all the inner workings of the domestic unit.

Becker (1965) started to unpack this box within the paradigms of neo-classical economics by producing a model that conceptualised the household as both a producer and consumer within the market place, and assumed the maximisation of a joint utility function. Within this model, goals are formulated by the household head, the 'benevolent dictator'. Behrman (1990), who accepts the 'black box' model of the household as a usable hypothesis, nevertheless points to the difficulties of determining whether some variables are exogenous or endogenous to the model. Production and consumption activities, for example, become more difficult to distinguish at the level of the household both with respect to material and non-material goods. More recent work within the New Household Economics school has tried to disaggregate further the activities of individuals within the household. (See for example the collection by Rogers and Schlossman, 1990.)

Positivist approaches to conceptualising the household have given rise to what Davidson sums up as 'rigid boundaries and harmonious goals' (1991, 15). Even given the relative sophistication of more recent models, they are restricted to a specific time and place, and they are highly constrained by the data available. Most importantly from the perspective of the analysis of change, they do not take into account the dynamic effects of structural and policy changes. Although such models now attempt to incorporate the economic endowments, needs and entitlements of individuals within the household, they do not try to take into account any non-economic ones. It is in this respect that the New Household Economics fails to address issues of power, sharing, reciprocity, nurturance and authority (see Folbre, 1986; 1994). Intra-household relations, gender, generation and conjugal status will all affect and be affected by the economic activity of the household.

Individuals benefit from opportunities and suffer constraints both as individuals and as members of the household and larger social groups. Such opportunities and constraints may arise from within the household. They will also be affected by the socio-cultural, political and economic environment. The multi-layered complexity of these factors and the position of individuals are described by Folbre:

> Individuals cannot be located by a single set of co-ordinates, because they operate in many different collective dimensions, within many different chosen and given groups. Nor can they be located by a list of all the given groups to which they belong, by a simple 'adding up' of separate positions. The interaction between different dimensions of collective identity affects the choices individuals make about which collective interests to pursue.
> (Folbre, 1994; 52)

How then, when such a variety of dimensions are pertinent, can the processes of change at the household level be analysed? How can we conceptualise the factors affecting the livelihood decisions of households? These issues are addressed in the next section as we develop a paradigm that moves away from the assumption of 'harmonious goals'. At this point we need to operationalise the concept of the household. In practice, rather than defining the household unit, it will be more useful to ask which social units perform the central activities concerned with living, budgeting, production, child care and cooking (Löfgren, 1974), and in the following section we examine the activities of household members and the reconceptualisation of work with this in mind. These issues are brought together in the final substantial section of this chapter when we pursue further the dynamic aspects of the model through the discussion of household livelihood strategies. What is clear is that the household is not useful when abstracted from the complex of relationships that extend beyond it (Evans, 1991). We can expect the character of these relationships to be specific to the locality in which people live. The locality will encompass specific social, cultural, economic and physical environments to produce a unique identity. This notion forms the basis for the comparative studies of Part III which bring out commonalities and differences of household behaviour in Britain and Norway.

The concept of the household is inevitably fluid, particularly at a time of rapid economic change. The institutionalist method ensures that these relations are incorporated into the analysis. Furthermore, it permits the explicit character of gender relations and the temporal characteristics of the object of the study to be explored.

Household flourishing

Let us imagine a household made up of individuals who have available to them an initial endowment of resources. Such resources include the capacity of different household members to work, whether inside or outside the labour market, and ownership of housing, land, tools or consumer durables. The household is embedded in a society which is itself composed of more aggregate orderings, including those of class, gender and age. We can further imagine the household at the centre of concentric areas accounting for the economic, political socio-cultural and physical environments. Changes in any of these environments may affect any or all of the other environments. The household objective is to sustain its members within this changing world. How is their income generated?

Wallerstein and Smith (1990) propose five different types of 'income' which the household uses in order to do this: wages, market sales, rent, transfers and subsistence. Wages, market sales and rent may generate cash or kind income and be generated by what we have referred to as the marketed sector in either the formal or the complementary economy. Transfers and subsistence move us into more rocky terrain. This classification does not entirely capture the value of the activities of the non-marketed economy.

As Wallerstein and Smith themselves note, transfers may not be pure income flows to the household at all, in that they are not necessarily a reward for work. They may be receipts that are part of gift giving, or reciprocal transactions that may or may not be obligatory. It then becomes relevant to ask whether such transfers should be classified as a production or consumption activity. The ability to participate in such essentially social activities in turn may be important in maintaining the status of the household within the community affecting its future productive and consumption opportunities. Further, the subsistence activities to which Wallerstein and Smith refer are not the primary activities of production, but activities to maintain the home and family. They give examples of food processing and home maintenance and improvements. Such activities can certainly be seen as producing 'income' for the household, but the motivations to carry them out may well not be economic.

However, activities presume organisation. How are these activities organised? All members of the household except the very young or the very old may participate in some or all of them. Certainly, all members of the household must be involved in consumption activities. Neo-classical models assume that consumption is an output of the household. Within New Household Economics, the household maximises a joint utility function which represents its welfare as measured by its consumption. But is consumption a satisfactory measure of the output of the household? Sen's (1985) model of capabilities points to the achievements or levels of functioning that consumption permits, as a more realistic indicator of well being.

Just as we have noted above that receiving gifts may not be straightwardly classed as an income flow into the household, so giving may not be a straightforward act of consumption. (See Douglas, 1982). Thus the 'income' generating activities that each individual participates in will be mediated by the desire for these subjective outcomes, as well as the (assumed) objective output of consumption. We would argue that the well-being of household members is also affected by factors such as recognition, appreciation, love by others, feelings of self-worth, participation in the community and so on. The management of household resources encompasses material and non-material needs. Both motivations and satisfactions may be non-material. Both sets of objectives can be comprehended in the concept of human flourishing[2].

So, individuals' endowments, intra-household relations, and status affect decisions over household labour use. But these factors will also affect the ability of the individual to achieve a given level of well-being through consumption. Initially the person's position within the household may affect their access to consumption goods, including those subjective characteristics mentioned above (Pahl, 1989). But even when goods are available to them, they still have to turn them into the achievement of a state of well-being or functioning. For example, a young unmarried woman within a household may be able to consume a number of years' education and graduate from high school or college. She may not, however, be able to achieve the well-being and self-fulfilment that she wishes from a well paid job because of social restrictions, observed by her family, that prohibit her from working outside the household. (See Sen, 1985).

There is a second class of models that do not assume altruism, but instead depend upon a bargaining approach. These models provide an alternative theoretical route to understanding decisions over the production, distribution and use of resources within the household. (See Manser and Brown, 1979). Such models enable us 'to produce accounts which encompass both structure and agency' (Seiz, 1991). Indeed, an institutionalist approach to household bargaining assumes that 'Behavioural outcomes are likely to reflect rights and obligations as well as economic incentives.' (Kabeer, 1993; 9). But such rights and obligations are not just objective entitlements. Sen (1990) has further developed the bargaining framework in his cooperative conflict model of the household. He emphasises the importance of perceptions in the information base of the individuals involved in the negotiating activity. For example, change in the formal (paid) economy, or the informal (unpaid) economy within which the household finds itself, will involve renegotiation of the contribution and entitlements of the household members. Such renegotiation is based not only on the direct effect of changes in their circumstances, but on the indirect effect via their perceptions of their roles. As we have already argued, changing environmental factors will give rise to and influence these renegotiations.

Changing meanings and values

We pointed out earlier in the chapter that an important principle illustrated by the cloverleaf diagram (Figure 2.1) is that production activities may shift from one circuit to another. Gershuny's (1978) ideas of a self-service economy, for example, mean that households purchase consumer durables from the market circuit, and substitute unpaid work using these household investment goods for purchased services. Ideas of Fordist mass consumption as a parallel to Fordist mass production, involves a shift in the opposite direction. Busy households where both partners go out to work in the labour market substitute purchased convenience foods, or meals out, for home-made meals, in a process of 'commoditisation'. The privatisation of state services spearheaded by right-wing governments, and now pursued by many countries throughout the world, shifts parts of education or health to the market circuit and subjects them to market principles. The same shift is going on with the re-privatisation process in former communist countries, sometimes dubbed 'marketisation'. The factors bringing about such shifts may be exogenous or endogenous to the household. In this section we examine the activities of the household and how institutional transformation takes place at the level of the household.

The household can be regarded as a 'moral community', referring to the individual's particular view of the moral duties and obligations they have towards those whom they consider to be household members (Gullestad, 1985; Eidheim, 1981). Cultural values and ideologies are important dimensions, for they influence the rights, duties and expectations involved in the relations between the household members. Practical and symbolic aspects of the household are interrelated. As Netting writes:

> 'They [households] are a primary arena for the expression of age and sex roles, kinship socialisation, and economic co-operation where the very stuff of culture is mediated and transformed into action.' (Netting, 1984; xxii)

The household is a social unit performing tasks to support family life. The organisation of tasks on the household level is linked to household members' connection to the labour market. Whether it is relations to the labour market, or the organisation of tasks within the household that is decisive for how household members allocate their time, both depend on gender and social class backgrounds. The difference between unskilled and educated women and their attitudes towards paid work is an illustration of this point. Educated women are more inclined to work full-time when they are participating in the labour market than are unskilled women.

If we look at the way in which people organise everyday life, it shows clearly how processes at the household level, in the labour market, and in the public sector are interrelated (Wadel, 1983). The organisation of work in the household and in the labour market influence each other and must be coordinated by household members. Not only money budgeting, but also allocation of time for alternative purposes and time budgeting are important in understanding household economic adaptation.

Householding tasks vary culturally, but these are central dimensions in the description of any household (Gullestad, 1984). In this context a division of the household into tasks and teams can be useful (Rudie, 1969/70; Yanagisako, 1979; Grønhaug, 1978). It is possible to discover the household's relationship to other households and the formal labour market through the forming of teams for different tasks, for example, child care and agricultural work. Thus grandparents or neighbours can be involved in child care in addition to public nursery schools. Adult daughters can help their mother with cooking and cleaning while a friend, son, nephew or a paid worker can help in agricultural work. A commuting father may be absent from home but participate through his economic contribution to the household economy. Such aspects of the organisation of household activities can be analysed using the concepts of tasks and teams. The study of change is thus broken down into looking at changes in the teams performing different tasks, as well as at changes in the tasks themselves.

Changes in the social organisation of production and household work reflect important aspects of social change related to the labour market, the economic system, conceptions of gender, work and household composition. The relationship between work in the household and the labour market concerns both structural questions, and social and cultural factors. Work as an analytical concept is quite problematic, especially since we are not only concerned with it as paid work defined by the labour market, but also as related to the maintenance of households. Instead of defining work as an objective category, it may be more useful to treat work as a socially constructed category. Thus Wadel writes:

> ...the activities we term work in our own society are continuously changing: new types of activities are continuously included under the concept, while others are excluded, and the way in which we characterise work activities and distinguish them from non-work activities are continuously changing. (Wadel, 1979; 365).

Wadel suggests that the analysis of work as a social construction must take account of a dialectical relation between changes in institutional arrangements (allocation of work activities) and cognition (characterisation of work activities). All the time, new kinds of activities, especially related to different kinds of services, are introduced as paid work. Work in the context of the household can be characterised as 'hidden work'. It is not public, nor is it wage work. (See for example, Himmelweit, 1994).

As with every other activity, work has an instrumental and a symbolic aspect. The instrumental aspect of work is related to the need to achieve something, whether material or non-material. Work as the organisation of tasks and teams is also connected to cultural values and ideology establishing identity: gender, class and lifestyle (Wallman, 1979). How work is codified is a cultural process, and tasks are codified according to gender relations and prestige. These aspects are often combined: tasks associated with women tend to carry less prestige than tasks associated with men, because they are evaluated in terms of power relations.

The tasks men and women perform vary both historically and culturally, but every society has a practice and ideology related to the gendered division of labour. This gender division of labour is confirmed in many contexts, and this gives it a character of naturalness. Gender is associated with specific properties and characteristics which are linked to different kinds of work and tasks. Identity is created not only by what you can do, but also by also what you cannot do. Indeed, neither competence nor incompetence in relation to different kinds of work is arbitrary. Not being competent is a way of showing who one is not, or, indirectly, who one is (Solheim, 1986). Competence and incompetence are questions of identity management related both to gender and social class or group. This affects which tasks men and women see as desirable. It thereby affects the economic behaviour of the household and is the answer to such questions as: 'how do working class kids get working class jobs?' (Willis, 1977).

Social mobility is a characteristic of modern society. Work, skills and competence then become crucial factors in the construction of individual identity. Making a lifestyle as the communicative aspect of a way of life is the modern individual's most important project. (Giddens, 1991; Berger, Berger and Kellner, 1974). Having waged or paid work is considered in western society as an important aspect of being an adult person because it enables the person to support him or herself. More recent literature sees this as applying to both men and women (see Stubbs and Wheelock, 1990 for example). Paid work is also the key to developing certain rights and benefits in the welfare system (see Chapter 3) and crucial in the construction of a social identity.

Gender is related to position in the social structure, and is a basic factor in the construction of identity. However, the household is an arena where management of gender identity is a central issue, both on the symbolic and practical levels in the definition of tasks and duties. Gender is a relational concept. What is considered male and female, man and woman, must be analysed in relation to each other within the household.

Ortner and Whitehead argue that aspects of both prestige and kinship-marriage organisation systematically influence cultural concepts of gender.

> More specifically, we find that the cultural construction of sex and gender tends everywhere to be stamped by the prestige considerations of socially dominant *male* actors. In effect, the way in which prestige is allocated, regulated, and expressed establishes a lens through which the sexes and their social relations are culturally viewed. (Ortner and Whitehead, 1981; 12).

This has implications for gender-based division of labour in the household and in the labour market where actions have instrumental and symbolic aspects, conveying meaning in different ways. The gender-based division of labour in households is not only a question of finding instrumental and pragmatic solutions to practical and economic challenges. Work and the contexts in which work tasks are carried out, convey meaning in terms of gender identity and chosen lifestyle.

Changes in farm work and housework can be used as examples showing how rights and duties have changed, affecting the social construction of the individual and the social organisation of work. (See Chapter 9). The gendered division of work in the labour market is related both to tasks and monetary rewards. Men's work is in general better paid than women's work. In addition, men's work historically has been full-time, while women's work is more likely to be part-time. In the unskilled and semi-skilled labour market, the gendered division of work is even more marked than in the skilled one. (See Chapter 4).

Institutional and anthropological analysis is concerned with the balance between the stability of institutions and their mutability. Economic restructuring implies new structural conditions as far as household income sources are concerned, changes which lead to new tasks being defined, with new teams set up in order to fulfil these tasks. These changing patterns of daily life impose transformations in the deeper, institutional setting.

Working towards the future

In Chapter 1 it was suggested that starting from the level of the household enables us to explore the interface between the formal economy and complementary economies, a boundary which is established in how production decisions within the household are made. A major theme of this book is the study of change. Although we describe the household as an institution, with the implication that it represents stability and continuity, it is also the place in which individuals must accommodate change.

Changes are taking place in all three circuits of the production cloverleaf. At the present time, in both Norway and Britain, market and state circuits of production and redistribution are shifting and altering. This in turn leads to changes in the significance of each in their contribution to household consumption, in their relation to each other, and in their relation to the non-market sphere. Within the household this will result in the negotiation and reinterpretation of the roles, tasks and opportunities that individuals face. In the process the household itself, as an institution, may change but individuals reconstruct their activities to recreate a sense of order, to provide continuity and stability. The adaptations that households make in the light of social and economic changes are widely discussed in the literature under the rubric of household work strategies.

How does the notion of a 'strategy' fit with the framework of economic change? Formal definitions of strategy include the ideas of rational decision-making, applied to long-term plans (See Anderson, Bechhofer and Gershuny, 1994). These concepts raise difficulties with respect to the study of households. Rationality requires comparison with a single dimensional yardstick. Yet, as has been pointed out, the activities of households are multidimensional: behaviour that is rational in economic terms may well not be rational for the nurturing objectives of the household. Similarly religious activity and commitment may be 'rational' within the cultural sphere, but not economically. Formal rationality, then, is not an appropriate criteria for defining household strategies.

A second consideration is that strategies may have different time horizons. The events and goals to which they relate may be known and certain; they may be improbable but possible events; likely or unlikely. For example: everyone has to eat tomorrow; there will be a harvest in seven months' time; we will die; children are likely to grow up, marry and have children of their own; the economy will improve for the foreseeable future; the demise of capitalism is imminent. Overlaying this, the opportunities that the domestic group has for ensuring and insuring its own provisioning will be strongly influenced by the kinds of goals it has, as well as its current constraints. The dynamic framework necessary for looking at economic change must therefore be able to accommodate different time horizons, and the speed and probability of change.

In Chapter 1, we saw how Weber distinguished between the substantive rationality of household based calculations of how best to fulfil needs, and the formal rationality of calculation in money terms. Modernisation and economic change mean institutional differentiation between households and firms which leads to differences in values, based on different forms of rationality. Alternative organisational forms are based on hybrids of the dilemma between the rationality of money calculus and capital accumulation and that of the direct fulfilment of human need, in its broadest terms.

These differences are described by Cheal (1989) as arising from the distinction between the moral economy and the political economy. The moral economy is described by Thompson (1971) and Scott (1976) as where: '...economic exchanges appear to be regulated by traditional norms that define both an individual's social status, and the support to which he or she is entitled in order to maintain an appropriate level of subsistence.' (Cheal 1989; 13). Cheal's political economy is the monetised, profit-maximising economy of the formal market. The moral economy of the household is, however, not just relevant to the non-monetised sector. The relationship between the culture of the moral economy and the political economy will affect decisions about the individual's and household's responses and actions within all three circuits of the cloverleaf of Figure 2.1. The relationship between behaviour in the moral and the political economies returns us to the question of the nature of the boundary surrounding the household, and the need to understand the decision making processes that take place within and without the household.

Household livelihood strategies must be analysed in relation to the kinds of alternatives members consider: moving to other localities, commuting, reducing their living standards, dependence on unemployment benefits, spending more time in the labour market and so on. Households with the most limited resources just 'get by' with no surplus from current needs to invest in a strategy. (Wolf, 1991; Anderson, Bechhofer and Gershuny, 1994). Investment of time and economic resources is a joint venture of the household, although not an activity necessarily reached through consensus. Nor can the household be distinguished from the ideas people have of the domestic group and the symbolic aspects family and home represent. The rules of the household are culture-specific and set limits on the possible and desirable solutions to instrumental problems.

Yet despite the fact that the household can be viewed as a moral community, as we argued in the previous section, this does not imply that the household is a social unit with a common strategy. Becker has argued that within the household each person maximises their own utility by choosing the optimal allocation of time between market and household sectors (Becker, 1981). But the division of labour and the internal power relations between household members mean that the strategy and adaptation of the household must be seen as a result of negotiations, disagreement and bargaining. Cultural values are central to the choices people make, where lifestyle and social class are key contexts. The economic outcome of a household's decisions are often the result of discussions related to non-economic issues to do with the social and cultural values of the family and the household. But Wolf (1991) offers a timely warning here. Our expectations may be confounded in empirical research. Conflict and change within the household may bring about behaviour which contradicts our generalised understanding of the culture. Responses to economic change within some households may proceed much faster than in others, and these differences may be significant to our understanding of that process.

Most households do, to some degree, organise and plan resource use and exploitation. The question then becomes: how do they actually do their planning? Carrithers[3] has proposed that we can more fruitfully think of 'distributed strategies'. The decisions and plans for the management of household resources are not the function of the thinking of one individual but are the combination of thoughts, interests and objectives of the individuals of the household both as individuals and as members of the household group. Strategies may be explicitly negotiated within the household, or they may arise from established patterns and habits. The relative authority and weight given to the strategies of individuals will again depend upon their status and position within the household.

It is clear that there is a difference between choice, and acceptance of the circumstances facing the household (Crow, 1989); conscious and unconscious decisions (Wolf, 1991); and between planning for the future and getting by in the present. The ability to conceive and act upon a strategy depends upon the resources of the household. But the social, local, regional and environmental networks and contexts within which the household is embedded will contribute to determining the form that optimal behaviour takes. Most importantly, we can expect these contexts to change over time.

Conclusions

This chapter has been devoted to developing an institutionalist economics of the household, to help in understanding responses to economic change at the household level. We have drawn on other economic models, but have shown that in order to see how the household is embedded in its social, political and economic context, it is important to examine the economic character of the household empirically. The chapter has thus established a grounding for the research objectives of the case studies of Part III. For research at the household level is essential to any project hoping to understand how the whole economy functions (see also Wheelock, 1992a), where the household provides a key link between production, reproduction and consumption.

Chapter 2 has been careful to show that identifying the household is not always a straightforward matter. Indeed the impact of change at the household level can only be fully encompassed if the concept of the household is a fluid one. The boundaries of the household are inevitably porous and flexible, nor, despite its collective identity, do its members necessarily share the same goals. In practice, therefore, it is more useful to ask which social units perform the key activities involved in living, in budgeting, in production, in child care, and so on. Furthermore, true human flourishing can only be achieved if non-material needs are given attention as well as material ones.

Changing patterns of daily life in turn affect underlying institutional patterns - of gender work practices for example - and can thus transform power relations. Households and their members also anticipate the future to a greater or lesser extent. They accommodate to the future through livelihood strategies that are moulded not only by changes in the political economy, but also by interaction with the moral economy of the household itself.

Notes

1. Parts of this chapter draw on the arguments in Wheelock and Oughton, 1996

2. The term 'human flourishing' was suggested to us by Chang-Woo Lee based on the use of this Korean term in his PhD thesis. We are grateful for this contribution.

3. Personal communication.

CHAPTER 3

SOCIAL SECURITY, EMPLOYMENT AND THE HOUSEHOLD

Michael Hill

Introduction: institutional stresses

How are changes in employment opportunities, household structure and female labour market participation affecting European social security systems? This chapter explores the stresses that are emerging in the respective roles of insurance and assistance, and how these affect social divisions. Social security systems fall broadly into three categories: those based upon simple entitlement (child benefit without means testing, for example), those which rely upon insurance principles, and those which use means tests. Typically European countries combine the three systems; the first type plays a comparatively minor role, and the other two are mixed in ways which emphasise either insurance or means tests. As far as the two countries studied in depth in this book are concerned, in Norway social insurance is dominant, in Britain means testing has to a large extent replaced insurance as the central element.

The principle embodied in the social insurance ideal was one of 'solidarity' between the mass of regular labour market participants and the minority not so fortunate. Comparative studies in social policy contrast national systems in terms of a solidarity defined by the extent to which social security coverage is universal, and high income replacement ratios protect the old, the sick and the unemployed from poverty (Esping-Andersen, 1990). A contrast is then made between the high solidarity of Scandinavian social security, the differentiation between social groups in the Bismarckian schemes characteristic in the mid-European countries (particularly Germany and Austria), and the patchy nature of the provisions in the Anglo-Saxon countries (particularly Britain, dominated by a limited 'Beveridge' social insurance model).

That contrast is heightened by differences in the treatment of women (Sainsbury, 1993). This is probably partly explained by the different views of dominant national ideologies about family life and equality between the genders. However, the strong position of women in the Scandinavian model is certainly linked with, if not explained by, their high labour market participation. The British Beveridge scheme by contrast was not designed for high female participation. It has not adapted well to the increased number of women in the labour market, nor to changes in family life since 1946.

The principles which lie at the heart of social insurance schemes depend upon high labour market participation overall. The weaknesses in the British schemes have been exposed by changes in the labour market: the rise of unemployment and part-time employment. The worrying underlying question which arises from the British experience is to what extent will other - apparently stronger and more solidarity-based schemes like Norway's - survive a similar onslaught from economic change?

It was concern to protect workers against changing economic fortunes that was one of the main influences on the development of social security systems. Yet, the use of an insurance model presupposed that misfortunes would be individual rather than collective: that in a general context of economic security, individuals could be protected from the consequences of their temporary unemployment or sickness. Even in the early days of social security schemes it became evident that a substantial and prolonged national recession would have an undermining effect. In Britain, in the 1920s, governments were forced, when faced by mass unemployment, to adjust their social security policies in ways which undermined the original insurance principles (Gilbert, 1970). Subsequent to those early set-backs some countries were able to establish strong insurance based schemes in the post-Second World War period, in a context of full employment.

In both Britain and Scandinavia social assistance schemes fulfilled a 'safety net' role for those inadequately protected by social insurance. In the British case, the decline of insurance has generated a situation in which the 'safety net' has become increasingly the main form of social security.

Assistance schemes seem to offer solutions to the difficulties social insurance has in adapting to mass unemployment. They also appear to respond to the needs of women. For women may prove ill-protected by the 'dependency' provisions in the Beveridge social insurance model largely because of marriage breakdown. Their own social insurance may also prove inadequate, because it is difficult for women to achieve levels of labour market participation high enough to ensure full protection. But social assistance brings with it another set of problems because it is means tested. It is likely to create household 'dependencies'. These arise from rules about contributions of individual income to households, assumptions about female dependence upon males and sometimes vice versa, etc. Social assistance also engenders disincentive effects for individuals, for example through the creation of 'poverty traps', disincentives to saving and difficulties about informal work solutions to income problems.

The foregoing creates the underlying questions for this chapter. Has the British approach to social insurance collapsed because of its intrinsic weaknesses? Or has the particular way in which household and economic change have interacted contributed to that collapse? If the latter, are there lessons for others in this experience? Does the assistance alternative - which Britain has *de facto* adopted - offer a satisfactory alternative model? Or are there other, more acceptable, ways in which social security can evolve? To explore these questions the chapter will first outline the contrasts between the insurance and assistance alternatives, and then relate these social policy models to social structure to examine the ways in which social change and social security change interact to affect social divisions.

Social insurance as a basis for income maintenance

Social insurance, with entitlement to benefits depending upon previous contributions, occupies a central role in many income maintenance systems. Countries have developed schemes for pensions, protection for widows, sickness benefits and unemployment benefits along social insurance lines. Some add maternity benefits and benefits to provide for parental absence from work.

However, the umbrella term 'social insurance' covers a multitude of possibilities. Some remain close to the commercial insurance ideas upon which social insurance was originally based, some even involving private organisations in the system (Germany, Switzerland). If it is to remain solvent, commercial insurance requires methods to ensure that contributions match the likelihood that claims will be made. This may lead to the rejection of some potential customers as 'bad risks'. Social insurance departs from this hard-headed commercialism by pooling risks much more radically. It gets over the problem that 'good risks' may subsidise 'bad risks' to a degree that may deter the former from purchasing a commercial insurance. Compulsory inclusion deals with this. At the same time state 'underwriting' of social insurance is expected to eliminate the other commercial problem: that too many 'bad risks' may bankrupt a business.

In fact in many social insurance schemes the risk-pooling is taken further. They also require contributions from employers, and build contributions from the state into the system. On top of this most social insurance schemes are not actually 'funded' in the way commercial schemes must be. Funding means making long-term calculations which accept that, to cope with periods when demands upon an insurance scheme will exceed income, there must be other periods when income exceeds outgoings, with the surplus invested to protect against future demands. Only very exceptionally have governments sustained funded schemes, the main example of which is in Singapore. Instead, government provides cash contributions to running costs on an *ad hoc* basis each year.

In reality, social insurance schemes are thus generally 'pay as you go' schemes, where current income funds current outgoings. Over the long run this practice has inevitably led to many specific decisions based upon short-run expediency, when responses are needed to meet exceptional demands. So whilst social insurance is modelled upon private insurance, a range of political concerns leads to an evolution away from that model. The insurance contribution then functions as no more than a social security tax.

What does this mean for the principle of 'solidarity' in social insurance? The answer to this question may prove very complex in practice. First, remember that there may be three contributors to social insurance: the insured person, his or her employer and the state. The insured person may pay a large or a small proportion. Second, contributions may be flat rate, they may be related to income, or they may be some combination of the two. Third, 'risks' vary between groups, so that certain demands upon social insurance schemes are likely to come more from the worse off than the better off. Likelihood of unemployment is strongly skewed towards the worse off, likelihood of sickness is similarly, but less strongly, skewed. Conversely the better off are likely to live longer, making greater demands upon pensions schemes. Fourth, this socio-economic skewing of claims may be affected by entitlements. Some benefit schemes provide flat-rate payments; others contain adjustments to take into account previous incomes. If the latter applies, clearly the better off claimants will, proportionately to their numbers of claims, take more out.

To make an overall judgement about how far any social insurance scheme is redistributive there is a need to look at all these issues. Other things being equal, a scheme with graduated contributions but flat rate benefits will be highly redistributive. A scheme with both graduated contributions and graduated benefits will achieve a comparable rate of income replacement across the income groups. A scheme with flat rate contributions and graduated benefits - an improbable combination - would be regressive. Real country cases can demonstrate very complex mixes, but solidarity is most clearly embodied in schemes which cover the whole population and redistribute effectively. It is least embodied in situations in which different economic or social status groups are differently protected, often through separate schemes (as in Germany; see Clasen and Freeman, 1994).

However, whilst solidarity may well equate with egalitarianism, it does not necessarily do so. What form of distribution does the scheme attempt? Is it between individuals, between generations, or within individual lifetimes (see Hills, 1993 pp.15-21)? At what level is the minimum benefit set? To what extent is any egalitarianism of the social insurance scheme offset by strong incentives to the better off to make separate provision? In the British case, the egalitarianism of a flat rate pension scheme funded by graduated contributions is undermined by the fact that a low basic pension is supplemented by an earnings related scheme, in which strong incentives (including relief from contributions) are provided to better off individuals to 'opt out' into private schemes. By contrast, in Sweden and Norway effective, but graduated state schemes make additional separate arrangements a comparative rarity.

Let us now turn to the way the solidarity principle is applied to the different work experiences of men and women. A scheme will tend to offer inferior benefits for women if there is no regard for women's different work opportunities and earning levels, and no compensation in the calculation of entitlement for periods spent outside the formal workforce in caring roles. Compensation via the contributions of 'partners' has the paradoxical implication that whilst perhaps reducing disadvantage, it reinforces another form of dependency, dependency within the family (see Sainsbury, 1994).

In many countries - Sweden, Finland, France and Italy, for example - employers provide the majority of the income for social insurance schemes. Hatland suggests that historically workers' organisations have seen employers' contributions as a way of making 'capital' pay for social security but that '...today there is widespread agreement among economists that employers have plenty of opportunity to pass the costs on to others through price and wage determination' (Hatland, 1984; 178). It is important to recognise that social insurance contributions are a form of tax upon the size of the workforce for an employer. This may be a factor, at the margin, in choices about whether tasks should be performed in capital intensive or labour intensive ways. In some countries (Belgium, for example) deliberate manipulation of levels of employers contributions is used as an economy management tool, to try to influence levels of unemployment or inflation.

It is also the case that quite specific rules may affect employment practices. Examples of this kind include rules that part-time employees working less than a specific number hours a week need not be insurance contributors; exemptions of employers from any responsibility for self-employed workers' contributions may offer an incentive to forms of sub-contracting. Contribution rules may also make it cheaper to offer existing staff overtime rather than to take on new staff, while exceptionally onerous rules about contributions (plus the administrative complications coming with them) may be a factor in the evasion of requirements to register staff for tax and social insurance purposes (informal economy practices in short). As a number of these examples suggest, these issues need to be seen in a wider context. This includes the stance of government towards different employment practices, taxation and the collection of social security contributions, and the ways in which entrepreneurial activity is organised.

Social assistance and means tests: equality with efficiency?

The provision of income maintenance through schemes involving tests of means has a long history in many societies. At first glance this approach seems to satisfy the requirements of both a desire for equality and a commitment to efficiency. Equality, because means testing is generally designed to concentrate help upon those in greatest need. Efficiency, because such 'targeting' is designed to keep expenditure to a minimum. But a deeper examination of means testing reveals problems which may undermine these two goals.

Concentrating help on those with least at any point in time, means that those who have squandered resources will get help, whilst those who have saved or made some other kind of private provision for adversity will not. This may operate as a disincentive to self-protection. The position is made more complicated because means testing systems are likely to look at more than individual resources. Logically if children and a spouse are deemed to be the 'dependants' of a benefit claimant, then their resources will also be taken into account. Many means tests also consider the resources of other household members, particularly if they are related.

The household approach to means testing has historically been the product of a view that family life involves dependencies. Though views may now be different, it remains difficult and costly to adapt means tested schemes to individual needs. A particular difficulty arises where housing costs are taken into account in determining entitlement, for these apply to the whole household unit.

Means tests may trap people in poverty by the disincentives they provide to self-help. They are likely to be seen as very unfair to those who secure earned incomes slightly above the guaranteed benefit level. Achievement of a job with pay a very modest amount above that level implies going to work for a minute real reward, if a comparison is made with the benefit available to the workless. Unfavourable comparison is likely to be encouraged by the unpleasant and onerous nature of many of the lowest paid jobs. Provisions that enable means tested support to taper off gradually above the guaranteed income level may help to avoid invidious comparison, but much depends upon the rate at which the tapering off occurs. If it is rapid then it will resemble a draconian tax on earnings. This is the case with the British system - the phenomenon is described as a 'poverty trap'.

Disincentive effects undermine the efficiency of means testing. They also create incentives to fraud, as people may be able to conceal resources in order to secure help. If a small increase in income undermines benefit entitlement, there will be a strong incentive to conceal it. These issues about fraud feed into administrative concerns. Means testing makes claims complex. It requires proof that an individual has an income deficiency, a lack of savings and no help from other family members. Payment must then be accurately tailored to available resources and to the family (and perhaps housing cost) commitments of the applicant. If the scope for fraud is extensive, then assessment of the claim will require a costly investigation. Once the benefit is in payment, high administrative costs are likely to continue. Changes of circumstances will necessitate re-assessment and the continued risk of fraud may be deemed to necessitate surveillance procedures over the lives of beneficiaries.

In the light of disincentive effects, assumed family obligations and administrative surveillance, the process of obtaining and retaining means tested assistance will be regarded as degrading and stigmatising to applicants. Of course this may be seen, by those not in need of help, as a desirable feature, deterring claims to benefit, keeping costs down and counteracting the characteristics which seem to discourage self-help. However, this attempt to define means test recipients as the 'undeserving poor' has provoked a political reaction, with strong demands that benefits be provided in a non-stigmatising way.

Institutional inconsistencies

Hostility to means testing from politically active low to middle income people (what used to be widely called 'the respectable working-class') has led to the creation of two-tier income maintenance systems in many countries. Contributory benefits meet many contingencies - particularly those deemed to arise through no fault of the claimant. These are then accompanied by means tested 'safety net schemes' for those not protected by contributory benefits, but with a tendency to see such schemes as the appropriate form of support for less 'respectable' categories of need, likely to include single parents and the long-term unemployed for example.

Such dualism of contributory benefits underpinned by means tested benefits is widespread. But with very different principles for the determination of benefit operating side by side, there is a danger that inconsistencies in the income maintenance system as a whole will develop. This is particularly so if the level of income guaranteed by a means test is similar to that provided by contributory benefits. It creates situations where many people, despite entitlements to contributory benefits, find that means tests determine their final income. This erodes support for the contributory principle. It engenders the possibility that individuals will see it as unnecessary to make contributions - evading them by working in the 'informal economy' - on the grounds that if they lose their work the state will protect them just the same. Britain is a country where these issues have particularly arisen - from the relative frugality of insurance benefit rates, the desire to provide comprehensive protection through means tests, the fact that the latter take into account housing costs but the former do not, the poor protection for women, the provision that insurance support for the unemployed exhausts after six months out of work, and the encouragement given by governments (since 1980) to self-employment. Many other countries have avoided getting into such difficulties by ensuring a wider gap between contributory and means tested benefits either through the generosity of the former (the Scandinavian countries), or the meanness of the latter (the United States).

National systems, as a whole, always involve some sort of mix of types. It is not intended to suggest that one can 'fit' types to countries but it is possible to classify countries in terms of the popularity of the various options, and the relative importance of insurance or assistance. In the Scandinavian countries a strong emphasis on insurance is found, but with principles of solidarity strongly developed. Few people are left out, and schemes come so close to universal that there are grounds for wondering whether the term 'insurance' is still really appropriate. In these countries means tests are in a genuine residual role. However, at the margin they may be crucial, and with the potential for undermining the insurance approach. One particularly critical circumstance where this may occur is where support for social care costs is means tested, as in Norway. This is an issue of growing importance with the increase in the incidence of high dependency levels in old age.

In Germany, France and the United States less has been done to mitigate simple insurance principles with notions of solidarity. In these countries means tests are evident but harsh, the gap between insurance and means test benefits is wide, and long-run labour market attachment is crucial for the former. In Britain, as already noted, there is a muddle. The Netherlands keeps strong insurance and means tested schemes side by side; the generosity of insurance benefits largely protects the 'gap' between them and the latter schemes. The final example is Australia, which has placed a relatively generous and relative rule-based means testing system at the centre of its income maintenance system, and has largely avoided developing social insurance.

Income maintenance systems in practice: who gains and who loses?

How well do different groups do out of their particular national social security system? There has long been discussion about the link between policy systems and social divisions (Titmuss, 1968; Sinfield, 1978). How far do these divisions reflect, even reinforce, wider stratification divisions in society? If we combine together the effects of labour market situation, family or household patterns and male dominance, three broad groups of people with very different social security systems can be identified (see also Hill, 1990; 1996). These groups can be called simply (1), (2) and

(3). Let us look first of all at how labour market attachment affects each group. Complications with regard to gender will be followed up afterwards.

Group (1) can be defined as employed people unlikely to experience breaks in their working lives before retirement. If they are temporarily sick their employers will make up their pay. In practice, they may be unaware of entitlements to state insurance benefits when sick or unemployed. Once retired, private pensions schemes are likely to determine their income, and although they may have state insurance pensions too, in many societies these will be dwarfed by private scheme entitlements. This will apply as much to state employees as to private ones.

Group (2) comprise the main beneficiaries of insurance benefit systems. These schemes will be important in reducing the impact of temporary absences from work, and in providing support in retirement. There are some important differences in the extent to which different countries have ensured that public schemes provide high levels of income replacement for this group.

Group (3) are largely defined by contrast with group (2). Low wages and high levels of job insecurity will tend to undermine social insurance entitlements, so that means tests will very often determine their incomes. Indeed the 'poverty trap' may make it difficult to move away from a state determined minimal level in many societies. New and recent entrants to the labour force will tend, because they have not built up rights to private or contributory benefits, to find themselves in this group. If they are young people, they may be protected from the full implications of this by the resources of their family of origin. Immigrants or migrant workers, by contrast, are likely to be particularly disadvantaged by an absence of insurance rights and difficulties in securing satisfactory labour market attachments (Castles and Miller, 1993; Ch.8).

Group (3) is the group that is sometimes called the 'underclass' (Field, 1989). But this usage has been linked with arguments about the behavioural characteristics of the disadvantaged, emphasising not social but psychological processes (Murray, 1984; 1990). Mann condemns the attempt to identify the economic and social forces that create this division as 'sloppy' sociology (Mann, 1994; 94), encouraging a popular media usage which blames the victims and derives harsh policy prescriptions from its focus on behaviour. Moore similarly argues that the pejorative connotations of the term 'underclass' create problems for a realistic analysis of the issues. He analyses the situation of this group in terms of the concept of 'citizenship', where the absence of work opportunities leads to exclusion from full social participation (Moore in Coenen and Leisink, 1993). Comparisons between societies suggest that such exclusion is more likely in economies with high unemployment and low wages, particularly where specific areas of the manual labour market have collapsed.

This three group model provides a tool with which to generalise across industrial societies. In devising the model the author was inevitably influenced by his own country, Britain, where the advance of the 'welfare state' originally accompanied, and contributed to the erosion of the old divide between non-manual and manual. This movement towards classlessness was then undermined by two things. The massive advance of unemployment and economic insecurity created a very large group (3). In Britain today nearly 12 million people live in families at or below the income level provided by the means tested 'income support' benefit (Hills, 1993; 35). There was a widening of the income gap between these people and those at the top of the income distribution during the 1980s:

> While average income for the population as a whole rose by 36 per cent, the real income of the bottom tenth **fell** by 14 per cent. Meanwhile the incomes of the top tenth rose by 62 per cent (*Ibid.* p. 37).

The availability of secure employment is particularly important for the prevention of the growth of a large group (3). Many European countries, other than Britain, have comparatively small numbers in this group, because of a combination of minimum wages laws, measures to combat part-time and insecure employment and policies to try to avoid concentrating the burden of unemployment. In the United States, on the other hand, the phenomenon of the 'dual labour market' (Doeringer and Piore, 1971), with a significant group who have very poorly paid and insecure work, has been recognised for a long while.

Income maintenance policies can reinforce or counteract stratification; a great deal turns upon how social insurance has developed. In countries such as Norway and Sweden, great efforts were made to make it a scheme for all, with sufficiently good pension arrangements to ensure participation at the top end of the income distribution, and the 'insurance' element muted to prevent people with weak labour market attachments from falling out of the scheme. Such a scheme plays an integrating role, minimising divisions between groups. But this success of these countries' programmes in keeping people in the labour market in turn reinforces their inclusive approach to income maintenance.

Households, gender divisions and the 'group' model

Once we look at family and household relationships, it becomes clear that the advantages possessed by group (1) may not extend to women. If women are not in well-paid employment themselves, they derive any advantage at second hand, through their dependent position. The distribution of resources within the household may not only leave women in a vulnerable position, but actually deprived of opportunities to benefit from the privileges and wealth of the family unit (Pahl in Walker and Parker,1988). Widowhood and divorce is likely to 'relegate' women from group (1) to group (2), without any corresponding impact upon males. This exposes weaknesses in a model of private provision which is very much employment linked - private pensions, employer help with health and education expenses and so on.

Many of the things that have been said about women in group (1) also apply to group (2), but income maintenance issues are rather different. The key issue is in the link made between labour market participation and social insurance. Women will be disadvantaged when sick, unemployed or retired if the pattern of female labour market participation is less complete than the norm for adequate insurance protection. An unavoidable fact of nature - that women bear children - and social assumptions -

which of course the women involved may cheerfully choose to accept - about women's roles in the care of those children combine in producing this problem. Social assumptions about other caring roles make matters worse for women. All is compounded by male expectations, as both husbands and employers, about who should make the adjustments to work patterns when caring tasks arise. It is feasible to devise income maintenance systems which give due weight to caring withdrawal from the labour force, and this is an important feature of the evolution of some social insurance systems away from rigid insurance assumptions (Sainsbury, 1994).

Many of the early social insurance systems, designed in a more patriarchal age and one in which female labour market participation was much lower, dealt with these issues by regarding married women as the dependants of their husbands. The author should not need to spell out the objection to this. However, as a system of social protection which linked female fortunes to those of male breadwinners, this approach did have the merit of protecting the widows of men in group (2), so that loss of the breadwinner through death had no more serious economic consequences than if he became unemployed. Indeed, if the man was mean about handing over money, his death might be less devastating than his unemployment, financially speaking! However, the relative longevity of working-class women relative to men, once the dangers of childbirth were past, was likely to result in exceptionally long periods of benefit dependency for women. Insurance provision for widows in traditional schemes did not extend to separated or divorced women, or to women whose dependant status was in a partnership rather than a formal marriage. The consequence of relationship breakdown, for female non-labour market participants, is likely to be a relegation into group (3). Even when labour market participants, such women will often be in casual, part-time, temporary and/or low-paid employment. The termination of a relationship then has much the same consequences as if they had no work at all.

Group (3) is thus likely to contain a disproportionate number of women. The combination of disadvantages and discrimination in the labour market, and the weaknesses of social protection schemes will tend to mean that many women who are unprotected by relationships with men, or particularly who lose that protection, are likely to be in this group.

Conclusions

This chapter has related general issues about social stratification to specific issues about income maintenance policy, contrasting the effects of social insurance and social assistance. The main beneficiaries of 'welfare states' are the white male workers (both manual and non-manual) found in Group (2), (Bryson, 1992). Their security is maintained so long as their attachment to the labour market is kept up. Women's fortunes in this system are linked to men's. This implies a reliance upon egalitarian behaviour within the family. Family breakdown undermines the support system for women. Female labour market participation offers an alternative route to security within group (2), yet low wages, temporary work and inadequate support for caring tasks make this impossible for many.

The role of group (1) in the dynamic of social protection should not be forgotten. Those who make the rules for the social protection system are likely to be in this group. The more they perceive the comparatively universal benefits provided for group (2) as extravagant and in need of better targeting, the more they accelerate the processes under which economically weaker individuals drop into group (3). Devices that impose means tests or limit state help for the needy such as health care, legal aid, social housing, and diminish incentives to participate in insurance schemes, tend to sort the occupants of group (2) into those who can make the strenuous efforts necessary to join the privately protected in group (1) and those who drop down into (3).

Social stratification systems are dynamic. This chapter has shown how social policy can play a role in contributing to the growing rift between the secure and the insecure in the labour market. Robust inclusive protection schemes mitigate the factors which lead to the growth of group (3). Conversely, an outright attack on universalist social policies could polarise a social structure much more profoundly, into simply groups (1) and (3).

It seems likely that secure and stable forms of labour market participation will be harder to sustain in the future. Social insurance, if it is to survive, must evolve in a way which makes labour market attachment tests much less salient. It must develop ways of ensuring that young people trying to enter the labour force have adequate benefits, notwithstanding that they have paid no insurance contributions. It must offer long-run protection to the long-term unemployed. It must provide satisfactory ways of covering periods spent outside the labour force in caring roles. It must offer satisfactory benefit entitlements to part-time workers. More radically, it may need to attend to ways in which benefits can subsidise part-time work.

If it can do these things it will offer a simple and non-stigmatising approach to the support of *individuals* enabling them to participate in *households* undergoing processes of economic and social change in ways that will not impose pressures upon the survival strategies adopted by other household members. The benefits to individuals will not be contingent (as they are both in insurance systems premised upon family assumptions and in most means tests) upon absence of work or resources on the part of others in the household.

This takes 'social insurance' a long way from 'insurance' in the commercial sense of the term, and a substantial way towards the concept of 'basic' or 'citizen's income', (Parker, 1989, 1993). Basic income implies a benefit for all regardless of employment status, a tax-funded entitlement like child benefit. An alternative halfway house is that that all who fulfil certain specific contingencies (Atkinson, 1993) - old age, sickness, unemployment, caring, part-time work - should get a standard benefit regardless of either means or past contribution record.

Is the acceptance of the necessary substantial transfer of resources from taxation to those in need a tenable scenario (OECD, 1994)? There are two less radical alternatives. One is to ensure a high level of employment. This too has public expenditure implications, but it may be politically easier to develop and sustain a system of public employment and/or publicly subsidised private employment, than to support high levels of income transfers from those in work to those out of work.

The other alternative is means testing, despite its built in disincentives to individual initiatives. But is may be possible to construct taper systems so that all but the very well off are included, and the poverty trap is mitigated (this is, arguably, achieved in Australia). It is possible to avoid asset testing, with its deterrent effect upon saving (some parts of the Dutch social assistance scheme do this).

Above all it may be possible to means test on an individual basis rather than a family basis (this is also on the agenda in Australia, see Briggs 1994). However, this is a costly alternative. The easy option, made attractive by economic restructuring and the ageing of the population, is to push the costs of support for those unable to participate in the labour force back upon the family and household. This is justified as 'targeting' help, with means tests stressing wide responsibility. Bringing in other household members is an ideal device for states eager to limit state support to the young unemployed, to single parents, to the vulnerable elderly and so on. Indeed, the definition of the responsible household can be widened to include parents who have moved on to new households, as with the Child Support Act in Britain.

In explicitly comparing Britain and Norway it may be utopian to expect Britain to pull away from the social assistance road; it is perhaps better to concentrate on improving that road. But as far as Norway is concerned the extension and reinforcement of the principle of solidarity, along the lines suggested above is still a feasible option. The problem is that political leaders are unprepared to grasp the implications for social security of changing labour markets. Eric Hobsbawm, at the end of his splendid analysis of twentieth-century history says:

> Suppose - the scenario is not utterly fantastic - present trends continued, and led to economies in which one quarter of the population worked gainfully, and three quarters did not, but after twenty years the economy produced a national income per capita twice as large as before. Who, except public authority, would and could ensure a minimum of income and welfare for all? (Hobsbawm, 1994; 577)

Who indeed? But the fear implicit in the analysis of this chapter, is that public authorities will do it reluctantly and grudgingly, exacerbating social divisions in the process.

PART II

ECONOMIC RESTRUCTURING, LABOUR MARKET CHANGE AND THE HOUSEHOLD

Åge Mariussen and Ian Stone

This second part of our book compares labour market outcomes of restructuring as a response to global economic change in two localities: Mo in northern Norway and Wearside in North-East England. In Wearside, restructuring has been market-led, as opposed to the more corporatist, Scandinavian restructuring of Mo. What are the implications of these national institutional differences in labour market response, in terms of employment, gender and household? In answering this question, other factors, such as size, resource dependency and how peripheral the local economy is, have to be considered.

The two localities each cover an area which roughly corresponds to a local labour market. While Mo is larger in terms of territorial extent, daily commuting by car from all points within the area is possible. Nevertheless, in terms of population, Wearside with its population of 296,400 in 1991 is very considerably larger than Mo (24,650 in 1990).

Both areas share a history of resource dependency. In the North East, mining of coal and its distribution has traditionally been at the core of the regional production system, providing an initial impetus to the development of shipping, steel, shipbuilding, and related heavy engineering. Fifty per cent of Wearside's 1973 employment was in industry (including coalmining); 38 per cent in manufacturing (mainly mechanical, electrical and marine engineering) (See Table II.1). In Mo, steel played a role comparable to that of coal and shipbuilding in Wearside, some 40 per cent of the workforce was engaged in manufacturing in 1970. The smaller Mo economy was noticeably less diversified than Wearside's, with the bulk of its manufacturing workforce employed in the integrated steel facility.

In their own national contexts, both areas are spatially distant not only from national loci of economic activity, but from the large population concentrations of Europe. Wearside is somewhat better placed in this respect, given its relatively easy access to a large domestic market via a network of rail, air and road communications and its east coast location (and its own port) gives it a sea connection to continental markets. Mo i Rana, located just south of the Polar Circle, is remote from both national market centres and particularly from those in neighbouring countries in north-west Europe.

Administrative and political dependence on outside decision-makers is a further dimension of being peripheral. On the face of it, one might expect the larger, more diversified and centrally-located economy of Wearside to adjust to the changing external environment more easily than the smaller, less diversified and comparatively isolated economy of Mo. However, this does not take into account the fact that the respective economies are 'embedded' within two very different national institutional contexts. Restructuring in both countries was necessitated by the acceleration of global market changes which followed the oil crisis of the early 1970s. The payments crisis experienced by the UK in the mid-1970s - and the consequent influence of the IMF in national economic affairs - gave rise to stringent expenditure cuts even before the coming to power of the first of a succession of Conservative governments under Mrs Thatcher. The old Keynesian consensus crumbled during the second half of the 1970s and policy shifted decisively away from state intervention and maintenance of employment towards a greater role for market forces and control of inflation. The Wearside economy was exposed to the full force of the early 1980s recession. In the Norwegian case, changes were mediated by national-level policies, as well as national-level economics, where the Norwegian oil-lubricated economy laid the basis for a prolonged Keynesianism, which postponed Mo's restructuring for more than a decade. Transfers from state budgets cushioned the effects of global economic shifts. The need to confront the problems head-on and to restructure the economy was according only accepted relatively late in the day.

National labour market policies differed as well. In Britain, labour market flexibility was considered an important element in the restructuring strategy, both in terms of the attraction of inward investment and the achievement of competitiveness in domestic firms. 'Restructuring' was something for the market to undertake. It was the state's role to sweep away any obstacles, provide (temporary and minimal) support for those affected, and help them adjust to the new circumstances. In Norway, on the other hand, the labour market was nationally regulated by a number of interventionist measures. Also, vertical cooperation between the local municipality, local unions and central government was institutionalised.

In Chapters 4 and 5 below, the experiences of these respective local economies are examined. With a view to addressing the issue of how differing national strategies have impacted upon the local population in Mo and Wearside, labour market outcomes of the different approaches to restructuring will be compared in a short conclusion to both chapters in Part II.

Table II.1 Changing employment structure in Wearside and Mo i Rana, selected years (percentage of total for selected years)

SIC division/sector	Wearside				Mo i Rana		
	1973	1981	1991		1970	1980	1990
0 Agriculture & fishing	219 (0.2)	125 (0.1)	200 (0.2)		688 (6.5)	470 (3.7)	439 (3.6)
1 Mining and utilities	10,965 (9.8)	5,807 (6.0)	2,767 (2.8)		475 (4.5)	429 (3.4)	305 (2.5)
2-4 Manufacturing	42,231 (37.7)	25,447 (26.5)	25,064 (25.5)		4,279 (40.2)	4,821 (38.1)	2,668 (22.2)
5 Construction	7,975 (7.1)	4,563 (4.7)	5,148 (5.2)		873 (8.1)	835 (6.6)	1,028 (8.5)
6-9 Services	50,593 (45.2)	60,124 (62.5)	64,905 (66.2)		4,350 (40.9)	6,095 (48.2)	7,603 (63.1)
Total Employees	111,983	96,191	98,084		10,662	12,712	12,043
Of which Public Sector	*31,250 (28.0)*	*36,900 (38.0)*	*26,400 (27.0)*				

Sources:
Wearside: Compiled from standardised Annual Census of Employment data; figures for the public sector are derived from Wearside Industrial Database (industry) and a count of selected SIC Activities (Services and Utilities)
Mo i Rana: SSB: Population census, 1970, 1980 and 1990

Table II.2 Employment change comparisons (percentage change) Wearside/Great Britain and Mo i Rana/Norway, selected years

Employment change comparisons, Wearside and Great Britain 1973-91*				Employment change comparison, Mo i Rana and Norway, 1980 and 1990		
	Wearside		Great Britain	Mo i Rana		Norway
Male employees	-17,725	-26.6	-16.2%	-1,044	-15.4%	+0.5%
Full-time	-19,063	-29.3	-18.6%	-768	-13.0%	+5.3%
Part-time	+1,339		+60.0%	-60	-11.1%	-2.4%
Female Employees	+3,826	+8.5	+24.3%	+1,051	+30.1%	+24.8%
Full-time	-4,401	-14.4	+5.4%	+1,089	+58.8%	+42.2%
Part-time	-8,227	+55.9	+99.8%	-93	-5.0%	+14.0%
Total employees	-13,899	-12.4	-0.1%			

*GB figures relate to 1972-91
Source: derived from Table II.1 and Employment Gazette

Source: SSB: Population census, 1980 and 1990

Table II.3 Major Industrial Sectors (percentages of total manufacturing employment) Wearside and Mo i Rana, selected year

Wearside						Mo i Rana			
SIC 1990	1973	SIC		1991	SIC			1970	SIC
Mechanical eng.	18%	Mechanical eng.	19%		Metal manufacture			74.8%	Metal manufacture 54.4%
Electrical eng.	18%	Motor vehicles	13%		Chemicals, Coal			8.5%	Fabricated metals 14.9%
Shipbuilding/marine eng.	18%	Clothing	13%		Fabricated metals			1.8%	Food 8.6%
Clothing	12%	Paper/printing	11%		Food			2.8%	Paper, printing 8.3%
Glass/non-metalic minerals	10%	Electrical eng.	11%		Paper, printing			3.2%	Wood, wood products 7.2%
Employment share of largest five sectors	76%		6%					91.1%	93.4%

Source: Wearside, Stone, 1994b; Mo, SSB Census of population 1980 and 1990

Table II.4 Employment in Wearside and Mo i Rana: gender and part-time/full-time breakdown, selected years (percentages of total for each year)

	Wearside				Mo i Rana	
	1973	1981	1987	1991	1980	1990
Male employees	66,715 (59.6)	50,249 (52.2)	46,430 (50.1)	48,990 (49.9)	6,795 (66.1)	5,751 (55.9)
Full-time	65,147*	48,136	43,035	46,084	5,910	5,142
Part-time	1,567*	2,113	3,395	2,906	539	479
Female employees	45,268 (40.4)	45,942 (47.8)	46,290 (49.9)	49,094 (50.1)	3,488 (33.9)	4,553 (44.1)
Full-time	30,556*	24,880	23,941	26,155	1,851	2,940
Part-time	14,712*	21,062	22,350	22,939	1,501	1,400
Total employees	111,983	96,191	92,721	98,084	-	-
Proportion part-time	*14.5%*	*24.1%*	*27.8%*	*26.4%*		

* Full- and part-time figures based on 1971 proportions for Wearside TTTWA

Source: Wearside: Annual Census of Employment, figures for Sunderland Borough, Mo, SSB Population census, 1980, 1990

CHAPTER 4

BRITISH MARKET-LED RESTRUCTURING: A CASE STUDY OF WEARSIDE

Ian Stone

Introduction

The UK economy has, since the 1970s, undergone far-reaching change arising out of de-industrialisation and government-led attempts to create a more flexible and market-responsive economy, particularly with respect to the labour market. This experience, though generally shared by western European economies confronting the effects of global restructuring since the 1970s (Sengenberger and Campbell, 1994), has been especially pronounced in the UK, reflecting the early onset and extent of de-industrialisation and the determination of a succession of Conservative governments to improve the economy's competitiveness. The most dramatic experiences of restructuring are found in the old industrial areas of the UK, where de-industrialisation has been especially sharp due to the extent of contraction among the traditional industries and newer branch factory implants. One such area is the North East of England, which has traditionally displayed economic and employment features similar to those of other peripheral regions in terms of its industrial structure, poorly developed service sector, high incidence of external ownership, low rates of new firm formation, low labour activity rates and above average rates of unemployment and long-term unemployment.

However, in the 1980s, while peripheral economies generally struggled to find a source of new jobs, the North East performed better than any other in terms of attracting foreign investment (Stone and Peck, 1996), which has helped to diversify the local economic base and boost exports. The region's manufacturing sector as a whole revealed a robustness in the face of the early 1990s recession which contrasted sharply with its dismal performance in previous market downturns (Cambridge Econometrics, 1993). These achievements, and the confidence they have engendered, are widely ascribed to a radical change in labour attitudes since the early 1980s, including a willingness to embrace new employment practices, a reduced commitment to unionisation and replacement of adversarial forms of industrial relations with more 'harmonious' ones. Government has hailed the transformation as a vindication of their policies of reduced state intervention in industry and supply-side policies, especially the freeing-up of the labour market.

Wearside, as the recipient of much of this new investment - including the prestigious Nissan car plant and its satellite factories - is a part of this 'new' North East. For many, the area's economic transformation is symbolised by two historically juxtaposed events: the closure of Sunderland's last remaining shipyard and the development of the Nissan factory. A remnant of an industry identified with public subsidy, workforce inflexibility and a culture of unionisation has been replaced by a cluster of new internationally-competitive activities based around vehicle manufacture using state-of-the-art production techniques and employment practices. This is a showpiece economy - an example of the way in which it is possible to modernise and diversify an old industrial area through inward investment attracted by (and contributing to) a transformed industrial relations climate and flexible labour force. It would be difficult to find an old industrial area which has experienced more change - both in terms of disinvestment and of regeneration via new public and private investment - than Wearside. It is thus an appropriate case study through which to provide a framework of reference relating to economic restructuring and labour market change, within which individual household and group responses to evolving labour market situations can be considered.

This chapter begins with an outline of the economic and policy context in which local restructuring takes place. This is followed by an analysis of structural change since the early 1970s, including an assessment of the character of the economy which is emerging and of the shifting labour market requirements. The third section uses Population Census data to help reveal how changing levels and patterns of demand for labour has been accommodated. It shows how the largely exogenously-determined changes affecting demand for labour have had a dramatic labour market impact, both in the aggregate and in terms of conditions of individuals and households. The principal indication of economic hardship - the growth in unemployment - is one of the dimensions of this accommodation. Others include the formal (such as the number on government schemes) and the informal (the increase in the permanently sick, early retirement, acceptance of part-time work, out-migration). Processes of exclusion and differentiation have implications for households, and for gender.

Economic and policy context

Macro-economic policy since the late 1970s has shifted radically away from interventionism and demand management primarily aimed at achieving full employment, towards monetary measures designed principally to control inflation. Emphasis has been placed on improving the supply-side of the economy and extending market-based resource allocation (Stone, 1994a). Thus the 1980s saw anti-union legislation and other measures to make the labour market more responsive to price signals, increased support for innovation and small businesses, privatisation of state enterprises, and government unwillingness to support loss-making activities. UK governments in the 1980s not only operated a 'hands-off' policy in relation to industry, but generally showed scant concern for its needs where these conflicted with other priorities, particularly inflation. Regional policy subsidies were reduced sharply;

remaining aid has been made more discretionary, with employment a key criteria; and greater emphasis than previously is placed on service industries and the development of indigenous potential. In relation to industrial regeneration, much emphasis has been placed upon attracting inward investment. The ready availability of labour combined with wage adjustments to reflect job scarcity is regarded as important in attracting such investment to areas of high unemployment. Government's resistance of European Union attempts to establish common policies on employment (on the grounds that they put up labour costs) has meshed with its labour market reforms to make the UK the prime European location for foreign capital in the 1980s (Thomsen and Woolcock, 1993).

Within the confines of this external environment, changes in any local economy are conditioned by local structures and processes. This underlies the debate on the nature of recent change within capitalist economies and its local manifestations (e.g. Piore and Sabel, 1984; Storper and Scott, 1988; Hudson, 1991; Scott, 1988; Amin and Thrift, 1994a). The extent and pattern of the rationalisation of the industrial stock in local economies is influenced by the nature of those establishments - ownership, age of plant and equipment, range of on-site functions, labour relations, products, markets and skills - and the specific rationalisation outcomes for these plants reflect complex processes of interaction between external and local factors. The process of industrial renewal, whether through modernisation of existing plants, incoming greenfield investments or new start-ups, is similarly influenced by an area's industrial past and its restructuring experience. De-industrialisation and re-industrialisation are thus not discrete processes, but ones which are linked in a complex way. Earlier investment phases in a local economy combine to give rise to particular forms of social and economic structure, which in turn condition the character of subsequent waves (Massey, 1984). Local policy intervention is limited - particularly in the short-to-medium term - in its ability to alter fundamentally these conditioning factors. Thus, the emerging character of a local economy's industrial activities, and the nature the flow of new investments, cannot be understood without reference to the specific history of the locality in terms of its industrial structure and related labour market characteristics. These are important in determining the role the area plays in the broader spatial division of labour, not just in relation to industry but increasingly also to 'footloose' tertiary activity.

Wearside: background

The Wearside part of the conurbation of Tyne and Wear is synonymous with Sunderland City, made up of the older urban settlement of Sunderland itself (population 191,000), Washington New Town (60,000), and the mainly rural former coalfield zone of Hetton-le-Hole and Houghton-le-Spring (45,000). The core of the area is the industrial urban centre of Sunderland itself, originally a coalfield port which, during the nineteenth century developed a range of industries linked to production, shipment or use of coal - shipbuilding, heavy engineering and glass manufacture. Its industrial specialisation gave rise to severe problems in the inter-war period, and attempts at diversification date from that period. Eligibility for regional aid and available labour reserves helped Wearside attract substantial mobile investment during the 1950s to early 1970s. The earlier branch plant investments were located on the industrial estates created in the older industrial zones; subsequently the focus shifted to industrial estates developed on the outer edges of Sunderland and in Washington New Town. Diversifying investments also began to locate in new industrial estates in the coalfield zone - something previously discouraged by the National Coal Board to restrict competition for local male labour (Hudson, quoted in Massey, 1984).

The influx of light engineering branch plants counteracted the steady contraction of jobs in traditional activities, thus continuing Wearside's specialisation as an industrial economy. In the early 1970s nearly 50 per cent of the workforce was engaged in manufacturing and mining (compared to 42 per cent in the region). The establishment of branch plants by non-local companies combined with takeovers of existing firms to steadily increase external control: in 1973 over 80 per cent of manufacturing employees worked in externally-owned plants. In spite of the spatial dispersal of new manufacturing investment, Sunderland still had an overwhelmingly dominant share of Wearside's manufacturing jobs. The new branch factories opened up employment opportunities for women in an area where the traditional heavy industries continued to rely overwhelmingly upon male, mainly skilled, labour. Women increasingly entered the labour market in this period, as semi-skilled operatives in the new factories and in the expanding private and public service sector. Services, which were also initially centred upon Sunderland itself, accounted for a smaller share of Wearside's employment than in the region generally their growth limited in extent and type by the overshadowing effect of the nearby regional capital, Newcastle.

Local regeneration policies

Up until the late 1970s, there was little locally-based economic development activity in Wearside. The centrally-operated regional policy measures were the main influence over industrial development; development agencies of various kinds were yet to proliferate. Local authority involvement amounted to little more than workshop provision for small firms. It was the employment collapse accompanying accelerated de-industrialisation which prompted a locally-focused policy response involving the build-up of an institutional framework in order to attract inward investment. The main effort - capitalising upon Nissan's decision to come to Wearside - focuses upon re-industrialisation; hence the promotion of Wearside under the banner of the 'Advanced Manufacturing Centre of the North'.

State intervention in Wearside has reflected both the commitment to market-led economic restructuring and the form of government prevailing in the UK. There is no tier of (regional) government between the local authority and the centre. The UK political system is highly centralised. The autonomy and revenue-raising capacity of local government is heavily circumscribed. Moreover, unlike Scotland and Wales, the North has not had the benefit of a fully-fledged and properly-resourced development agency to construct and put into effect a regional strategy (the success of the

Northern Development Company in the role of attracting inward investment, notwithstanding). Thus the state's input to the restructuring process on Wearside has largely been through appointed agencies which are not necessarily representative of the local community and are accountable to central government (which provides their funding) rather than the locality. Government explicitly rejected corporatist responses to de-industrialisation. Quangos and regional offices of government departments assumed in the 1980s a prominent role in policy formulation; the local authorities were just one agency among several, while unions have played only a minor role alongside that of business. Development agencies such as the Tyne and Wear Development Corporation, together with local government, have worked with the Northern Development Company to market the area to potential inward investors and have also carried out a major physical rehabilitation programme, using public funds to 'lever-in' private investment. They have developed a diverse range of sites to suit different kinds of inward investor, from metal-bashing through to hi-technology activities and business services. The physical transformation of the old riverside industrial zone in Sunderland has both created new industrial and commercial space and improved the physical image of the place as a location for investment. Further financial and practical inducements to investors are embodied in the Enterprise Zone - conceded by government as part of the 'price' of shipyard closure - which covers both riverside areas of Sunderland and an outlying greenfield site (Doxford International Park) (for details, see Stone, 1995).

Labour market change is both an outcome and a driving force behind the restructuring of Wearside's economy over past two decades, illustrating Massey's contention that earlier phases of investment condition subsequent waves. The local availability of unemployed reserves of labour with manufacturing skills - workers released onto the market by large-scale disinvestment during the 1980s - has been an acknowledged influence on the location decisions of inward investors. This was the case in the economic boom of the second half of the 1980s, when labour was scarce in many areas of the UK. More than this, however, the shock of employment collapse in the North East is thought to have made labour more flexible and amenable to new working practices.

Deindustrialisation and labour market shock

De-industrialisation - an absolute and proportional decline in industrial employment - is central to any analysis of the longer-term process of industrial change affecting urban areas since 1970. Nationally, the phenomenon was in evidence from 1966 (Rowthorn, 1986; Caslin, 1987), but redistribution via regional policy of the new job creations favoured assisted areas like the North East where the sector was broadly stable up to the early 1970s, in spite of contraction in traditional manufacturing (NRST, 1977). The adverse macro-economic environment of the following decade or so, saw enhanced levels of contraction and closure and a dramatic fall in mobile industrial investment. Wearside began the period with 38 per cent of its employment in manufacturing, which was substantially above the figure for the UK (32 per cent) and represented an unambiguous specialisation in manufacturing. By 1990 it had fallen to 25 per cent, which is barely above the national and regional average for 1991 (both 24 per cent). In overall terms, manufacturing employment in Wearside declined dramatically over 1973-1990, falling by 43 per cent from 43,150 to 24,580.[1] (See Table II.1.) The contraction was greater than that which occurred nationally (a fall of one third), but very much par for an industrial district within a conurbation in northern Britain (Townsend and Champion, 1990). In net terms, forces for industrial contraction were such that, even in the expansionary late 1980s, re-industrialisation was not taking place. Over half the 1973 stock of 330 establishments had closed by the late 1980s, entailing the loss of over 19,000 jobs (Stone, 1994b). Further losses resulted from net *in situ* change: surviving establishments contracted overall by 6,600. New creations, of which there were nearly 300, were the chief source of replacement jobs, but contributed only 7,400 new jobs. This was equivalent to only a quarter of the net decline of almost 26,000 jobs in the original stock of manufacturing establishments over the period to the late 1980s. The main element in the contraction has been the collapse of the non-locally-owned UK sector, employment within which fell from 28,000 to under 10,000 over the period 1973-90. Employment contraction has been greatest among large plants and in specific sectors, resulting in a less specialised economy, increasingly characterised by small units (average employment size declined from 131 to 55).

Shipbuilding and marine engineering

At the heart of the 'traditional' sector of Wearside manufacturing was the integrated shipbuilding and marine engineering complex which in 1973 accounted directly for over 9,000 jobs (mostly skilled full-time jobs for males). In the early 1970s Wearside still possessed a comprehensive merchant shipbuilding capacity consisting of five shipbuilding yards, a repair and refit yard, two marine engine building facilities, a marine electrical installation, propshaft and propeller service unit, and a specialist marine coatings factory. Numerous small firms specialising in supplying castings and componentry and outfitting services were clustered along the banks of the Wear. This industry effectively disappeared during the period, which was marked by a prolonged recession in merchant shipbuilding markets. Nationalisation in 1977 was originally conceived as a means by which the industry could be rationalised, consolidated and strengthened; when power shifted to Conservative governments seeking to withdraw from involvement in industry it became a vehicle for rationalising the industry virtually out of existence. When an orders crisis subsequently arose, attempts to find a private buyer became enmeshed in the financial arrangements of the sale of a Scottish yard and European Commission subsidy rules, culminating in the controversial decision to close NESL in 1989, with the loss of 2,000 jobs (Hinde, 1994).

UK and overseas owned branch plants

The UK sector performed dismally over the period under review, reflecting the contraction of British manufacturing in general. There were few new inward investments from UK sources and the branch factories which had been established since the 1950s proved vulnerable to recession. More than 10,000 job losses were recorded during 1973-87 in closure and contraction affecting just seven plants engaged in electrical assembly, components and made-to-measure suits. Many of the jobs lost were occupied by women full-time (Stone and Stevens, 1986).

The main contribution by way of inward investment during the period has been from overseas sources. Thanks to the recent influx of new greenfield investments this sector's employment increased to 9,800 in 1993 (compared to 6,800 in 1973), accounting for well over a third of total manufacturing jobs (up from 15 per cent in 1973). This level of concentration is well above the current equivalent figure for the Region (22 per cent), and strikingly in excess of that for the UK (6.5 per cent in 1989). The bulk of the investment has gone towards the creation of an entirely new industry based around the Nissan car assembly plant, which bears some similarity to the pre-1980s agglomerative production system centred on shipbuilding. The developing network of suppliers around Nissan has been encouraged by 'local content' agreements, and by synchronised production in vehicle components plants needing to make frequent deliveries to Nissan's factory through the day (Peck, 1990). A new industrial district, based upon and driven by inward investment, is emerging, the integrated nature of which contrasts with earlier branch plant investments. Wearside has thus been increasingly incorporated into the broader division of labour by foreign rather than domestic investment, and has had to conform, both socially and politically, to the requirements of foreign capital to maintain its development impetus. Incoming companies are altering the social aspects of production through their new managerial techniques and personnel practices, usually involving changes in the status and role of trade unions (Peck and Stone, 1992). These changes have been facilitated by the fact that de-industrialisation has increased the pool of unemployed to an extent which has made labour (and unions) much more acquiescent than formerly. Smaller plants especially are likely to be operating as non-union workplaces, while some of the large plants have opted for single union agreements with a circumscribed union's role (Peck and Stone, 1992a).

Although a large proportion of jobs created by recent foreign investments have been full-time, skilled and for males - and thus nominally replace jobs lost in the yards and mines - many have been filled from outside Wearside's boundaries, while the vast majority of shipyard-related employment was for Wearsiders. The specific labour force requirements of Nissan, in particular, has by no means matched the profile of workers released from the shipyards and mines (Peck and Stone, 1993). In this sense, the new industry is significantly less embedded in the immediate local community than was the case with shipbuilding.

Indigenous firms

The other chief source of new manufacturing jobs on Wearside has been small firms. The period 1973 to 1987 saw the creation of 238 new surviving indigenous (Wearside-owned) firms employing over 3,800 workers. The small firms sector (with less than 50 employees) was the only size category within manufacturing to record

78   Ian Stone

net employment growth over the period. Although located in a region which has performed relatively poorly in terms of small firm growth, employment in the Wearside small firms sector grew during 1986-90 at over 11 per cent annually - substantially above its counterpart in other local economies for which comparable data is available (NIERC, 1992). A core of new small indigenous businesses has emerged on Wearside making products for niche markets beyond the region, including abroad. Many are sectorally linked to the past industrial structure. Where they have their 'own' products, they are largely in markets sheltered from overseas competition. Many remain reliant upon major firms for orders, have no design capability, and neglect marketing.

Coalmining

Coalmining has traditionally been a key industry in and around Wearside. Although the closure of the smaller and worked-out pits proceeded steadily through the 1960s, the number of Wearside residents employed in the industry was still substantial (12,000 in the early 1970s). Amalgamations and closure of the higher-cost pits meant that by 1984 there were just three mines with 4,360 employees, and the only pit to survive into the 1990s - Wearmouth Colliery, one of a handful of North East 'superpits' tunnelling under the North Sea for their reserves - succumbed in 1993 to a combination of factors which accelerated falling demand for deep-mined steam-raising coal.

Services

Services has been the only major Wearside sector to expand since the early 1970s (Table II.2). While this follows national trends, the extent of growth in Wearside has been comparatively limited. In the early 1970s a smaller share of its population was engaged in services (45 per cent) compared to that of the UK (54 per cent). Although this gap has narrowed substantially, this is more to do with the overall decline in Wearside's total employment, since the growth rates in service employment have been greater nationally (35 per cent) than in Wearside, where the increase of 14,300 jobs since 1973 equates to only a 22 per cent rise. The sector is dominated by female employees, whose share of total services employment (63 per cent) has not changed since 1973. More than half (53 per cent) the women working in this sector are part-timers.

A large sector which has nationally shown moderate employment growth, distribution, hotels and catering, has locally remained static at just over 20,000, reflecting the comparatively slow growth of local income (and spending), a shift towards larger-scale more efficient retail operators, and Wearside's general unsuitability for significant development of tourism. New supermarkets and retail units - largely developed outside Sunderland itself - have been particularly active agents in the shift towards part-time working, particularly for young females. Growth in banking, insurance and business services (2,300 to 7,300 over the period) has exceeded that achieved at national level. It started, however, from a low base and its employment share remains well short of the UK figure of 12 per cent, reflecting the national pattern of concentration of these activities in the South East and major provincial cities, including nearby Newcastle, and the essentially 'branch office' nature of those activities which are in Wearside (Richardson and Gentle, 1993). The development of tradeable services, which is an important way of generating employment in a local economy, was in general limited in Wearside up to the early 1990s.

Labour market adjustment to economic restructuring

The net effect of the restructuring process in terms of changes in the demand for labour in the main industrial sectors is given in Table II.1. It shows the huge structural shift occurring between 1973 and 1991. In particular, the production industries (manufacturing, mining and utilities) have contracted dramatically in both absolute and relative terms. Wearside, in spite of the publicity given to its new industry, patently relies mainly upon services. Yet the increase in demand for employees in the services sector has not been sufficient to outweigh the employment contraction occurring in the former staple industries.

Tables II.2 and II.3 depict the fall in demand for labour which has accompanied the loss of industrial jobs and the failure of services to compensate. This contrasts with the experience of the national economy, where service sector growth over the period has been sufficient to maintain the overall level of demand for labour in terms of crude job numbers. The fall in male full-time employment in Wearside is particularly noticeable - nearly half as great again as the fall in total employment, and higher than that experienced at national level - and is not in any way counterbalanced by the small absolute rise in the number of male part-time employees (See Table II.4). The way the benefits system operates, in combination with the nature of new jobs, provides possible explanations for the fact that relatively few males have entered (or re-entered) the labour market on this basis, although the general lack of full-time opportunities may account for higher growth in part-time work by males compared with the country at large.

Nationally, the rise in female employment since the 1970s has been substantial. This applies to both full-time and part-time employment, but particularly to the latter, which has doubled since 1972. Sectoral characteristics of employment growth have combined with specific strategies of workforce organisation by firms to produce a rapid rise in part-time work opportunities for women. However, while Wearside's economy has exhibited the same bias as that found nationally in terms of generating jobs for women rather than men - to the extent that females are now marginally ahead of males in terms of numbers employed - the gains made by females have been small in absolute terms, and fall short of filling the gap left by the reduction in male employment. Full-time employment for women in Wearside has actually fallen, and the rise in part-time employment among females has fallen proportionately well short of that achieved nationally.

It must not be forgotten that the overall balance of change in employment numbers - both nationally and within Wearside - conceals a downward bias in terms of hours worked. Bearing this in mind, the static position of aggregate employment (males and females) in the UK is in reality a significant fall, as part-time working has risen by 2.1 million, or 60 per cent. In Wearside, the rise in part-time working among Wearside women (+56 per cent), barely outweighs the fall which has occurred in full-time employment among females alone, let alone making up for the collapse in male employment. This is because within the defined limit of 30 hours, many part-time jobs involve only a few hours per week. Accepting the ratio used elsewhere (e.g. Townsend, 1985/86) of 2 to 1 as the appropriate fraction of full-time to part-time, on a full-time equivalent basis there is no case for arguing that female employment has increased at all. (A similar point might be made regarding aggregate income from employment, given the generally lower levels of pay associated with female and part-time work.)

Numbers in employment

The number of Wearside residents of working age in employment - either full-time, part-time or self-employed has fallen over the period 1971-91. The Population Census-derived figure for those 'in employment' fell from 116,870 in 1971, to 112,710 in 1981, and then to 103,850 by 1991 (including 7,900 self-employed). This fall of over 13,000 jobs (equivalent to 11 per cent) is consistent with the picture given above derived from Annual Census of Employment data, and suggests that neither the growth of self-employment nor net flows of commuters significantly affect the extent of the contraction in employment opportunities available to Wearside residents. As would be expected given the size of Wearside's economy relative to that of the rest of Tyne and Wear, there is a small net outward flow of commuters in favour of the former. However, with numbers in employment in the nearby Tyneside economy showing an even greater contraction (16 per cent) over the two decades, the increased competition for jobs in the area is marked, and employment opportunities for Wearsiders in the rest of the conurbation is restricted to those with specific skills. In terms of full-time equivalents, the overall fall in employment in Wearside is understated in the figures given above, since the ratio of part-time to all employment rose from 14 to 26 per cent over the period.

Population change

One response to worsening local employment opportunities is outmigration. Indeed, in spite of the obstacles to movement presented by the housing market (Muellbauer and Murphy, 1991), the relatively poor economic performance by the region as a whole has given rise to a decline in the North's population since the early 1970s. Between 1971-91 it fell by 1.4 per cent, compared to a national population increase of almost 3 per cent. This is largely a reflection of limited economic opportunities in the North compared with other areas of the UK, and especially the regions of the South. The North's balance of births over deaths (natural population change) has been positive; population decline since the early 1970s has been due to a persistent balance of out-migration over in-migration (amounting to 64,000 during the 1981-91). The net outflow has consisted disproportionately of the more mobile members of the community, particularly younger working-age groups, in search of education or jobs elsewhere. It has thus had the effect of altering the local balance of age groups and increasing proportionally the dependent population (the old and children).

While compared with the region a sharper population decline (6.7 per cent) is observable for the Tyne and Wear connurbation as a whole, Wearside's population has moved *against* the trend, actually growing by 1.1 per cent during 1971-91. The important point is that the adjustment to a contracting demand for labour in Wearside is not one of a net shrinkage of population of working age, as has been found to be the case in UK coalfield areas suffering mine closures (Beatty and Fothergill, 1996); rather this has risen in Wearside, *ceteris paribus* increasing the pressure for labour market adjustment.

Economically active population

One possible labour market response in this situation is for a reduction to occur in the number of people participating in the labour market. The activity rate, that is the proportion of residents aged 16-64 (for males) and 16-59 (females) who are employed, self-employed, on a government training scheme or seeking work, has in overall terms remained surprisingly constant, showing only a slight reduction (from 73 to 72 per cent). The number of economically active people in Wearside has actually increased by nearly 3,000 (from 124,270 to 127,010). This reflects the rise in both total population and the proportion of Wearside residents of working age.

These figures, in fact, conceal a large discrepancy between males and females. While the activity rate for Wearside males fell over the two decades from 92.4 to 81.1 per cent, in contrast, the rate for women increased (from 52.6 to 62.4 per cent). These changes are very similar to those occurring in the conurbation as a whole (92.2 to 82.4 per cent for males; 54.4 to 64.9 per cent for females). However, the 1991 rates are significantly below those recorded nationally (males 86.6 per cent, females 67.6 per cent). Indeed, figures for 1981-91 show Wearside performing poorly relative to the national trends (males down by 8.1 percentage points, females up by 4.3, compared to -3.8 and +6.7 respectively for GB), with those for the Northern Region lying somewhere between the two.

In absolute terms, the number of economically active males in Wearside contracted from 82,370 to 72,750 over the whole period. The fall in activity rates for men has been particularly marked among those in the older age groups, a substantial proportion of whom are 'discouraged' workers and have taken early retirement or registered as 'permanently sick'. The 1991 Census revealed that a quarter (24.8 per cent) of Wearside men aged 45-64 are describing themselves as 'permanently sick'; a figure which is well above that for Tyne and Wear (20.7 per cent) and the North (18.3 per cent), and more than twice as high as for the nation as a whole (11.1 per cent). Economically active females have increased from 45,280 to 54,260; the extent of the increase has been held back by a lack of job opportunities.

For males, the extent of the fall in the numbers economically active has been influenced by the general shortage of vacancies which are appropriate to their skills, age, background and sex.

Unemployment

Overall, therefore, population increase, an increase in the proportion of Wearside residents of working age, and an increase in economic activity among women have outweighed the fall in activity rates among men to produce an increase in the size of the labour force over the period 1971-91. In the context of a sharp fall in demand for labour, and in the absence of substantially increased net outcommuting, a rise in unemployment is inevitable. Census figures for unemployment differ from the Employment Department's claimant count, being based essentially on self-reported status rather than on eligibility for benefits. Nonetheless, it could be argued that they are a more accurate measure of those seeking work. It has been shown that the Census figures are close to those of the Employment Department as far as males overall are concerned, while in relation to females it exceeds the claimant count. This is not a problem in that the claimant count underestimates the number of women seeking work, by omitting those (particularly married women) who do not qualify for benefit (Tyne and Wear R and I Unit, 1994).

Wearside unemployment in 1971 stood at just under 7,950 for males and 2,650 for females, equivalent to 9.8 per cent and 6.2 per cent respectively. By 1991 the totals had risen to 13,500 and 5,400, representing 19 per cent and 9.8 per cent of the male and female workforce respectively. These figures, and their change since 1971, are only slightly 'worse' than those for Tyne and Wear as a whole. Current levels of unemployment in Wearside are, however, substantially above those in the Region (14.5 per cent and 7.8 per cent), and - for males in particular - exceed, even more markedly, national figures (11.3 per cent and 7 per cent). Furthermore, these figures take no account of government schemes (mainly work experience for younger age groups) the numbers on which have increased sharply in recent years (to nearly 3,000 for males and 1,350 for females, 4.1 per cent and 2.5 per cent of the labour force respectively in 1991). Proportionately, such placements are more in evidence in Wearside than in Tyne and Wear (2.5 per cent and 1.4 per cent). Indeed, the proportion of the 16-24 age group which is either unemployed or on a government scheme is higher in Wearside (32.5 per cent) than anywhere in Tyne and Wear (29.4 per cent) and, again, well above the national average of 19.6 per cent.

The rates of unemployment would plainly be higher in Wearside but for the labour supply adjustment of 'discouraged workers' opting for early retirement or permanently sick status, particularly by males of 45 and over. In their recent study of labour market adjustment in coalfield areas, Beatty and Fothergill (1996) calculate what they term the 'real' rate of unemployment. They argue that this can be measured by adding the Census unemployed to those on government schemes (who would almost all take a 'real' job if they could obtain one), and the hidden unemployed, that is, the 'sick' and 'retired' unemployed who are the excess over the proportions of male residents aged 16-64 that are recorded as 'permanently sick' and 'early retired' in the South East of England.

The reasoning behind this is that in the context of a severe jobs shortage, males who rate their chances of obtaining employment as low may be able to use an ailment to register 'permanently sick' as an alternative to long-term unemployment.

Some males, if they have a pension from a former employer, might opt for early retirement, even though their age and health would enable them to take a job if one were available. Social security rules, here also, are favourable to the family with an early-retired male in allowing the wife to earn without incurring benefit deductions. The result is a boost to the numbers in the sick and retired categories in areas of job shortage. Beatty and Fothergill argue that the 1991 rates of permanent sickness and early retirements found in the South East - then a near fully-employed economy - are a better reflection of the true levels. Applying these rates (3.4 per cent and 2.2 per cent respectively) to the Wearside figures, and adding the numbers on government schemes, produces a 'real' male unemployment figure of 23,880 or 32.8 per cent. The rate is especially high among young male workers (16-24 years), where, including those on government schemes, the figure reaches 38 per cent.

The above figures relate to individuals; they say nothing about how restructuring affects households. Further detailed calculations based on Census data yields a picture of how the joblessness problem affects such units. Excluding those beyond official retirement age, there are some 22,000 households (a quarter of the total) without a single person in employment. This phenomenon is especially pronounced in Sunderland itself, where the proportion reaches 28 per cent.

Conclusions

This chapter has analysed and set in context the process of industrial restructuring experienced by a local economy situated in a peripheral old industrial region and the effects on the labour market. It has shown that, even in a local economy which was the recipient of a large share of the inflow of inward investment into the region - an inflow which during the 1980s was higher than that into any of the UK's assisted regions - and an economy which, in addition, performed relatively well in terms of the growth of its indigenous manufacturing firms sector, it has proved barely possible to balance the scale of job losses affecting manufacturing alone, leaving aside those incurred as a result of coalmining closures. The depressed level of local spending as a result of the contraction in the main industries, and the failure to attract a larger number of investments in tradeable service activities, has meant that the new employment generated in the services sector has lagged behind national rates, producing a significant overall contraction in employment opportunities, even before taking into account the growth in the proportion of part-time jobs in the total. This aspect of change in the area gives credence to the arguments of those writers who question the extent to which the North East has been transformed (Hudson, 1991; Robinson and Shaw, 1991).

The chapter has also shown how the changing level and pattern of demand for labour in the Wearside economy has been accommodated locally. This has involved relating the specific changes in the structure of the local economy to the demand for and supply of labour, both in aggregate and in terms of different gender and age categories. It is beyond the scope of the chapter to examine this response in terms of local willingness to accept employment which is less secure, more poorly paid and involves a lower degree of skill than that prevailing either nationally or previously.

(This does not apply to 'flagship' developments, but the increased proportion of Wearsiders working in small non-unionised workplaces - and the increased number of part-timers - does suggest this is an important issue). Within the confines of this analysis it is shown that the principal indication of economic hardship, that of the growth in unemployment, is just one dimension to the employment problem affecting Wearsiders. Other adjustments, formal (such as the number on government schemes) and informal (e.g. opting for classification as 'permanently sick', early retirement, acceptance of part-time work, out-migration), have been made to bring the supply of labour into line with demand. Such adjustments clearly have important implications for households and for gender roles.

The examination of trends in the Wearside economy does not suggest any radical reversal of recent trends. It is possible that the manufacturing sector will grow slightly over the coming years, based mainly on continued development of the motor industry. A number of local firms may experience significant growth through developing as suppliers. Some of the jobs will continue to go to outsiders, however, and employment opportunities for males in Sunderland wards will continue to be limited. The service sector cannot be expected to expand *ad infinitum*; the 'catch-up' component of its growth has largely taken place. Any new service jobs attracted by current investments in infrastructure and buildings will, as before, be predominantly for females and largely part-time. Even if the rate of job generation were to be increased, Wearside would find that the unemployment rate would be slow to fall, since improved employment prospects would attract the re-entry of people who have opted out of the labour market.

Wearside's jobs crisis is just part of a wider problem affecting all industrial countries, and which is now receiving serious attention from the European Commission. British attempts to deal with unemployment through freeing up the labour market has undoubtedly created jobs, though of a particular kind; the more regulated labour markets of other European economies have not only impaired job generation but diverted inward investors from outside Europe towards the UK, with its lower labour costs. In the context of a trade and technology-induced fall in demand for unskilled labour, a de-regulated labour market and restricted unemployment and welfare benefits (which provide the necessary incentives for the effective operation of the labour market), undoubtedly produces greater employment. This much is clear from the experience of the USA. The problem is that it also tends to sharply widen income differentials and push low-wage workers towards poverty.

At some stage, rethinking both tax incentives to employers and the question of how employment is to be defined and shared among the population will be seen as a viable alternative to running ever harder in an attempt to meet conventional job targets. The 'household' has an important place in that debate.

Notes

1. Unless otherwise specified, figures presented in this section are drawn from the author's Wearside Industrial Database, which covers all establishments operating in the period 1973-90. For a more detailed account of industrial restructuring see Stone, 1995.

CHAPTER 5

CORPORATIST RESTRUCTURING: A SCANDINAVIAN CASE STUDY

Åge Mariussen

Scandinavia is different from continental Europe. A northern Scandinavian country like Norway is certainly different from the UK. The fertile European and UK soil, ideal for agricultural production, and the layers of coal under British soil, are not found in northern Scandinavia. Instead, Norway has other natural resources, such as hydroelectric power, iron, oil, fish, timber and natural gas.

Institutional structures embed the northern Scandinavian economy in ways which are different from the UK. Norwegian political economy is more corporatist, with a stronger emphasis on vertical cooperation and bottom-up influence, in contrast with the more liberal, market dominated economy of Britain. Contemporary corporatist institutional structures were created over more than a century of Norwegian history, where the political movements of peasants, fishermen and industrial workers have dominated the scene. These mass movements gained parliamentary power through the organisation of liberal, rural and social democratic political parties. Here, they constructed the institutional structures which still embed the national economy today. The result of the 'Norwegian' way is a state with redistributive and regulative mechanisms, and vertical channels of cooperation, co-optation and bottom-up control.

Contemporary restructuring may be regarded as an attempt to divert the path laid down by these institutional structures, to turn the 'Norwegian way' in a direction that is more in line with 'mainstream Europe', as a response to the tensions created by trying to reconcile the outcomes of this 'way' with global economic trends. Today, deregulation, privatisation and market-led restructuring policies are central to the Norwegian agenda. Corporatism is under pressure. At the same time, these very processes of deregulation, privatisation and growing flexibility have been initiated inside corporatist institutions, and decisively shaped by them (Mariussen, Karlsen and Anderson, 1996).

In this chapter, the tale of the privatisation and restructuring of one of the flagships of national industrial development policy, the steel industry of Mo, is told. In order to tell this small story of Mo, however, the larger story of the construction of the path of Norwegian corporatism, must be briefly sketched. This larger story gives a context without which restructuring in Mo cannot be understood. In Section 1 below, this is done by means of a 'flashback' to some of the major trends in Norwegian institutional development. These cast light on the smaller story of the restructuring of the steel industry. Following on from this we can then discuss some of the outcomes of restructuring in Mo, in terms of labour market and gender.

Flashback: constructing corporatism

The distinction between a Norwegian and a Dane was encapsulated at the end of the eighteenth century, when Norway was still a Danish province. It was based on a romantic picture of a 'giant', a free Norwegian peasant, a unique character constructed in contrast to the unfree peasants of Denmark, along with other countries in Europe with a feudal history. The free Norwegian peasant was supposed to carry the heritage of the allegedly glorious Norwegian Vikings into the somewhat more modest present. This heroic picture of the free peasant was eagerly adopted by the Norwegian peasants themselves, in organising a social and political mass movement, which, in alliance with liberal intellectuals, in 1884 was able to establish parliamentary democracy, inspired by the British example. Eventually, in 1905, national sovereignty was also achieved in Sweden through a similar alliance, when the Swedish king was peacefully forced to resign. However, national level democracy and independence had been preceded by a goal with even higher priority: that of local independence and control. A law on municipal democracy had been laid down as early as 1836.

In 1905, Norway, with some minor industrialised exceptions, was backward and rural, dominated by small-scale farmers and fishermen living in sparsely populated areas, on small strips of land surrounded by vast, uninhabitable mountains, fjords, woods and rivers. What today are towns were then villages, connecting rural areas with the outside world through their harbours, visited by coastal liners. The main local lines of communication were fjords, connecting populated pockets of habitable land. The economy was based on the extraction of natural resources. In Norway, modernisation, industrialisation and urbanisation were twentieth-century processes, which, broadly speaking, occurred more than a century after Britain. In Norway these processess - modernisation, industrialisation and urbanisation - were to be shaped by political movements, which were at that very time constructing central national power structures.

In fishing, modernisation and capital accumulation were initiated through the introduction of new, large-scale technology at the turn of the century. However, most Norwegian fishermen were independent, small-scale, coastal fishers. The new large-scale technology was a threat to the independence of these fishermen. Their main strategy was to resist capital concentration. Through a decentralised system of regulation, laid down by law, small-scale fisheries were protected from the competition of large-scale fisheries in rich, coastal fishing grounds (Hallenstvedt, 1982). Another potential basis for capital concentration was the on-shore fishing industry. From 1937, fish markets became controlled by fishermen's cooperatives, the authority delegated by central government to approve fish buyers and control fish prices. The fishermen's cooperatives used this control to strengthen their position in relation to the fishing industry, preventing capital and spatial concentration as well as on-shore industrial control over the fishing fleet. These regulations largely preserved fishing as a predominantly small-scale, rural industry. Small-scale fishermen often embed their fishing in a flexible peasant household economy, combining it with farming.

In agriculture, farmers developed an even stronger position. They controlled the food industry through integration into state administrative structures. Farmers' cooperatives were both 'bottom-up' membership organisations, and had governmental administrative functions at the same time, which controlled domestic food distribution, the food industry and food imports. In short, this sectorally organised segment controlled the domestic food market (Jacobsen, 1965; Hernes, 1978; Almås, 1993). This control is used to preserve a diversified farm structure and to protect Norwegian farming and its food industry from foreign competition. Modernisation in such a closed national food market leads to problems of over production - and requires the regulation of production. Modernisation is thus a gradual process of transition, where small-scale farmers are slowly marginalised, but still cope, through the embedding of farming in household economies with other sources of income. The Norwegian food industry, controlled as it is by farmers' cooperatives, and operating in a protected, national food market, is - by European standards - small-scale and decentralised.

Thus, the structure of Norwegian rural society is defined through the regulation of the markets for fish and agricultural products. Fishermen's and farmers' cooperatives, integrated into the state administrative structures, have considerable influence over these regulations. Control is used to prevent capital and spatial concentration. The result is plain to be seen in the map of Norway, as an extremely decentralised population pattern. Cities and towns are small; a large part of the population lives in rural areas. Here, production is mostly small-scale and flexible, within rural labour-markets where people combine different jobs in different industries. Flexible households, where different industries are combined, make a central organisational unit (Brox, 1966; 1986). These flexible, independent, small-scale rural producers are protected by corporatist organisations, through which they control public administration and the regulation of their industries as well as their domestic markets.

Urban industrial life is regulated by corporatist structures as well. National regulation of electricity and labour are central in this respect. In particular, the regulation of electricity explains aspects of Norway's industrial geography. At the turn of the century, a number of innovations made industrial utilisation of electricity prospectively highly profitable. However, the new source of energy was not available in large quantities everywhere. The eyes of industrialists from all over the world fell on Norwegian waterfalls as a potential energy source. The young state wanted to protect national waterfalls from foreign influence. The answer was local control of waterfall rights, combined with national control over its industrial utilisation.

Regulations were developed in the period 1906-1917, which delegated responsibility for development and distribution of this valuable energy source to the local, municipal level. Energy-based industries were controlled by central government, through a system of licensing. A dual price system, where energy-intensive industries got favourable contracts, securing rights to cheap electricity in large quantities, was developed. After the Second World War, the social democratic government launched an ambitious scheme of modernisation and industrial development, where the dual price system was used to initiate energy-intensive industry (Thue, 1995; Kaiser and Hedin, 1995). Under an institutional regime which gave the local municipality control over energy, and in the absence of a national distribution system of electricity, such industrial development took place in isolated localities close to waterfalls. Industrial development was, to a large extent, a joint venture between government and local authorities, sometimes joined by inward investors of foreign capital, attracted by cheap energy.

This led to the development of geographically isolated 'one-company towns', based on cheap energy in large quantities, often combined with minerals, as a basis for metal processing or other energy-based industries. In these small, isolated industrial villages and towns, the labour market was based on work in the factory, and in public and private services. Such towns had boom periods, with former fishing or farming families migrating in, transforming their lives from peasants living in a household economy, to modern industrial workers (Berg, 1965; Sande, 1991). These industries developed in isolated locations, surrounded by rural villages, sparsely populated areas and uninhabitable mountains.

Traditions in Scandinavian working life are characterised by a large degree of union participation and union-management consultation. This is regulated both by national law, and by agreement between the Federation of Trade Unions and the Norwegian Employers' Confederation. National agreements involve an institutionalised national system with strong government participation for solving conflicts. Corporatist labour market regulations are strong; government law protects against flexible working conditions and 'unfair dismissals'. It is only as a result of rationalisation and by the principle of seniority (last in first out) that employment can be terminated. The National Federation and the Employers' Confederation can be called in to settle disputes. Disputes over redundancy can be brought before an industrial tribunal. All employees in an enterprise must be treated equally.

Employees have direct representation on the board of their firms assured by law. The Norwegian Federation of Trade Unions comprises twenty-nine different trade unions, amongst which the Norwegian Iron and Metalworkers' Union has been the most powerful. The post-war period has been distinguished by close cooperation between the Federation of Trade Unions and the Norwegian Labour Party Government. Matters such as the working environment and conditions of employment are regulated by national laws. Unemployment benefits and employees' rights are safeguarded by public bodies such as the Department of Labour market Services and the Labour Inspectorate. These institutional systems and government control give employees a high degree of job security.

Thus, the modern, industrial society which developed in small industrial towns during the 1950s and 1960s was stable and well-organised, determined by institutional structures defined by corporatist national level regulation affecting electricity and labour. To the people who migrated to such towns, the major attraction of urban life was a stable, predictable and well organised job, with regulated work hours, a regulated, fixed salary and a regulated holiday. Norwegian energy-based manufacturing industry was, in sum, regulated, well organised, and 'Fordist'.

The close links between unions and government were laid down in labour laws drawn up by social democrats, but respected by most political parties. Modern industrial society offered formalised rights for each employee, protected by the government, in industrial structures which depended on the competitive advantages of cheap and easily available resources, also guaranteed and regulated by government. In other words, modernisation in Norwegian working life was synonymous with regulation, formalisation and job security guaranteed by government. Fordism in Norway was corporatist. Job security was ultimately guaranteed by government. In the organisation of production industries, stability, rather than flexibility, was the ideal for which both unions and industrial managers and owners cooperated to put in place. Where stability was threatened, unions and managers asked jointly for government support.

Like other western countries, Norway was hit by the decline of production industries during the 1970s. Unlike Britain however, Norwegian restructuring was delayed for a decade. This delay was due to two closely interconnected counter-policies: growth of the public service sector, and Keynesian regulation financed by petroleum revenue.

In Norway, a large part of service sector growth consisted of public sector services. Municipal services, which, during the 1970s, had been based on principles of national standards, were decentralised. It was changes in the financing of the municipalities during the 1980s, that placed the stronger emphasis on decentralised responsibility. However, any financial disadvantages arising from decentralisation to municipal service production were compensated by additional transfers from central government. This meant that levels of public services in more peripheral localities were brought into line with service levels in central regions, using national laws and regulation. Public sector employment created new job opportunities at the periphery; municipal services made for expanding opportunities in rural areas.

In rural areas, public sector jobs for women became additional sources of income for household economies with a male working in agriculture or fishing. Expansion of the public sector at the periphery, and the development of public and social services integrated rural areas into the national arena. They were, to use Wiborg's expression, 'nationalised' (Wiborg, 1995). Such 'nationalisation' meant that agriculture and other peripheral resource industries gradually began - albeit indirectly - to depend more and more on the female employment created by the public sector.

Another counter-policy was Keynesian-based. In the growth period of industrial development subsequent to the Second World War, small cyclical variations were easily handled by Keynesian regulations. When the deeper troughs of the 1970s occurred, they too were interpreted as cyclical. And it happened that these troughs coincided with a gift of God, as the national budget benefitted from a new source of income: petroleum revenue. The solution appeared obvious: a counter-cyclical,

Keynesian-inspired policy, financed by petroleum income. Public budgets supported agriculture, mining, steel - and some other industries which were not doing too well. Public wealth was also - to a large extent - spent on expanding the public sector, and on industrial development programmes. Thanks to such counter-policies, employment was maintained at high levels during the 1970s and into the beginning of the 1980s. Then, things started to change.

As the turbulence of the global economy continued, prices of Norwegian raw material exports dropped. As the 1980s wore on, the situation gradually began to be perceived in terms of a structural problem. The shock waves from the new, downward trend in oil prices from 1986 onwards, made an important contribution to this redefinition among central policy-makers. New questions were asked. If the problem were a structural one, subsidies and transfers from state budgets to particular industrial branches and firms might just preserve a structure which the market would otherwise rule out. Perhaps the old industrial resource-based structures were 'sunset industries', which needed to be replaced by new industries? Huge redistributive budgets, with money transfers into agriculture, fishing and other industries, began to be questioned. These budgets, however, were the lifeblood of corporatist structures.

Subsidies and transfers should be removed and markets should rule, to bring about an industrial structure compatible with demand in the world economy. Norway should become more 'mainstream European'. A rather more liberal line was introduced during the last part of the 1980s, and a number of political initiatives were taken, in several areas, all of which pointed in the same direction: adjustment to the structural demands of the world economy. Industrial restructuring was finally put on the Norwegian agenda a decade after Britain.

Further interpretation of this flashback shows that timing was not the only difference, however. For the requirements of global restructuring were interpreted in a Norwegian corporatist context, where governments continued to guarantee job safety. A policy of 'restructuring in safety' was devised, quite different from British and US neo-liberal policies of flexibility. Or was it? Surely restructuring must mean more flexibility? How could any government link safety to a policy of industrial restructuring? We will return to this conundrum in the smaller story of Mo, told below.

A further, closely connected, central problem was that of industrial geography. The restructuring debate highlighted the obvious disadvantages of a number of Norwegian industrial areas, with a peripheral, geographically isolated location and their one-sided dependency on certain core industries. There was a widespread conviction that 'market-led' restructuring under these conditions would produce intolerable social and demographic consequences for these isolated islands of industrial production. The answer produced was not surprising, given Norwegian traditions of corporatist organisation and planning. Restructuring had to be organised, with cooperation between local industry, unions, and local and central authorities. Norwegian restructuring not only came a decade after British policies, it took a different form: that of corporatist restructuring.

Contemporary Norwegian restructuring policies span a wide array of industries, as well as parts of the public sector. Public sector functions are being privatised, fishing regulations are being reformed, agriculture and the food industry are slowly being deregulated. In the primary industries, however, questions of restructuring have been politicised, connected with the larger question of Norwegian European Union membership. In manufacturing industries, things have been moving faster, and one case where the corporatist restructuring trend was particularly pronounced, was in the privatisation and restructuring of the steel industry of Mo.

Corporatist restructuring

Mo is the administrative centre in the municipality of Rana, which makes up the daily commuting area around Mo. The town is often referred to as 'Mo i Rana'. It is situated just south of the Arctic Circle in the northern part of Norway. Historically, the market in Mo was a meeting place for farmers, hunters, Lapps, fishermen from the islands further off the coast and producers of small-scale fishing boats. Here, fish, agricultural products, reindeer meat, fishing boats - and other products of more distant origins - were bought, sold and bartered. Mo has a long history as a rural market village, and as a production site for fishing boats. Some of the established firms in the town today were founded during this rural period. However, the mountains around rural Mo contained iron, with waterfalls on their rivers.

Iron ore was first extracted in 1902 by the British company, Dunderland Iron Ore Company Ltd. During the Second World War, the Germans built a railway to Mo, as a part of their attempt to improve wartime logistics to support their northern front against the Soviet Union. After the war, the need for nationally-based steel production came high on the political agenda. It was argued that, to secure supplies, Norway required its own steel production facilities. A heated debate as to where these should be located resulted in the selection of Mo. A state-owned steel works was built in the early 1950s. The Norwegian government took control of the iron mines, nationalised the steel industry, and built an integrated iron, charcoal and steel works during the period 1946-65, the Norse Jernverk AS. Mo became urbanised, as population increased from 9,000 inhabitants in 1946 to 26,000 in 1972. Over 4,000 people were directly employed in the state owned companies. The work force was recruited from primary industry in the surrounding rural district. Fishermen and farmers previously dependent to a large extent on subsistence activites became industrial workers. By 1980, industry accounted for 49 per cent of jobs in the area.

Norse Jernverk AS in Mo remained an integrated, state-owned company which, until 1988, was directly controlled by government, with the Minister for Trade and Industry as chairman of the board. The board of directors was to a great extent made up of politicians. The company was, of course, a member of the National Employers' Confederation. Both production and company leadership became deeply rooted in the local community. Executives and employees alike had strong work and family ties in the town. Company executives were, therefore, loyal both to the local community and to the Ministry of Trade and Industry as owners. The company's organisation was characterised by a strong bureaucracy and central leadership combined with employee participation.

Until 1988, the ironworks in Mo made up the largest section within the

Norwegian Iron and Metalworkers' Union. In a town of 25,000 inhabitants, there were 8,000 trade union members. Over the post-war period, both the trade union federation and the local union influenced the development of a nationally determined wage level, forming agreements and introducing reforms in working conditions. Competent shop stewards at the ironworks were recruited as foremen, administrative employees and staff managers. The Labour Party, the local council and the federation recruited members from amongst the shop stewards in this government consortium. Mo i Rana and Norse Jernverk AS developed a close network of social democrats in positions as owners, managers, trade union leaders, and town mayor. Inhabitants and employees voted Labour at both general and local elections. This Labour Party dominated political system had close, direct connections with government, consortium and trade union federation management.

Policies to restructure geographically isolated industrial towns were discussed during the 1980s. Subsidies were reduced; unprofitable mines closed down; industry was made more efficient. In Mo i Rana, the steel mill - based on local cheap electricity, local iron ore and coal from Spitsbergen - was subjected to processes to ensure higher efficiency, but within a continuing institutional framework of state ownership. The results did not satisfy its owner, the Ministry of Industry. A more fundamental restructuring - implying layoff of 2,000 state employees from the mill - was planned. These plans met with strong local opposition. Workers at the steel mill were tightly organised in a strong union with high levels of involvement. Union leaders were members of the same political party as the Minister. Negotiations were carried out in an atmosphere of close, personal contact between the parties.

The Ministry of Local Government and Labour instructed the consortium to set up a new restructuring plan. The strategy was debated on the board, in the Ministry, and in parliament during 1987. The proposals were strongly opposed by both the trade union and local actors. The trade union's aim was to maintain an integrated state-owned production system in the municipality, securing jobs for everyone, while the government plan for privatisation would lead to the loss of 2,000 jobs and an extremely uncertain future. There were fears of grave consequences for so small an industrial town. In the run-up to the parliamentary decision of 9 June 1988, the trade union movement organised massive opposition to the proposals, with a solid alliance to confront the government. Only the consortium management and the employers' confederation supported the proposals.

The history of political organisation in Mo put the alliance in a strong position *vis-a-vis* the Labour government. Union leaders in Rana changed their tactics. Once the restructuring process began, the overwhelming opposition to the restructuring proposals was used to commit the government to statutory measures for the local community. Negotiations over the content of these measures found the union in a strong position. In Mo, restructuring was gradually redefined from being a long-term disaster, to becoming a short-term effort which demanded sacrifices, but which would also open up possibilities for rewards. 'Restructuring' was reinterpreted as *dugnad*, a coordinated effort demanding participation from all. The negotiations resulted in a compromise between the government and the union, approved by the parliament in the restructuring decision of June 1988.

This compromise consisted in a number of elements, namely:

i) Reorganisation of the consortium as a holding company
ii) Winding up and segregating unprofitable activity
iii) Centralisation of production in Mo i Rana
iv) 2,000 redundancies among employees in Norse Jernverk AS
v) NOK 500 million in a reorganisation grant to the Rana authorities
vi) Special work schemes for those made redundant
vii) NOK 1 billion for consortium restructuring
viii) Establishment of new government activity in Mo i Rana
ix) Early retirement for all industrial workers over the age of 60.

Another central element of the compromise, which proved very significant for local employment generation, was the preservation of rights to cheap hydroelectric energy for local firms. When the ore-based steelmill was closed down, this released large amounts of cheap electricity, which were then available locally for industrial purposes. The government, as supplier of energy, transferred these rights to new local firms, so allowing the maintainenance of metal production as a basic local industry.

The assistance measures defined by this compromise were, then, substantial, and indeed larger than those obtained by other industrial regions in similar situations. Union and industrial leaders felt they had obtained the best deal possible, and there was a widely held opinion that the strong political position of the union had enabled it to extract an acceptable compromise from the government. It was on this basis that union leaders decided to participate in the restructuring process.

In the ensuing debates within the union, members followed their leaders' advice, with the parliamentary decision increasing the legitimacy of this process. The tradition of the trade union movement and of social democracy is to respect a democratic resolution. The process put in train in 1988 was interpreted as a *dugnad* - a time limited common task, demanding sacrifices of everyone - and promising rewards, through compromise. The values of equality and individual sacrifice for the benefit of all were strongly present. Local identity - defining oneself as a member of the union and as an inhabitant of Mo - was strongly developed not just in the work force, but among the citizens of Mo. When restructuring came on the agenda, values of solidarity and cooperation through *dugnad* were already well established. The financial resources put on the negotiating table by government, further tempted the union. By including the local trade unions and local authorities in the process of developing new jobs and allocating new benefits, support, loyalty and effort were encouraged.

Restructuring of the existing steel industry took high priority. Consortium reorganisation was underpinned with 1 billion NOK. The central role played by local actors and the unions meant a conservative emphasis. Other values of the existing industrial tradition were respected: changes were organised and carried out so that new phenomena could be interpreted and managed within the framework of familiar paradigms, by actors with local legitimacy. An important value of this kind was the principle of seniority.

Seniority had been a central issue in agreements and in working conditions. Though the principle was modified, it was still used as the basis for allocating new jobs. Older employees were given the first option of new jobs at the expense of the younger employees. This was generally accepted - and it legitimised the process of reorganisation. Such interpretation and modification of traditional values made it possible to maintain an image of equal exposure to external threat: faced with the legitimate and objective criteria which regulated priority in the allocation of jobs and welfare benefits, all were equals. The process could thereby lay claim to support and cooperation from everyone.

The benefits for each employee were controlled by objective criteria worked out by negotiation. The dismissal of an employee had an objective external cause: state restructuring and personal seniority. The distribution process was managed and supervised by known and legitimate local actors. All were equals, given that the right to new jobs and welfare benefits were distributed according to principles and procedures accepted through negotiation. These principles corresponded to the traditional values and laws of the old industrial system: well-known, and respected by all.

Thanks to the cheap local electricity, two new metallurgical firms, a chemical firm and two small firms producing steel were established in the wake of consortium restructuring (Seierstad 1992; Andersen, 1996). The service division at the steel mill became twenty small, independent firms, supplying industrial services to the parent industry. After fission, some of these firms also developed other markets (Karlsen, 1996a). Today, the former steel works has become an industrial centre made up of seventy firms, with more than 2,000 employees between them. This fission process was an organised one, in which *ad hoc* organisations set up by steel mill staff set out to develop new firms.

Mo had been a union dominated town, dominated by union values. It was not a place anyone would expect to find 'entrepreneurial spirit'. Restructuring in Mo was organised as an attempt to promote indigenous entrepreneurship, despite this obvious lack of entrepreneurs. A 'firm forum' was established, where section leaders in each branch plant were called upon - through discussions with external consultants - to define and establish new firms. These were to handle the tasks of the particular branch plant section as an independent, small, and more efficient firm. Such plans for new firms were developed, evaluated, and implemented with the support of resources made available from government.

The transformation from a section within a branch plant into an independent firm raised problems. It was difficult for the individuals involved, particularly because it entailed a transformation from the safety of working in a state-owned factory, into working in a small firm, subject to market competition. What had been administrative contacts between people, became market contacts. The major change, in the first phase, was that a hierarchical relation within the corporation was replaced by a market relation. The individual who had been the section leader now met his former superiors as the leader of a small supplying firm, negotiating a contract. It was no longer possible to raise the topic of departmental running costs, for instead a supply price had to be negotiated. Competition with external firms became implicit, as buyers made use of price competition to increase efficiency and cut costs.

The transition to a market regime was tightly organised, but employees still perceived the change as profound. Those who had migrated from rural coastal communities into the growing industrial town of Mo, had chosen industrial work in contrast to a rurally-based livelihood. For them, flexible market adaptations had been left behind. The attractions of modern rural industrial life lay precisely in a stable and well-organised existence as an employee in a state-owned factory, with the legal, organisational and political protection of job safety and stability.

The metal industry has been reorganised into a 'leaner' and more competitive industrial system, based on cooperation between local resources and external firms, where the latter have taken over ownership of some of the small firms. Another element was the encouragement of inward investment, through support to private investors and the allocation of public sector jobs to Mo. One such public sector allocation was a national library. However, attracting inward investment proved hard. Labour market flexibility as a basis for attracting inward investments was precluded by the policy of restructuring in safety adopted in Mo. Labour market dynamics were limited by corporate regulations, where central government, local municipality, union, and local *ad hoc* agencies, were central actors. Restructuring was planned in public documents, which defined goals in terms of labour market outcomes, whose fulfilment was monitored and evaluated by the Department of Industry.

Structural changes

Sande (Sande, 1991) has pointed out that the gendering of work in Rana's steel workers' households was a case of institutional diffusion. The first generation of steel workers migrated into Rana from the surrounding rural and coastal villages, translating rural classifications of gender into urban ones. In rural society, the line of division between 'dirty' male work (handling the earth, wood, animals and fish) and 'clean' women's work (handling milk, meat, water, fish meat and other things to eat) was clear and could not be crossed. Work at the steel mill was dirty, consequently it was men's work. Women married to steel workers stayed at home. The result was, by Norwegian standards, extremely low rates of female employment. By 1970, as few as 36 per cent of women between 16 and 65 were employed, compared to 90 per cent of the men. The subsequent growth of the service sector in Mo was a part of the modernisation of gender definitions. Women in Mo caught up with the rest of Norway.

As Table II.1 indicates, employment in Rana increased from 10,662 in 1970 to 12,712 in 1980. Even employment in manufacturing grew - from 4,279 in 1970 to 4,821 in 1980. Restructuring, which took place during the 1980s, was followed by a decrease in total employment from 12,712 in 1980 to to 12,043 in 1990. The loss in manufacturing in this same period was much greater, however: from 4,821 in 1980 to 2,668 in 1990. Primary industries - agriculture, fishing and mining - also decreased: from 1,163 to 744.

Assuming that the service sector in a regional economy depends on export oriented primary and manufacturing industries, it could be expected that this drop in manufacturing and primary industries would result in a loss of service sector employment. The opposite was the case, however. Services continued to grow at a strong rate: from 4,350 in 1970 to 7,603 by 1990. This persistent and strong growth in services is not arrested, as might be expected, by the sharp decline in manufacturing from 1980 to 1990.

There are several reasons for this. One is the growth in services which results from the fission process. Here, industrial services which used to be produced inside a company, are instead outsourced and and bought in as services. Another is that restructuring in safety implied disposable income, some of which was spent in Mo. Public services grew, because public institutions were located to Mo, some of which export national services out of the region: one example of this is a library. Other jobs were created as a result of programmes generated by restructuring. To a certain extent, the Norwegian municipal sector is independent of tax reductions, which are compensated by government transfers.

In contrast with Britain, growth in services was not the cause of more part-time work among women. This is confirmed by Table II.4, which shows that part-time employment actually decreased during the 1980s, among both men and women. Despite growth of 14 per cent in part-time employment among women in Norway in 1980 to 1990, part-time employment in Mo decreased by 5 per cent between 1980 and 1990 (See Table II.4). The explanation for this is obvious: restructuring in Mo took place at the same time as female employment increased from 3,488 to 4,539. The number of full-time jobs for women grew by 1,089! Women were reaping the benefit of service-sector growth, and increased their employment - from 36 per cent employed in the adult (16-66) female population in 1970, to 65 per cent in 1990. At the same time, the number of full-time jobs for men fell by 1,044, from 6,795 to 5,751. Men lost employment, from 90 per cent in 1970 to 78 per cent in 1990.

Assuming that levels of part-time work make a reliable indicator of growing flexibility, it is fair to conclude that employment growth among women in Mo was not 'bought' by accepting 'flexible' work contracts. And indeed why should they, as long as they enjoyed the new opportunities opened by a growing service-sector with regulated, full-time employment? In this respect, however, women in Mo have been somewhat better off than Norwegian women in general, for amongst the latter, part-time employment rose by 14 per cent between 1980 and 1990.

It is worth noting, however, that men in Mo, who lost 1,044 jobs over the decade from 1980 to 1990, did not increase their part-time employment either. The British strategy of part-time work to cope with job losses, which Stone describes in Chapter 4, is not significant in Mo. There is a national level explanation for this: restructuring in Norway has not so far included policies of deregulating the labour market, while in addition the Norwegian government has expanded schemes for unemployed.

Although unemployment grew in Mo, both among men and women, all things considered, the result was a relatively high level of participation in the formal economy, whether as employed, unemployed seeking jobs, or as participants on programmes. In 1990, only 15.7 per cent of the population of working age was not economically active. Yet 1990 was an early phase in the restructuring in Mo; what may still be to come, given a region where long-term unemployment remains a persistent problem, is an increasing number of permanently economically inactive people of working age. We are already seeing a more pronounced emphasis on labour market flexibility, albeit within the limits set by Norwegian labour market regulations, and this is further discussed by Karlsen in Chapter 8.

PART II: CONCLUSIONS

CORPORATIST AND MARKET-LED RESTRUCTURING COMPARED

Åge Mariussen and Ian Stone

Considering the differences in point of departure and strategies pursued in the respective sub-regions, the case studies reveal striking similarities in terms of the structural changes which have taken place. There are, to be sure, differences, but they only emerge on close inspection.

Seen from the perspective of the 1980s debate in Norway on the problems of restructuring, the extent of similarity is reassuring. In that debate, it was argued that more centrally located and larger labour markets would largely manage restructuring by themselves, whereas smaller and geographically-isolated labour markets, such as Mo i Rana's, were poorly placed in this respect and would require corporatist rather than market-based solutions.

In terms of employment change, Mo has clearly benefited from restructuring, justifying the strategy adapted. While Wearside saw its employment fall by 12 per cent over 1973-91, Mo recorded an increase of 13 per cent in employment in the period 1970-90. Mo also lost proportionately fewer manufacturing jobs (37.8 per cent compared with 43 per cent in Wearside), although as a proportion of total employment - given the rise in its employment overall - Mo has seen a relatively greater fall in its *share* of total employment in manufacturing, falling from 40 per cent to just over 22 per cent over the period, compared to 38.7 per cent to 25.5 per cent in the case of Wearside. Both Mo and Wearside thus share the experience of de-industrialisation, losing (at least in terms of employment share) their previous specialisation in manufacturing and undergoing a shift towards service industry. The greater fall in the importance of manufacturing in Mo is perhaps predictable, given its remote location and lack of industrial diversity.

The changing character of the manufacturing sectors in the respective sub-regions reflects the contrasting strategies for restructuring. As might be expected, the corporatist approach taken in the case of Mo was inherently more conservative than in Wearside, since it was based upon cooperation between local interests. Finding ways of saving *existing* industries was given priority over the creation of something altogether new, and Table II.1 and II.3, comparing changes in industrial sectors in the respective local economies, offer support for this line of reasoning. Mo has substantially preserved its old core industry, metal manufacture, through a state-supported process of reorganisation.

The local stock of skills in the metal industry has been retained for use in an industry which, in addition to the advantage it continues to provide in the form of cheap electricity, has been made more market-competitive through fission and privatisation. As a result, metal production still retains its dominant position within Mo's manufacturing economy, providing 54.4 per cent of the employment in 1990. Another of Mo's 1970s industries, chemicals, has disappeared - again largely a government instituted change linked to the closure of a charcoal factory. Fabricated metals, food and paper have become proportionately more important, and timber products have emerged to replace chemicals.

In Wearside, the core manufacturing industry, shipbuilding, has gone, and - beyond maunfacturing - coal production has similarly closed down. The availability in Wearside of reserves of flexible labour and its tradition of 'metal bashing' helped attract inward investments which have established an entirely new industry, car manufacturing. By 1993, over a third of Wearside's manufacturing employment was in foreign-owned plants (compared with 15.8 per cent in 1973). Inward investments from UK and overseas sources since 1990 - not all linked to the car complex - have included a number of significant electronic plants, replacing much of the capacity lost in electronic engineering. The absence of such inward investments substantially accounts for the fact that restructuring did not bring wholly new activities to Mo. Governnment subsidies were available to investors seeking to locate in the area, but most inward investment has been in the form of acquisition of existing plants rather than greenfield projects. Those investments which have involved new branch facilities have proved to be speculative and short-lived.

The relative decline of male-dominated manufacturing industries in both case study areas has been paralleled by growth in services, where women have occupied a stronger position. Thus the experience of restructuring among males has differed markedly from that of females. As Table II.2 shows, in both Wearside and Mo, the trend has been for employment among men to fall while women have been expanding their role within the labour-market. Among males, the largest contraction was found in Wearside, where the fall in the proportion of males of working age with a job fell from 83 per cent to 63 per cent over the periode 1973-1991. In Mo, where the initial employment among men was higher (90 per cent in 1970), the fall was somewhat less dramatic, reaching 78 per cent in 1990.

Wearside began the period with 53 per cent of its working-age females in employment. Compared with both Wearside and the Norwegian average, employment among women, at just 36 per cent, was strikingly low in Mo in 1970. The figure has risen sharply, however, to reach 65 per cent in 1990. This is actually higher than the Wearside equivalent (63 per cent). While in Mo the gender gap has narrowed dramatically, a difference of 13 per centage points still remains. In Wearside, the dramatic fall in male employment has meant that, even with modest growth in overall female employment, men and women are now on a par in terms of crude employment numbers.

While there are certain structural similarities in terms of the direction of these identified trends, the differences in terms of overall magnitudes of change become greater when allowance is made for the effect of part-time work. A sharp increase in this form of employment has accompanied restructuring in both case study areas, and its growth is largely confined to the female part of the workforce. While the proportion for men has risen slightly, at the beginning of the 1990s, part-time work still constituted only 8.3 per cent in Mo and 5.9 per cent in Wearside. The equivalent figures for women, however, were 31 per cent (Mo) and 46.7 per cent (Wearside). It has been argued in relation to Wearside that the growth in female employment, when allowance is made for the shift towards part-time working, is virtually non-existent in terms of number of hours worked, and that it thus fails altogether to compensate for the large fall in male employment. Mo is more fortunate in this respect. A greater proportion of Mo's employed female contingent is in full-time work. Real growth has occured in terms of both crude numbers employed and hours worked; moreover, the number of jobs lost among men has been smaller, reinforcing the overall picture of a genuine increase in the number employed over the period.

This contrast in employment outcome of restructuring in the two areas is also reflected in the extent of non-participation in the labour-market. Non-participation may be a result of different life strategies, such as full-time housework, education or other options. In many cases however, non-participation may be regarded as an indication of social exclusion. The proportion of the population of working age in Wearside which was not employed, not on government schemes, and not seeking employment was 27.9 per cent in 1991, compared with 15.7 per cent in Mo. The difference, 12.2 per cent points of the population of working age, indicates that processes of social differentiation and exclusion from the labour-market have been stronger in Wearside than in Mo. Among men, 18.7 per cent of the population in Wearside was economically inactive, as compared to 13.6 per cent in Mo. The difference is, again, in favor of Mo, with the share of the economically active male population 5.1 per centage points larger than Wearside.

There may be several explanations for this difference. The *scale* of government intervention in Mo, not just the choice of strategy, is important in explaining the result. Strategies of market-led restructuring plainly have a cost in terms of the larger numbers of people experiencing difficulties as a result of being left outside, or only casually connected to, the labour force. In the corporatist approach to restructuring, these costs are less borne by individuals than by the state (e.g. through transfers for subsidies) and by those in employment (e.g. through higher taxation or wage restraint). The issue comes down, at least in part, to one of how the burden of restructuring is distributed within the population.

The choice between the two approaches is arguably not a free one. Mo's remoteness and small size made it unsuitable for the kind of flexibility strategy pursued in Wearside. It was hardly a location likely to find favour with Far Eastern capital, while its size - and the political and social traditions of the country - made it a feasible option to explore an alternative means of restructuring. Withdrawal of state support and full exposure to market forces may well have led to a wholesale exodus and the disintegration of the Mo community. Similarly, faced with numerous collapsing industrial economies as in Wearside, state support on the same scale as applied in Mo was hardly an option for the British government. The important point to make is that this does not mean that choices did not exist. Different mixtures of liberal flexibilisation and the more Scandinavian corporatist organisation and planning might have been explored in relation to the task of restructuring these and other local economies. Corporatist restructuring would have demanded government resources. But market-led flexibilisation creates costs as well, in terms of a larger part of the population being economically inactive, with all this implies in terms of wasted resources and personal and social problems.

There is another difference between the two strategies. In the case of Mo, corporatist restructuring implied a public demonstration of central government respect for local actors' traditions and institutions. A fundamental concern of the union, respect for older union members, was transformed into a principle of organisation in the creation of the new, more competitive industrial structure, as new jobs in 'fission' firms were distributed according to the principle of 'Rana seniority'. Those who lost their jobs did so not because they were not competitive in a flexible labour market, but because they submitted to a union value, the seniority principle. Many of those who did lose their jobs, preferred unemployment or government programmes to flexible work. Corporatism restricts the operation of the market. Corporatist restructuring is a policy where the market is set free gradually, and within limits which are monitored, controlled and regulated.

PART III: CHANGING LIVES AND LIVELIHOODS: SECTION A

HOUSEHOLD RESPONSES TO INDUSTRIAL CHANGE AND UNEMPLOYMENT

Jane Wheelock

We turn, in the third part of this book, to Norwegian and British case studies which show how changes in sources of livelihood affect the lives of people in households. In this opening section we see the ways in which the benefits of flexibility for employers may translate into costs for the household. Redundancy and unemployment for sections of their labour force, and the shift away from standard labour contracts, provide a buffer of flexibility for employers faced with change and uncertainty in their opportunities for making profits. Management strategies of flexibility in labour markets - including labour markets internal to the firm - are mirrored in strategies for flexibility within households. Flexibility involves a shift in the balance of power between market-based firms and individual labour market participants and members of their household. The household must make economic adaptations. The state benefit system may provide the household with some protection against this process.

The following chapters can be read as testimony to the varied ways in which households adapt to sustain the human flourishing of their members, in the face of growing labour market flexibility. They show the household as a flexible institution which sustains the human and economic needs of its members, preserving their dignity to the best of its ability. The process of restructuring is one which differentiates between workers as individuals. Unsurprisingly, a diversity of household strategies and responses to this pressure on individual members are apparent. This diversity can be interpreted in the light of the meanings that people give to work.

For the shifting balance of power between markets and households means that people's understanding of work changes, and in particular that gendered understandings of what constitutes women's and men's work alters. Traditionally, power relations between men and women are brokered through men's work involving a breadwinning role while women's work sets the parameters for standards of care and maintenance inside the household. Fundamental to how households adapt is that gender identities affect responses; they affect the form that household flexibility takes.

Recent economic restructuring in both Norway and Britain has tended to dissolve the traditionally gender linked domains of paid work and home, albeit in a partial manner. Taken together, the three chapters here make up a story where households may combine changes in the division of labour between women and men with maintenance of those divisions. What work is seen to consist in by both men and women can change along two dimensions. Firstly, the work tasks to be done inside and outside the home can change, and this can lead to the formation of different working teams between men and women in undertaking them. Secondly, men's and women's identities can be affected by changes in the work they do. This means that household flexibility in response restructuring takes two different forms: flexibility of tasks and teams and flexibility of gender identity. The two are related to each other through the household's moral economy.

Restructuring processes have tended to undermine the household power base of men as breadwinners, thanks to the loss of traditional industrial employment. Interestingly, those small number of women who had been able to penetrate this relatively high waged sector, despite strategies to exclude them, have also diminished in importance. Instead, women are drawn into the still expanding state and service sector employment available. As Sande and Wheelock point out in Chapters 6 and 7 respectively, this challenges gender power relations within the home, but in a limited way, because female employment is often both part-time and low-paid. In addition, this type of employment still fits the domestic stereotype of women's work as caring. These two chapters nevertheless show that male unemployment alongside continuing female employment, whether in Britain or in Norway, can result in real changes in who does what inside the home. Wheelock concentrates on developing a classification of the gender divison of domestic labour which can be used as a benchmark in judging the amount of change. Sande brings out issues of changing women's and men's identities mediated by the household's moral economy.

In general, the empirical material reported on in Chapter 8 indicates considerably less modification to the traditional division of domestic labour than Wheelock and Sande report. The more temporary character of the unemployment experienced by the workers reported on in Karlsen's study underlies this difference. None of the workers he interviewed looked upon themselves as retired - forcibly or otherwise. They all had aspirations for more paid work. As Pahl (1984) maintains, there is more room for flexibility and relaxation of gender roles as couples grow older, and especially once children have left home. The selection of workers in the studies of Sande and Wheelock include older workers.

The chapters in this section highlight the shortcomings of the individualised rational economic man approach to economic change. People do not just behave in labour markets on the basis of their individualised preferences and incentives. They are concerned that both they and their household should flourish as best they may. Dignity is sufficiently important to outweigh purely economic concerns, at least in some cases. This underlines the importance of taking a household-level approach and incorporating consideration of a household moral economy, rather than starting from individual economic maximisers.

Inevitably, people find themselves and their households affected in different ways by the economic restrucuring process. These chapters point up both winners and losers. Households who retain a permanent worker in their midst are better off than those who rely on temporary workers. Of the latter however, Karlsen points out that loyal workers, so reliable for their employer under the old standard Fordist labour contract, put themselves at a disadvantage by maintaining that loyalty when only bound by a temporary contract. Faced with temporary employment, it is those who show reflexive adaptablility who are likely to gain, particularly if their household, backed by provisions from the state, is flexible enough to provide an economic cushion. Reflexive workers, posits Karlsen, are those who see their identities based on competence in coping with a changing labour market, and not just on their qualifications. Section B picks up on those who have followed the route of setting up in business.

The evidence from these chapters tends to show more flexibility on the part of women to economic change than men: it is wives who provide more of a cushion for the household than their husbands. The evidence also shows how tough being flexible can prove for household members, and here it is perhaps men who are at a greater disadvantage. It takes time to learn new tasks, and adapt to new roles and identities. As Sande points out, the incompetence of men when it comes to domestic tasks displays not only male identity, but resistence to the loss of male power. The household must usually also adapt to a lower income. This puts pressure on households and the people in them, and may lead to serious illness and depression or even to household breakup. All households are likely to experience pressure in the form of shorter-term horizons over which they can make plans for the future, such as investing in housing or taking holidays.

These pressures can be alleviated in a number of ways. Adjusting the boundaries of the household can be significant, and the use of networks of friends or relatives can extend opportunities to obtain work or more informal sources of income and support. But the chapters show that pressures are often mediated by individual characteristics. Gender has already been discussed. Generation can be particularly significant in terms of time of entry onto the labour market. Allan Sande shows the older generation of Norwegian men with direct experience of the transition from countryside to town during industrialisation, so that traditional fishing, hunting and farming activities are still familiar to them as a possible partial substitute way of providing for their own flourishing. The life options open to younger men are more restricted, and the case studies of Section C highlight the particular pressures on young men and women with very recent entry times into the labour-market and their effects on household transitions.

State benefits systems can of course impact on the process of household change. The comparative evidence of household behaviour in Britain and Norway which comes out from the following chapters does much to confirm the analysis presented in Chapter 3. As a predominantly individual insurance based system, Norwegian benefits cushion the economic impact of restructuring on households and widen the choice of strategies for household members. True, relatively generous unemployment provision may encourage wives to keep low-paid part-time jobs as a top up to household income, but generally speaking such a system acts as a very real buffer for households facing the effects of restructuring. The increasingly means tested British system is more likely to do one of two things. Either households are structured into unemployment of all household members once the breadwinner looses his job, because the unemployment trap and women's low wages combine to convice members that it is not economically worth while to take up employment at all. Research during the early 1980s into the division of domestic labour under these circumstances indicated that this also seems to maintain, or even to reinforce, traditional gender roles (Morris, 1985; McKee and Bell, 1985). The alternative scenario, presented in Chapter 7, is that wives actually keep up their employment despite the disincentives of low pay and the benefit system. In doing so, they help to preserve the dignity of the household. In the latter scenario the state provides no cushion at all, in the former, a strictly limited one. While the British benefit system may continue to provide a minimal income safety net for households affected by unemployment, it makes little contribution to household flourishing.

CHAPTER 6

THE FAMILY AND THE SOCIAL DIVISION OF LABOUR DURING INDUSTRIAL RESTRUCTURING

Allan Sande

What happens to the social division of labour when the main factory, the cornerstone of the local community, is forced to carry out drastic reorganisation leading to redundancies in the labour force? What happens to the sharing of household chores between men and women when the 'breadwinner' become unemployed?

This problem is an important one which affects everyday life in the many small towns entirely dependent on one single industry in Norway. As described in Chapter 5, in the local district of Rana, the state-owned iron and steel industry was reorganised and privatized during the period between 1988 and 1993. The restructuring process in this iron town of 25,000 citizens provided an opportunity to observe changes taking place in domestic work in the household and family. By interviewing members of 24 households that were affected by this restructuring process, we discovered new divisions of labour in the local labour market, and new patterns of sharing household chores between the sexes.

As a result of the reorganisation in the state-owned company, 2,000 of the 4,000 jobs in the industry disappeared between 1980 and 1990. In 1989 alone the restructuring process made 900 industrial workers redundant. Many households were affected by this change due to loss of work and early retirement, and because some former employees were classified as occupationally disabled. The total employment rate in Rana declined by 5.5 per cent between 1980 and 1990. But for men in full-time employment it declined 16.4 per cent in a mere five year period between 1985 and 1990. Women, on the other hand, increased their share of part-time and full-time employment by 4 per cent and 6 per cent respectively during the same period. The new jobs created by government were given to younger women (Høydahl, 1992). These labour market changes meant that men were squeezed out of jobs and found themselves unemployed.

This chapter shows that the response to changing conditions in the labour market was that unemployed men took on responsibility for domestic duties, while women went out to work or educated themselves. The changes that took place implied both change and maintenance in the division of labour between men and women at home and in the labour market (see also Sande, 1994; 1995a).

Local historical and cultural contexts

Household-based production on small farms and in seasonal fishing formed the basis for an increase in the population in the northern part of Norway, with natural conditions also maintaining a traditional adjustment to subsistence economy in the county of Nordland until the 1950s (Fulsås, 1987). The characteristic features of the traditional fisherman-cum-farmer society were the strict functional division of labour between the sexes, and the fact that production was carried out in a household-based barter economy. Women did all the work connected with the house and took care of the livestock, while the men took part in seasonal fishing, farm-work and seasonal wage labour to provide the household with the necessary cash to buy consumer and capital goods. Living conditions along the coast and the way work was organised in the community gave women considerable equality in relation to men. Women in the local community pooled their efforts to carry out environmental tasks connected with their surroundings, while men formed crews for the seasonal fishery activities. Both men and women enjoyed a great deal of independence in their ability to carry out specialised tasks in the household-based production system. In the local community, labour and skills were administered through parameters of age and sex.

The household-based economy and its associated patterns of gender roles changed radically with the introduction of commercialised consumer goods and the increasing mechanisation of farming and fishing in the 1960s (Flakstad 1984; Saugestad 1984). The progress of modern everyday life in local communities led to increased specialisation and to capital-intensive farming and fishing. The result was a decline in the combined farming economy, and a withdrawal of women from productive labour on the farm (see also Chapter 9). Men took over the capital intensive farming and fishing, while women withdrew to a position as housewives responsible for domestic work in the home. Women's labour power for agricultural production became redundant (Flakstad 1984).

This introduction of more mechanised production in primary production occurred simultaneously with the development of industry in northern Norway. It is in relation to the traditional fishermen-farmer communities that the increase in the number of single-income families among industrial workers in Rana during the 1960s must be understood. This same pattern of gender roles was applied to the organisation of household work that developed in the industrial town of Mo i Rana. In other words, men occupied jobs in industry, while women did housework and took care of the children. The result was an even more rigid specialisation and gender-based division of labour in everyday life than had been the case in rural areas, where there had been a degree of complementarity. Women could find only two kinds of work in industry: cleaning, or serving food in the canteen. Men did not participate in caring for the children or other home tasks. A 'traditional' division of labour between the sexes was maintained in this industrialised community.

The effects of industrial restructuring on everyday life

The first generation ironworkers in Mo worked hard and acquired a relatively good standard of living, especially in terms of housing. Many originated from modest fishing villages and farming communities situated at the peripheries of Nordland county. During their initial stay in Mo couples divided responsibilities between themselves, with the woman staying at home as a full-time housewife while the man worked in the factory. The woman took care of the children, cooked the food, washed the clothes, and did all the other household chores. The man was responsible for household repairs, the gardening, the repair of technical equipment, and all heavy work in addition to wage labour. In the 1970s, when their children had became teenagers, housewives took part-time jobs in shops or in the public health service. But none of the men took over any of the women's household duties, even though the women became wage earners. During their free time and at weekends, men went fishing, hunting or on other trips to the countryside and mountains to provide the household with firewood, berries, fish, grouse and game.

During 1988-89, a number of older male workers took early retirement. They stayed at home all day, and many started to do women's work in the domestic domain. As time passed, men took over most of the daily housework which had traditionally been their wives' responsibility. These early-retired men looked after (grand)children for the first time in their lives - and found pleasure in doing it. Traditional male activities like work in the garden, and at the country cabin, continued to be the man's responsibility. Housework was carried out in terms of a gift from husband to wife. He did the housework while she was out, and she could not interfere with the ways in which he performed it.

The second generation inhabitants - those between 20 and 40 years of age - adjusted to the changes in other ways when the household was affected by the fact that the main breadwinner became redundant in the labour market. In most of these households, the couple worked or studied full-time to make ends meet. Grandparents looked after the children during the day. Otherwise, whoever had time off, stayed at home and looked after the children. Some of the men who lost their jobs, or those who were classified as occupationally disabled at a relatively early age, took over the child care and the housework on a full-time basis.

Contrary to the situation of their parents, and traditional opinions of gender roles, lively discussions over the division of labour and the ways work should be carried out took place in many homes. The most serious discussions concerned standards of hygiene and orderliness in the house. Women criticised the way in which the work was done when they came home. Men were denied access to certain areas of housework, such as sorting out the dirty clothes and starting the washing machine, baking bread or serving food at family gatherings. Women tried to disqualify the men from such tasks in order to maintain their identity as women, and so men were regarded as incapable of carrying them out.

Domestic life, then, was subject to relatively great changes in the division of labour between men and women. At home, the traditional gender-linked domains of responsibility were dissolved. Women started to take a greater part in working life and higher education, while men went in the opposite direction, and became more active in domestic work. In households where the husband was jobless and received social benefits or retired early, the couple swapped roles. However, women were still responsible for, and managed, work within the house. The former industrial worker stayed at home all day, and it was the men's own choice to carry out most of the customary duties in the home.

Gender identity and the division of labour

The negotiations and conflicts found in the home imply a close and complementary relationship between men's work in industry and women's work in the home. In the factory men had reacted negatively to the appearance of women in industrial jobs during the 1970s, as well as to the ways in which they carried out this work. Productive jobs had been protected by (male) workers, through common admission rules for new employees, and informal systems for assessing seniority and qualifications in connection with different jobs. After a lengthy discussion in the trade unions, work such as cleaning and cooking were finally accepted as equal to work in the production process carried out by men. However, it was not acceptable for men to carry out work within traditional female-dominated areas.

Once they found themselves based at home, and entered traditional female areas of work, men met the same criticisms they had levelled at women in the factory. And women responded in the same way that men in the factory had done: women protected their domain by not sharing their skills and experience with men. They maintained their control within the domestic domain, although they allowed men to undertake the strenuous, time-consuming aspects of housework.

Men's status and identity had been determined by their place in the production process in the factory. Degrees of cleanliness and disorderliness were used to rank people of the same gender according to responsibility and degree of authority. Women manage their gender identity by means of cleanliness and tidiness at home. Conflicts arose at home when one gender trespassed into the other's traditional labour domains. Gender-related personal identity was also based on carrying out gender-linked work related with gender-associated aesthetics.

Homes had a sense of order, both inside and out, contrary to men's work in the factory. The majority of the houses had attractive, well-kept gardens. Almost all families owned their own flat or house, inside which they showed orderliness with plants, family photographs, pictures of the places they had come from, bookshelves and furniture. The home and its interior decorations were given high priority, and this was particularly the case during the reorganisation of the steel industry. The home shows the influence of a 'woman' through her aesthetic rules and preferences for the interior.

Food, and dust and cleanliness in the house were matters which caused the greatest disagreements between couples. Grime and food in work and leisure became cultural codes for expressing equality, difference, rank and autonomy, so that gender identity could be maintained and compared between workmates and couples. The reproduction of such complementary identities was based on a rigid division of labour at home and at work.

The effects of reorganisation were most obvious in the performance of household duties. Men kept their 'hegemony' at the steel factory, but they lost access to the new job opportunities in the service-providing sector. Older men began to take part in the daily domestic work in the house in an attempt to create a new and meaningful life for themselves outside the factory, while their wives took up wage labour in service-provision. Women took greater part in working life and contributed substantially towards the household's total income. This change came about along with organisational changes in trade and industry. The dynamics can be analysed by studying the development of gender-based divisions of labour in an area of capitalistic market economy and the household's internal 'moral economy'.

Continuity and change in gender roles

The overall effect of the labour market changes in Mo has been a decline in the possiblities for supporting a family on one income alone. Service employment is mainly available for newcomers to the labour market, and most of these are women. Their escape from the home was encouraged by their husband's drop in real income, his physical presence at home, and increasing uncertainty over access to permanent employment. Households have had to adjust to a situation where both parents have to have an income to enabling the family to survive in a community increasingly reliant upon the service sector.

New - and lower paid - jobs in private and public services have replaced many industrial job opportunities. Access to these jobs has given women new opportunities as an alternative to men's hegemonic role in the old and dirty heavy industry. The welfare state and its system of social benefits has given households reasonable economic conditions in which to survive during the period of industrial restructuring. By combining social benefits and part-time work for women with domestic work at home, households survived quite well economically.

In Norway, payment of unemployment benefits is not regulated by the husband's or wife's income but regarded as an individual right. The interplay of these factors makes Norwegian households flexible in combining social benefits and wages. Norwegian men do not lose their unemployment benefits when their wives have a steady income. The family's and local community's moral obligations and normative guidelines force men to perform 'inferior' work at home. The change in gender roles and domestic work is a result of identity management within the framework of the moral obligations of family in the context of the industrial restructuring in the local community.

These changes mean that household members must find new conditions and circumstances to live by. Those excluded from working life, too old to take on retraining and education, have retreated to the domestic sphere to find a new meaning in life. Housework and care for the children has gradually been taken over by the unemployed and by prematurely retired men. The family's moral obligations and outstanding claims in the household's 'moral economy' has forced men into complementary duties at home once they no longer had 'work'.

Women's traditional independence and gender identity was produced by means of autonomy and sole responsibility for housework. Her identity as an independent woman was threatened when her husband began to perform these duties. Men's roles as 'housekeepers' threatens women's autonomy, skill and responsibility in the household. Women's gender-related identity was maintained by reallocating some of the duties to be performed, while protecting their essential skill and responsibility for the domestic domain. This did not entirely change the social division of labour, and led only to a partial transformation of gender roles.

The dynamics of negotiation over work and duties differed substantially according to generation. The older generation - those who settled first in Mo - experienced a less painful process, where husband and wife adjusted easily to the new division of household chores without the need of deliberate negotiations. The younger generation experienced more conflict during the same process of change, along with a disintegration of the traditional gender-role pattern.

The first generation's adjustment must be understood in relation to the interplay between factors such as exclusion from working life due to seniority, life cycle and their historical background from subsistence economy in rural areas. The identity of men and women was tied to duties which in an industrial context, were regarded as hobbies; in the kitchen, the garden, hobby room or the summer cabin. More time for leisure meant greater possibility for developing oneself through hobbies. Natural conditions before the industrial transformation in Mo had required a great deal of flexibility in relation to traditional gender roles. Organisational changes in working life could be met with pragmatic solutions in the domestic domain in order to maintain home and family.

Modern relationships between younger married couples and household members based on the consumption of goods and income from labour, underwent a more painful process, where women made men feel incapable of performing certain household duties. Equality was more difficult to achieve in areas of responsibility and skill concerning relationships defined by love and affection. Equality at work and within the home broke with the cultural grammar for realising different gender identities through everyday life.

Government-controlled restructuring of the national steel company did not lead to cultural discontinuity, but strengthened the common family values in everyday life. The home and the family were given high priority during the readjustments in Rana. However, a moderate change in the traditional gender-role pattern in the domestic domain occurred. Identity management and the social division of labour in the affected households showed a large degree of continuity, even though the gender-specific pattern in everyday labour changed character.

CHAPTER 7

GENDER RESPONSES TO MALE UNEMPLOYMENT; OR, IS ANDY CAPP DEAD?

Jane Wheelock

Introduction

This chapter is based on a study - undertaken in the mid-1980s - of Wearside households where wives continued with paid work when their husbands were no longer in the labour force.[1] The outcome was unexpected: male unemployment was leading to quite substantial changes in who was doing what work in the household. Some of the new gender roles being adopted were far from representative of the Andy Capp image; Andy Capp, the North East cartoon character who fulfils so many of the stereotypes of the working-class male chauvinist. Chapter 4 has already suggested that the North East of England in general, and the Wearside economy in particular, have traditionally displayed employment features similar to those of other peripheral regional economies. Indeed, the history of Wearside since 1971 provides one of the most dramatic experiences of economic restructuring to be found in any traditional industrial area of the UK. This reasoning underlay the choice of locality, on the grounds that the impact of social and class restructuring and of gender recomposition at the level of the household could be established, specifically in terms of any changes in the divisions of labour inside the home.

As Chapter 3 points out, for reasons associated with the British state benefit system, households with wives continuing to work while their husbands are no longer in the labour market are relatively few in the population as a whole. Yet such households were representative of the Wearside situation at the time of the study in a double sense. Whilst the employment opportunites for male manual workers had declined, the prospects for low-paid women workers remained relatively buoyant (see Chapter 4). Other studies of the effects of unemployment on who does what domestic and child care tasks had generally concluded that male unemployment does little to alter the division of household work, or indeed that it reinforces traditional gender roles within the family (McKee and Bell, 1985; Morris, 1985). Recently researchers involved in the Social Change and Economic Life Initiative (Gershuny, Godwin and Jones, 1994) have put forward the idea of 'lagged adaptation', with household negotiation of changing work roles taking place over many years, including across generations. They draw their conclusions principally from time budget studies.

I wanted to study households where changes in household gender roles were intuitively most likely to occur - where traditional breadwinner roles were being reversed, and where the presence of children made the burden of domestic work relatively high. At one level, it is therefore not so surprising that amongst the 30 couples interviewed there was a marked shift towards a less traditional division of household work. But the type of household chosen also provided the advantage of being able to observe the process of changing roles. It became possible to establish links between capital restructuring and the internal dynamics of the household. The study showed how, in certain conditions of economic change, the process of lagged adaptation can be telescoped into time periods of a year or two at most.

The research hypothesis, based on a 'changing roles' perspective (Pleck, 1979) was that under these household economic circumstances, the time available to undertake domestic tasks would be doubly altered. Men, not being in paid employment, would have more time to undertake domestic work; whilst women, being in the labour market, would have less. If there were also children in the family, the burden of domestic work would be relatively large, making changes both more imperative and more observable. In line with the changing roles perspective, the research looked at household situations that might bring changes in gender roles within the family. A sample of 30 husbands and wives were interviewed, using tape-recorded structured interviews which also contained a questionnaire element on domestic and child care tasks. A representative sample of the chosen household type was drawn from a project examining employment potential in what is now the City of Sunderland, where questionnaires had been carried out with a 10 per cent sample of households in selected areas.

In the event it was found difficult to identify a sufficient number of families with unemployed husbands, employed wives and with children under 16 from this survey. This meant that the sample was less homogeneous than was originally intended in two respects. Firstly, families with adult children still living at home were included, and secondly, so were families with non-employed men below retirement age. Thus 8 of the sample husbands were in fact sick, either temporarily or permanently. As Ian Stone argues in Chapter 4, supply-side adjustments to changes in the demand for labour in a deindustrialising economy mean that it is justifiable to include the sick as part of the total unemployed. The sample households were predominantly middle-aged, and the former occupations of husbands conformed to the occupational pattern of the Sunderland economy of the 1960s - skilled and unskilled manual work, with a sprinkling of service sector occupations, such as a salesperson.

Classifying differences

An initial problem that arose as the empirical data was analysed was that it was difficult to find details of how the division of domestic labour had been identified in other studies. McKee and Bell (1985) had found few changes, so a typology was not really required. Lydia Morris's distinctions between traditional rigid, traditional flexible and role reversal provided a useful starting point for categorising the organisation of domestic work, but did not encapsulate the finer gradations that seemed to be coming out from the Wearside interviews (Morris, 1985; Warde (1990); Gregson and Lowe (1993) have since made use of variations on the fourfold classification developed in this project distinguishing traditional rigid, traditional flexible, sharing and exchanged roles forms of organisation. This gave a picture of variations between different households at the time of interview, when husbands were not employed and their wives were. (Further details of how the classification was developed are given in Wheelock, 1990, Chapter 4.)

In the traditional rigid form of organisation, the husband performs almost no domestic tasks apart from some predominantly male gendered minor tasks - 'men's work' - such as mowing the lawn. In the traditional flexible household, the wife may still be busy at the weekend or regularly do housework before or after going to work, but her husband will undertake some non-traditionally male gendered minor tasks, as well as, perhaps, washing-up, a major gender-neutral task. In the case of sharing households, a range of tasks including some of the five major tasks (vacuuming, washing-up, making the main meal, washing and ironing) are shared between husband and wife, or may even be done by the husband. The sharing household often has an ideology of mutual support and company.

In exchanged roles, the husband does a substantial range of tasks, either alone or shared with his wife, whilst she is either the family breadwinner or has more or less full-time employment. Whilst the wife may have little to say about domestic matters, her husband may well describe his household routine in some detail, and will have substantial responsibility for the household, at least through the week. Although this form of organisation involves a much looser gender segregation than the others, there will still be residual elements of tradition. An exchanged role organisation implies just that; there has been some exchange of roles between husband and wife, but there is certainly not complete role reversal.

The 30 households fell fairly evenly between each of the four categories at the time of interview, with 8 households each in the sharing and traditional flexible categories, and 7 each in the exchange role and the traditional rigid group. As Table 7.1 shows, when husbands became unemployed, there was some change in organisation of domestic work in nearly half the families (8 from a traditional rigid to a traditional flexible form of organisation, 5 from traditional flexible to sharing), and there was substantial change in a further 6 families, with 3 families moving from traditional flexible to exchange roles and 2 from traditional rigid. In other words, 20 families (nearly 70 per cent of the sample) underwent change towards a less rigid division of labour within the household, while only 7 families (less than a quarter) did not.[2] This is a striking indication of the responsiveness of the gender organisation of households to the non-employment of husbands, although it must be kept in mind that even the change to exchanged roles means that there is still a core of household and child care tasks undertaken by the wife.

With regard to the process of change, time available proved crucial to the gender distribution of family work precisely in the double sense that was assumed when the

Table 7.1 The degree of change in the organisation of household work

Type of change	No. of families	% of families
Traditional Rigid and Regressive	3	10%
Traditional Rigid No Change	4	13%
Some Change TR to Traditional Flexible *and* Sharing to More Sharing	14	47%
Substantial Change TF to Exchange Roles	6	20%
Non-assessable*	3	10%
Totals	30	100%

* Either recently married, or husband unemployed for more than 10 years
Source: Wheelock (1990)

project was initiated. On the one hand, unemployment was a precondition for men taking on more work than is involved in a traditional flexible form of household organisation. If the wife is employed, male unemployment does indeed tend to lead to a positive change in gender distribution and only in a minority of cases will there be no change or a regressive change. On the other hand, the amount of change will tend to be related to the number of hours that wives work. It is nevertheless a far cry from the traditional and patriarchal image of North East households incorporated in the Andy Capp cartoons.

The Wearside sample was surprising in two further respects. Firstly, women were working despite the restrictions of the benefit system and their own low earnings. Secondly, the number of hours that some women were prepared to work was unexpectedly high. The popular conception of low-paid female workers is that they are uncommitted to the labour market. This was certainly not the case for the majority of women in the sample: not only were many prepared to work despite the disincentives, but also hours worked and length of time in current job indicated a substantial commitment to the labour market. Before moving on to a possible explanation for these unexpected findings, let me pause to present a case study. This indicates some of the mechanisms for change, but shows that adapting to economic change presents no easy option for a household.

No easy option

The Bradshaws are an example of a family who have changed from a traditional flexible to an exchanged roles form of organisation. Mr Bradshaw spent 23 years as a baker until his employer went bankrupt with a divorce settlement, and he loved his job despite the low pay. As a child his mother was not very reliable so that he and his brother learned to fend for themselves from an early age. When they were first married Mr and Mrs Bradshaw therefore decided that they would share the domestic tasks, at least until the children came along. At the time of interview they had two: a son of 15 and a daughter of 13, and since their birth Mr Bradshaw has always helped with the housework on a Sunday, something that is most unusual for the men in the sample. When her son was about two, Mrs Bradshaw started work again on the twilight shift in a mail-order firm, and this is why she says: 'he's always helped, taking on nightly duties.'

Just over two years before the interview Mr Bradshaw was made redundant, and only four or so months later Mrs Bradshaw got full-time work as a warden in sheltered accomodation for the elderly. Possibly because he has always been helpful in the house, both Mr and Mrs Bradshaw took a modest view of the amount of change that has taken place, but Mr Bradshaw points out that he now does housework through the week. Mrs Bradshaw says that she has 'much more free time now even though I'm working full-time, because he does most of the household tasks,' although she occasionally does some housework in the afternoon when she's finished work. 'He does the housework, while I do the hobbies,' she adds.

For Mr Bradshaw it's 'very belittling really. A man shouldn't do housework. I'll do it, that's it.' Of the major tasks he shares four of them (washing up, vacuuming, shopping and decorating) and he sometimes does the main meal. He does it because 'I've nothing else to do and it's nice to see a clean tidy house, but there's no financial reward,' though there are three tasks he won't do; windows, ironing and washing. Most unusually the three managerial tasks of planning the meals, making the shopping list and household budgeting are now all shared in the Bradshaw household. Mr Bradshaw also helps his wife with her job, taking out all the rubbish and getting up for difficult male residents in the night. Again he regrets that this is unpaid. It is worth adding that Mrs Bradshaw earns just enough for her husband to be unable to claim any state benefit at all.

She loves her job - 'we should do more for our older people' - and though she knows 'it doesn't pay me to work, he worked for me and the kids so why can't I work for him? I wouldn't like to have social workers in,' But the job is demanding, 'and that's why I need Malcolm around to depend on.' Mrs Bradshaw is most appreciative of what her husband does for her, but sees it as very difficult for him to adapt to his new role: 'It doesn't matter to me if I work or not. It's more important for men, it's been inbred into them.' Mr Bradshaw now bears a substantial domestic burden, but for him it's no substitute for being the breadwinner and though he's pleased that 'we're both independent of the state, at the end of the day we're pounds out of pocket.' It is obvious that Mr Bradshaw would dearly love financial recognition for his role in the house, and for the help he gives his wife in her job.

Dignity in the face of change

The flexibility and adaptability shown by the men in the sample was primarily based on a pragmatic response to practical circumstances. In general it was practical circumstances that lead to change rather than abstract attitudes to roles. Nevertheless there could be serious conflict between traditional, patriarchal attitudes, and practice; in which case the gender division of labour actually adopted within the household tended to be more liberal than attitudes. In other words, the complexities of adjustment and adaptation appear to be primarily practically based.

Now of course the Wearside families studied were in circumstances which negated much of the material basis for a patriarchal attitude: none of the husbands were in employment, and unemployment makes a nonsense of ideas of a male breadwinner and a family wage. Indeed, particularly wives in full-time employment, were often regarded as the breadwinner, whilst, as we have seen, a substantial proportion of husbands were taking on more domestic work than previously. Negotiations over the gender division of labour within and outside the household were thus subject to a conflict between the traditional, or patriarchal model and the rationality, or maximisation of economic interests model (see Yeandle, 1984).

The state exacerbates this possibility for conflict within the family in a number of ways. Firstly, there is the gender bias in the benefits system which derives from the assumptions underlying the Beveridge system, and which, as we have seen in Chapter 3, no longer correspond to the structural realities of the British economy. Thus paid employment no longer prevents financial poverty. Female heads of household in particular are likely to be low-paid; full-time work is no longer the norm, again predominantly for women; full employment for men is proving no longer feasible, particularly in the regions; and finally, married women who undertake paid employment are no longer appropriately regarded as financial appendages of their husbands or co-habitees.

Many of the families in the Wearside sample were subject to the 'poverty trap' - or more specifically the 'unemployment trap'.[3] It is the combination of the unemployment trap with women's low pay which undermines the incentive for families to move towards role reversal as a response to male unemployment, and encourages the polarisation of households into those where husbands and wives are both in employment, and households where neither are in employment. So why were wives prepared to work in the labour market?

The empirical evidence just examined suggests a third model for negotiations over the gender division of household work strategies in addition to the traditional and the economic rationality models: a model of dignity and self-respect. In a substantial proportion of the sample - some 10 families in all - wives continued to work despite the fact that the household was at best only very marginally better off, and in some cases was actually worse off as a result. Far from responsibility lying with individual households who are prepared to relapse into dependency on the welfare state - even to scrounge - state benefits and legislation actually encourage the traditional, patriarchal attitudes which undermine families' ability to act in an economically rational manner. Yet concern for dignity, in some of the sample families at least, was sufficiently strong to overcome both economic rationality and traditional attitudes.

Nevertheless, widespread evidence of perceptions of gender specific roles was apparent from the sample. Only one man ever did the ironing for example. Jobs perceived as 'women's work' and undertaken in public were rarely performed by men. Thus only one man cleaned the windows, something he explained by the fact that his father was a window cleaner by profession. There was a widespread view that men ought to be breadwinners. This was expressed most starkly by one interviewee - a cleaning supervisor, and the best-paid woman in the sample. She greeted me at the door to say that she had been looking forward to talking to me: 'let me put it this way,' she said of her unemployed electrician husband, 'to me he's not a man any more.' Personal identity itself can be brought into question when gender roles change. The strength of feeling amongst some couples that the gender changes they had adopted were alien to them was so great, that a small subcategory of 'reluctant' sharing and 'reluctant' traditional flexible was identified.

The potential for conflict within families where husbands are not working and their wives are in low-paid work is thus high. Not only are households the arena within which the gender conflict between the economic rationality demands of capitalism and the traditional demands of a patriarchal rationality is playing itself out; the household is also the focus for resolving the conflict between market rationality and the urge towards self-reliance and independence from the state. In households where men have become unemployed, it is wives who hold the key to the self-respect which the family can obtain by irrationally working in the labour market in order to avoid dependence on the welfare system, itself in conflict with traditional views of the gender division of labour. Despite Wearside men taking on new roles which by no means correspond to traditional stereotypes, adjustment to non-employment is not easy, since the potential for conflict within the household is large.

Household work strategies, then, and negotiations between the sexes over such strategies, are not merely adopted in response to market forces, but also to pressures from traditional views and from the state, these two reinforcing each other; as well as arising from the family's sense of dignity. Market forces themselves are in any case not purely economic in nature, but are affected by the historical development of the gender division of labour, which can both be reinforced by traditional ideology and actually masked by it. In seeking self-repect, families are on the one hand keeping the market at bay through the development of inter-personal relations within the household which lead to a household work strategy which conflicts with economic rationality. On the other hand, they are keeping the state at bay by attempting to avoid dependence on the welfare state as far as possible, where again the household work strategy conflicts with economic rationality, as well as with the traditional rationality incorporated in the benefit system. This can be seen as the adoption of a personalised family way of life, as opposed to a public one. Yet it is a process of personal privatisation not merely with respect to the state, but also with respect to the market. As Jahoda (1982) documents, people do indeed have a need to undertake purposive work.

Even in households where changes in gender roles were not taking place, people saw changes in their social networks and in public perceptions. Take one of the traditional rigid households interviewed - so traditional, that as the husband said: 'well, if I want a cup of coffee of an evening, the wife gets it.' Yet husband and wife commented in chorus: 'younger people don't do things like us any more do they?' It was noticeable that the wife had given up her part-time job which she had held for four years. Nobody said as much, but why should she continue to take on a double burden of work, while her husband took on no household tasks? As he himself acknowledged: 'I'm just looking after the budgie.' It remains true that from the evidence of this study, the response to economic change need not be as lagged as Gershuny, Godwin and Jones (1994) imply. One of the respondents pointed out that it was no longer impossible to let on at the working men's club that he did some of the housework - indeed the difficulties of vacuuming or getting the shopping done had become regular topics of conversation amongst men there. How sad that policy makers do not devise policies aimed at encouraging men and women to share both paid breadwinning and unpaid caring work.

Notes

1. I should like to thank the Equal Opportunities Commission for the grant which made this study possible, and for the generous cooperation of the Wearside families without whom the work could not have been undertaken.

2. Three families could not be assessed, either because they had been unemployed for such a prolonged period. or because husband and wife had only recently married.

3. Under the benefit rules in force at the time of the study, if spouses earned over £4 per week, claimants had a pound for pound deduction from their supplementary benefit. Benefit rule changes since 1985 have modified this situation, but poverty and unemployment traps have not been eliminated.

CHAPTER 8

REFLECTING FLEXIBILITY: FROM THE SECURITY OF REGULAR EMPLOYMENT TO COPING WITH CASUAL WORK

Asbjørn Karlsen

This chapter sets out to explain how the new, flexible employment policies of regional firms rely on the flexibility of the individual worker, of his or her household, and on the provisions of the welfare state. It is based on a study of two manufacturing locations: one is the steel plant in Mo i Rana situated in Northern Norway, the other, the woodworking and house prefabrication industry of Moelven in Ringsaker, in the south-east of Norway. Redundancy in manufacturing industries and changing manpower practices are new experiences for workers who until recently have considered their jobs permanent. How do individual workers and their households cope with the change from permanent employment to the insecurity of casual work and unemployment? Occupational identities are challenged in the transition from regular to temporary employment. Orientations and careers can be looked on as mediations between a changing labour market, the functioning of the household and identity management. How then are workers' identities bound up with their orientations and careers? The chapter examines how households cope when the main breadwinner loses a permanent job, and faces the prospect of casual work and unemployment, and how this relates to changes in the construction of identity.

The changing local economy

The development of a Fordist economy was a post-war phenomenon in Norway. Many manufacturing industries located in rural districts and small towns developed large-scale production with the support of the state (Karlsen 1996b). Localities such as Mo in northern Norway, and Moelven in the south-east, became one-company towns, almost totally dependent on the activities of a single company. The steel plant in Mo i Rana and the woodworking and house prefabrication industry of Moelven in Ringsaker employed mainly male labour power. When migrating rural families settled in such industrial towns, women left their position as productive workers in the peasant household, to become housewives in urban dwellings.

The Fordist economy meant a temporal and spatial separation of paid work and domestic work. A particular feature was the 'standard labour contract' which provided regular working hours and job security. Unskilled workers got permanent full-time jobs in local manufacturing industry, and this standard labour contract was soon taken for granted. Neither employers nor employees questioned the norm of regular full-time employment. Such employment opportunities in the local industrial complex were open to young males who had completed compulsory school. A job in local manufacturing industry was considered a job for life.

However since the late 1980s the industries of Mo i Rana and Moelven have faced an economic crisis, undergoing a process of restructuring. Production units were closed, many workers were laid off and unemployment rates increased. Government intervened to make the restructuring process smoother, because of the serious effects on local communities. Special employment and education programmes and public funds for industrial development, were allocated to municipalities. In the case of Rana, national public services were relocated to create new jobs as compensation for the loss of jobs in the manufacturing industry (see Chapter 5).

A new business idea among the restructuring agents and managers was for firms to concentrate on their basic activities and to outsource subordinate functions. Fission of integrated industrial production into independent units became part of the strategy. The relatively influential trade union which had been a dominant local actor for more than three decades, was similarly split up into several units. During this restructuring process, labour contracts were redefined. Unemployed workers who previously had regular employment, were engaged as casual labourers on short-term contracts.

Flexible firms, flexible households, reflexive workers?

There has been much scholarly debate on post-Fordism, flexible specialisation and the concept of flexibility in general. Here we pay attention to Atkinson (1984; 1985) who uses the flexible firm as a point of departure, and where flexibility is looked upon as a new managerial strategy. Atkinson makes a distinction between 'functional' and 'numerical' flexibility. Functional flexibility comes into operation when multiskilled employees move smoothly between different activities. Numerical flexibility is the ability to change the size of the workforce quickly and easily in response to changes in demand. This often implies policies with a less committed relationship between employer and employee; the latter may experience being hired to do a job and then weeded out.

Critics of Atkinson's model find that his analysis of flexibility provides a simplistic interpretation (Rainnie and Kraithmann, 1992; Lie 1994). Pollert (1988) points out that there have always been labourers with casual work and insecure jobs. Certainly this is not a new phenomenon within a broader perspective of history. There were more permanent jobs and less casual work among male industrial workers in our localities during the period 1960-90 than at both earlier and later times. We may indeed say that this period was an exceptional epoch.

More importantly Atkinson's model lacks an institutional perspective. First, the model does not take into account the significance of regulations in the labour market. One such regulation is the principle of seniority, which determines who will lose their job, who will continue and who will be recruited. Neither is the interplay between flexibility strategies and the national social security system taken into account. Secondly, Atkinson's model does not include the informal economy and particularly not the household level (see Chapter 11). The household is important for achieving increased flexibility both as a distribution and reproductive unit. With a focus on the household level, the role of domestic work in the daily and generational reproduction of labour power is included.

The notion of promoting a flexible work force raises important questions about identity management. Concepts from the debate on modernity by Beck (1992; 1994) and Giddens (1991; 1994b) are relevant for the broader analysis of this process. During the Fordist epoch workers experienced stability in everyday life. Their regular activities can be related to the concept 'ontological security'. Giddens (1991) maintains that day-to-day routine in social interaction keeps anxiety at bay. Due to new employment practices and general uncertainty in the labour market, this regularity is lost. With the title of his book Beck (1992) characterises the new modern society as a 'risk society'. Modern social life introduces new forms of risk which previous generations did not have to face (Giddens, 1991). The transition from the industrial to the risk period of modernity occurs as undesired, unseen and yet inevitable (Beck, 1994).

How do workers keep a sense of order in the world and achieve control over these changes? In our study, workers experienced the need to be more flexible. The concept of reflexivity is used to explain what happens. The reflexive project is to construct a coherent and yet continously revised biography. Since the risk society is not an option that one can choose or reject, reflexivity implies self-confrontation. The construction of identity is generally related to competence. With reflexive modernisation the value of traditional competencies, ways of thinking and lifestyle is taken over by universal forms of knowledge and language. This expansion of abstract systems is often met by re-educating. Identity is threatened by a deskilling process. Schooling will often mean choosing and planning one's own social biography (Beck, 1992).

Each person's biography is thus removed from the determinations given by local tradition, social class and the nuclear family. It is taken over by agencies and institutions which make the individual dependent upon fashions, social policy, economic cycles and national and global-level markets. In consciousness however, an image of individual control is established. The individual is put in a position where he or she may have to take a stand continually. Beck (1992) finds that the new modernity also generates tension at the level of the nuclear family. Men and women are released from traditional forms and prescribed roles in the search for a 'life on their own'. Conflicts are opened up because production and family work are subjected to contrary organisational principles. The former requires individual competition and mobility, while the latter necessitates sacrifice for other family members.

Work and household experiences for temporary workers

Our empirical material consists of interviews with 22 workers in Mo i Rana and

Ringsaker, all of whom had experienced a transition from regular to temporary employment. These workers were employed by six different firms. Since the manufacturing industries in the two localities are dominated by men, we interviewed just three female workers. Most of the workers were between 25 and 45 years old; due to the principle of seniority, those on short term contracts are to be found in this age group.

Exceptionally, there were a few young workers in their early twenties and a few older men on temporary contracts. Let us consider these first. Some of the young workers were recruited as apprentices. They lived with their parents, tending to postpone establishing their own household. As with the young men reported from the studies made by Magnussen (see Chapter 13) and Hollands (see Chapter 12) they face a delayed transition into permanent work and thereby also into adulthood. They found it difficult to save enough money to set up home and periods of unemployment created an undesired discontinuity in their everyday life.

A few of the older workers engaged in short-term work contracts; they had been working in manufacturing industry for many years, but had lost their seniority because of job changes. However, their domestic economy is relatively comfortable despite periods of unemployment, for their mortgages tend to be small and their children have usually left the household. Unemployment still shakes their judgement of their moral worth, and being without paid work represents a loss of dignity:

> I can't somehow accept that you work for three or four weeks and
> then you are out again. That you just drop in when they are in need
> of help and afterwards you are worth nothing.

Let us now focus on the main body of workers between their late twenties to late thirties with an established family household of their own. The social background, family and gender of workers appear to be significant factors in the choice of occupation. The fathers of most of these workers had been industrial workers, with their sons following in to the same firm. These second generation workers often lost their jobs at an age when their fathers had retained secure employment. Yet they were accustomed to high unemployment among their workmates, friends, kin, neighbours and other people in the locality. Being unemployed is no longer a social stigma, because so many are out of work that it becomes part of everyday life. Robert illustrates the changing attitudes to being unemployed:

> It lies heavier on my parents because they belong to a generation
> who thinks that work is the most desirable pastime on this earth.

Nevertheless, unemployment struck most of the workers we interviewed as a shock. They considered temporary employment as something that was forced upon them.

> I remember the days before the 1980s. We could pick and choose
> jobs.

The worst problems they face are those of making ends meet in the domestic economy, and the uncertainty for the future. For some, the shorter-term horizons make for problems of planning, of coordinating other jobs and organising family holidays. Periods of unemployment disrupt the time structure of the day as well. Just a very few are willing to admit that they have periods of depression. Yet despite these problems, many workers still cling to their former employers. Peter (43), for example, stays at home all day, close to the telephone, with nothing particular to do, until his wife comes home from her job, for:

> You never know what time they will call you and tell you to come to work.

Some workers find casual work elsewhere, breaking such reliance on a former employer. Others attend vocational training courses with a view to entering other segments of the labour market. Female workers appear to have more flexible attitudes in these regards than their male colleagues.

Let us now present the stories of four workers to illustrate the relationship between the changing labour process within the industry and the organisation of the household. These typical cases indicate how social background, former working experiences, and constraints and opportunities in the labour market help to shape workers' orientations and adaptations.

John (35), a steelworker seeking a new career

As soon as he left compulsory school John became a sailor, but after two years he followed in his father's footsteps and got a job in the steel industry. In order to learn different practical skills, John was prepared to move between different jobs. Over the nine years he worked in the industry, John found the number of workers at the ironworks continually reduced, as the production process was modernised and the working day intensified. He took the opportunity to get trained at work, and after a final examination received an 'iron and steel production' certificate. However, John discovered that this formal qualification was of little value when it came to job security. He therefore spent holidays and weekends attending courses directed to jobs offshore. Sure enough, in 1993 he got notice to quit, and from then on he was offered only casual jobs at the ironworks. John remained very active in sustaining the relationship with his former employer, but finds his job situation very difficult:

> It is getting worse. A permanent job is hardly likely... They didn't need me any more... I can't stand this. It's so insecure.

His dream is of a job on the oil rigs in the North Sea, and John puts a lot of energy into searching for such a job.

John and his wife Anne have three children. Anne attended a training course aimed at one of the newly created public jobs. A year after her husband lost his job, she was offered one. The considerable public efforts in creating new jobs in Rana proved very helpful for Anne and the household economy in general. The rent they receive from renting out a batchelor flat in their basement is a highly necessary supplement to their income, along with John's unemployment benefit. John had always taken some part in the domestic work of the household, but Anne's view was that she did most of the domestic work. When John lost his job, and his wife took up paid work, this division of domestic labour didn't change radically.

Henry (39), a joinery worker using skills in the informal economy

As a teenager, Henry started employment in the wood industry, working in sawmills and in construction work. In the middle of the 1970s he got a job at Moelven. He contrasted his own flexibility with other workers who were not willing to move between job activities. When Moelven was struck dramatically by a fall in market demand for prefabricated family houses, workers, among them Henry, lost their jobs. Soon he was offered temporary employment at his former workplace. Henry explained how the conditions of production changed as delivery deadlines became shorter and shorter. Much overtime work was put in. He reflected on the changes from the times when the local trade union had been strong, with everything carefully planned.

Since Henry lost his regular job, he has developed a sideline in the informal economy. His father was a joiner with well-rounded experience in the trade, and a good reputation in the local district. Henry had learned his practical skills as a joiner through an informal training with his father. When Henry lost his job, he invested in joiner's tools. During the summer many people now ask him to do work for them. He has developed in confidence, realising how fortunate he has been to have this work to rely upon. The short-time horizon of his formal work makes it difficult for Henry to plan his own business. He must be careful to not take on more work than he can cope with. Yet at the same time he finds it difficult to refuse a job offer, because he knows that work could be scarce at any time.

Henry misses being with the children when he has to work until late in the afternoon. He considers his wife's half-time job is ideal, as he believes it is not good for both parents have full-time jobs. Henry acknowledges that he takes no part in domestic work: 'she doesn't like me to meddle in her system'.

Heidi (32), a welder coping with casual work in different segments of the labour market

Heidi had three years education at a technical college. As a casual labourer in an engineering workshop she got the opportunity to take a welding certificate. After two years she became a welder at one of the engineering workshops which had the steel plant as its main market. She stayed there for six years until the firm went bankrupt and had to close. She had been comfortable at work:

> In some ways I have settled into men's work...I think it is normal for me.

Heidi is married to Hans, who, like her father, was employed at the charcoal factory. A fairly large, detached house and a private car mean a capital intensive domestic economy which depends on two wage incomes. When the government decided to close the charcoal factory in 1988, both her husband and father lost their jobs. since education was offered free of charge, Hans took the opportunity to requalify himself for a new service job. During his studies Hans received unemployment benefit, and he got job as a manager as soon as the new public service office was established.

Although the loss of her job came as a shock, Heidi soon got temporary employment at another engineering firm which was outsourced from the ironworks company, though there was plenty of labour power available, as several engineering workshops in the district had recently shut down. Employment of casual workers had become common, and Heidi benefitted from her welding certificate. In addition to the casual job in the engineering workshop, Heidi has two other jobs. One she obtained in a firm of industrial cleaners through an acquaintance; the other is a job as a subsititute in the kindergarden that her daughter attends. Heidi looks upon herself as a well-rounded worker, but prefers the job as welder.

> You just need to be prepared mentally. A job is a job.

Heidi's career sets her apart from most other woman in the locality. The paid work roles of Heidi and Hans turn the traditional roles of women and men upside down. This is also the case within the privacy of their own home: domestic work is shared between wife and husband in a non-traditional way. During the restructuring process, their household has become flexible in terms of both paid and unpaid work.

Martin (40), a carpenter tied to his workplace and hard hit by new manpower policies

After secondary school Martin took odd jobs until he was employed by a painting shop, where he worked twelve years before it went bankrupt. Later, in the mid 1980s, he was employed at Moelven. For more than ten years he was at the same place of work and found this continuity satisfying for: 'then you know what to do'. The production unit was hit hard by the closure of the two other company factories, and had a tough time developing new markets and products. During this process, half of the workforce, among them Martin, had to go. As with Henry, and other work mates, Martin is now a temporary worker at Moelven. As far as Martin remembers, he has had at least five periods out of work. Workers are surprised at these unaccustomed employment terms.

Martin and Maria have two children. Early in their marriage, they bought a detached house entirely financed by a bank loan. Maria stayed at home, though for a short period she got a job in a newly established firm, working in the evenings, which meant that Maria and Martin didn't spend much time together. There was a period when Martin stayed at home and Maria was out at work, when Martin took a greater part in the domestic responsibilities: 'you have to help when you have kids'.

They never discussed how to share domestic work between them, but Maria had higher standards when it came to the washing and cleaning.

The household economy came under severe hardship when Martin lost his job, and it was at this period that Maria and Martin divorced. They sold their house and each bought separate apartments. Martin had to take out an additional, high-interest loan, as well as paying child-support. His outgoings were so high that finally he had to resort to social security. He also had to change his patterns of consumption; it was even difficult to afford the food he had been accustomed to buying.

Martin does not see his periods of unemployment as an opportunity to become involved in other activities. He doesn't apply for jobs, finding few job advertisements in the newspapers. He cannot move, since he wants to live near his children. He does not consider taking a course. Occasionally he visits his former place of work, or a restaurant to have a chat with friends. Often he sleeps late in the morning, turning his days and nights upside down. He was not mentally prepared for his first lay-off; now he sometimes has difficulty sleeping, and this wears away at his nerves.

Household adaptations

Since most households had no savings set aside, the new economic situation usually forced them to make changes to the adaptation of the household to make ends meet. All of the case study workers received unemployment benefits during their periods of unemployment which compensated, to some degree, for the decrease in the flow of income into the household. However, mostly due to investment in housing, many households had become capital-intensive, relying on wage incomes from both partners. Without savings, capital intensive households become sensitive to any reduction in income flows. Newly established households found it hardest, having to make financial adjustments such as renegotiating bank loans or repayment terms. Those households which were hardest hit - including divorced couples - sold their houses to buy cheaper flats. Even two-income families still had to adjust their domestic economy by cutting down on extra expenses. Some households had to reduce their purchases of food and delay purchases of new clothes. Only two of the survey households which lost incomes from one regular employment, were able to compensate with more paid work by the partner. Couples seldom discussed the option of the female partner taking more paid work in these circumstances.

Unemployment among male workers raises important questions about gender indentity and the division of labour within households. The evidence showed that the traditional gender based division of labour in the domestic sphere was not seriously modified when the breadwinner lost his permanent job: many workers did not spend more time at home at all, because they either got other casual jobs, or attended a training course.

But let us concentrate on those who did spend more time at home. To a variable degree, they participated more in domestic work during their periods of unemployment. The two workers below represent contrasts. Peter, at home waiting for a call from his former employer, did not spend time on domestic work:

> It is a question of routines, you see...You are not allowed to touch anything in the house either.

Another explained that when he was in permanent work:

> I did not dislike domestic work...but you were perhaps exhausted and usually tired out. I very often was asked to do this and that, but I just postponed it, you see.

But when he became unemployed, things changed:

> I was not very clever with domestic work, but I became a 'housewife' and I learned things...such as baking bread which I still do.

On re-employment though:

> I have to some extent returned to my former habits. Because she is still in a full-time job...to ease my conscience, I have said that I'll buy her a dishwasher.

Most male workers interviewed fell somewhere between the positions of the two workers just cited. They participated domestically a little more during the periods of unemployment than before, but for most this lasted only until they became employed again, even in cases where the woman took up more paid work.

The restructuring process has done much to undermine the standard labour contract. By introducing new employment practices employers leave the reproduction of labour power to the individual worker to a greater extent, along with his or her household and to the welfare state. Flexibility requirements are transferred down the hierarchy from basic industry, to suppliers and down to the household. This last thus represents a productivity reserve for the former two. As Beck (1992) points out, this is a way of shifting entrepreneurial risk onto employees.

Our analysis of the process of flexibilisation points to the importance of the social security system for the reproduction of the workforce. At the level of the household, transactions to reduce housing expenditures and economising in the domestic economy, are common adaptations. To a lesser degree, the partners of workers increased their participation in the labour market as a household strategy to make ends meet.

We conclude that there exist mutual relations between the flexible strategies of firms, the general conditions in the labour market, the system of social security and the flexible functioning of the household. It is for this reason that we find Atkinson's focus on managerial strategies too narrow an interpretation of the way in which flexibility is implemented.

Reflecting flexibility

In general, our empirical material indicates less modification to the traditional division of domestic work than Sande and Wheelock have reported in Chapters 6 and 7 respectively. The more temporary character of unemployment in this study is the likely reason, where gender roles were very much taken for granted in the new situation of periodic bouts of unemployment. Yet growing flexibility is also a process of differentiation between workers affected by restructuring policy. The cases of John, Henry, Heidi and Martin illustrate four different adaptations to a situation where workers have lost regular employment and are left with casual work.

John finds it unthinkable to stay at home without work; an active life with paid work is crucial to his identity. His open attitude towards different sorts of work and his learning capacity form his labour market capital. When his job prospects started to decline, he realised the value of formal qualifications, but as a steelworker he had few obvious alternatives, since his skills were not transferable. With no mental barriers to a change of career, John's strategy was to retrain, as a first step towards moving to a different segment of the labour market. John has relied on different economic resources within the household during his periods of unemployment and retraining.

Though Henry does not find temporary employment desirable, he is able to cope with his new labour market situation through some self-employment. Henry is aware that his background, different work experiences and networks are resources that other workers do not possess. During the restructuring process, Henry revitalised the informal skills he had gained from his father. His identity as a self-employed craftsman is thus inherited. Nevertheless, there are high transaction costs from Henry's job combination. He spends long hours at work at the expense of family life. His adaptation is a way of securing a domestic economy by developing different options in the face of an uncertain future.

After the shock of losing her former place of work, Heidi's identity became more related to coping with different casual jobs. She made conscious use of social networks in her survival strategy. Though she looked upon herself as a welder who operated in a difficult segment of the labour market, she was self-confident and able to take up a variety of different jobs. In breaking away from traditional gender roles, the household was able to adapt in a flexible way to the changing labour market.

We interpret these three offensive strategies as products of reflexivity. Loyal workers like Martin, however, let all their hopes rest in the hands of their former employer. Martin had always been strongly tied to his place of work. He placed confidence in the routines of his working day. Even after being laid off, Martin still feels that he belongs to the workgang. In contrast with John, Henry and Heidi, Martin took no steps to establish a new career as his job situation worsened. He was soon in a vicious circle, hit by both a breakdown in his relationship to his regular job and to his partner. Social relations in both fundamental spheres of his life were lost. They were not compensated by other supporting networks, for Martin had few to resort to. He has ended up in social isolation, feeling that life has lost much of its meaning. It is loyal workers such as Martin who become the real losers as the requirements of flexibility are passed down from firm to household.

Workers' occupational identities are very much related to their qualifications. During the Fordist period when the standard labour contract prevailed, identity was connected to the employee's segmented job. As labour market changes and flexibility strategies are introduced, new occupational identities develop. Workers are put in a position where they must frequently take decisions regarding work, and perhaps reconsider their careers. From this the 'flexible worker' may emerge. These are workers whose identities are not related to her or his qualifications alone, but also to their capability to cope with an insecure and changing labour market. Such flexibility is partly dependent upon the household. Flexibility - and reflexivity - are less evident in regard to a gender-based division of labour. Couples do not automatically adapt to the different job opportunities available to men and women in the labour market irrespective of their traditional roles. Generally speaking, the husband is still looked upon as the main breadwinner and domestic work is mostly left to his wife.

SECTION B

CHANGES IN FAMILY AND HOUSEHOLD BASED PRODUCTION

Neil Ward and Agnete Wiborg

Household firms have symbolic significance in the national cultural identities of both Norway and the UK: the Norwegian farm or fishing household battling against harsh natural conditions provides the backbone of Norwegian national identity, while the British are sometimes referred to as 'a nation of shopkeepers'. Firms which are predominantly household or family enterprises also provide a useful focus for those studying the interplay between economic and social life with the household providing an arena for both economic activity and the construction and management of social identities. The chapters in this section thus explore the relationships between the organisation of economic activity and changing social relations within households in the context of economic restructuring in Britain and Norway. As a result, comparisons in this section not only straddle the divide between the British and Norwegian experiences, but also the divide between the rural and the urban, and between the agricultural and the non-agricultural. Some important distinctions should, however, be made at the outset between the different national contexts for household firms, be they urban or rural, in Britain and Norway. These contexual distinctions revolve around differences in the role of the public sector and the welfare state, the social geographies of town and country and different national agricultural structures and support policies.

The dominance of 'New Right' economic and social policies since the late 1970s in Britain has led to important shifts in the policy framework within which household firms are established and operate. Schemes such as the Enterprise Allowance Scheme have sought to encourage the establishment of new small firms and stimulate self-employment as part of a 'self-help' ethos. In Norway, employment generation has depended more in recent times on the development of a large public sector providing education, health care and social services while these activities have been the targets of budgetary squeezes in Britain. The Norwegian welfare state is still dominated by a system of social insurance, but with a strong sense of individual rights to benefits enshrined in that system (See Chapter 3). Moreover, the notion of individual rights to benefits means that unemployment is no great bar to geographical mobility in Norway. It is easy for the unemployed to remain in rural areas, or even for the urban unemployed to return to their rural origins. In Britain, the 1980s and 1990s have seen the erosion of the social insurance model and its replacement with social assistance (or 'means testing'). Household-oriented means testing has discouraged more flexible work strategies and concentrated the experiences of unemployment in 'unemployed households'. The move away to individual rights to benefits also accentuates a divide between the geographically mobile employed and the less mobile unemployed.

In Britain, it is primarily the employed who are moving to the countryside, often for lifestyle reasons, because the countryside is perceived as a pleasant place to live. This process, commonly called 'counter-urbanisation', has transformed the social geography of Britain in recent decades as members of the affluent middle-classes have moved from larger urban centres to smaller towns and rural regions. These rural in-migrants often, of course, continue to orient their working lives to the urban realm.

In Norway, counter-urbanisation trends have been less pronounced. Indeed, a major concern of rural policy has been to prevent the loss of population to urban areas through a system of state intervention, public sector support and regional policy. This is not to say that rural society in Norway is not experiencing important transformation processes, but rural transformation tends to be 'from within', rather than through the infusion of a post-urban, affluent middle-class bringing post-materialist environmental and lifestyle concerns into even the most peripheral rural areas, as has been the case in Britain.

Linked to the desire to prevent rural depopulation in Norway has been a strongly protectionist agricultural policy and an aim, pursued during the 1970s and 1980s, to guarantee comparable incomes between farmers and industrial workers. Hence levels of farm subsidies per hectare in the early 1990s were around four times higher in Norway than in the EU (OECD, 1991). Addressing rural and regional development objectives in Norway through support for agriculture has met with some success and has stimulated return migration and new investment in many marginal rural areas (Almås, 1990). In contrast, agricultural policy in Britain has been pinned to the EU's Common Agricultural Policy since the early 1970s with its repeated efforts since the early 1980s to address budgetary crises and reduce over-production and subsidies. Thus the movement towards world market prices for agricultural commodities began earlier and has developed further in Britain compared with Norway, prompting an earlier and deeper squeeze on farm household incomes.

Differences are also stark in the structure of the agricultural sectors of Norway and Britain. The average Norwegian farm has around 11 hectares of cultivated land, compared with an average of around 60 hectares in the UK. Dairy farms average 12 cows in Norway but nearer 70 in the UK. Moreover, Norwegian agriculture is dominated by part-time farming and multiple income sources characterise the vast majority of Norwegian farm households. Under a quarter of farm households derive more than 90 per cent of their income from agriculture (Almås and Ward, 1994), a proportion much lower than in Britain.

While household firms operate in distinct national political and economic environments in Norway and Britain, there are still useful comparisons between different responses to restructuring processes to be made, as the following chapters show. The chapters address these issues from different starting points - the newly formed household firm, the gender roles among farm families and the relationship between family, business and rural society - but each helps shed light on the relationships between economic activity and the household and between household change and economic restructuring processes. The household firms analysed in Chapter 10 were *established* in response to economic restructuring in a deindustrialising region. The two other chapters, focussing upon changes in established rural household businesses, illustrate the ways that household business and work strategies are being reshaped and renegotiated in the context of economic restructuring and the changing social relations of rural society.

From the three chapters, interesting comparative themes and insights emerge. Chapter 8 shows how the meanings associated with farm work are being transformed in rural Norway. Once agricultural work was shared between men and women and was understood to be an integral part of (shared) household work. But with the decline of primary industries and the increase in public sector employment in rural areas, gender roles are becoming separated and more distinct and both the idea and nature of agricultural work is shifting. Boundaries are changing and the team-work aspect of farm labour is being replaced by fragmententation and new gender codings for different tasks.

Chapter 9 develops a theme raised in Chapter 8, that of the heterogeneity of farm households. Even within a single locality, farm households do not make up a homogenous category. The chapter identifies three categories of dairy farmers in Britain on the basis of the environmental sensibilities they express about the problem of water pollution. The two extreme categories represent a traditional, 'business as usual' approach, while a more forward-looking, environmentally sensitive group seem much more amenable to the renegotiated 'rules of the game' in a rapidly changing rural society. These more 'radical' households are more likely to have moved away from a position wholly dependent upon income from agriculture and to have established tourist or other non-agricultural enterprises on their farms, sometimes with women or wives taking on the responsibilities for these new enterprises. The traditional, more environmentally 'sceptical' farm households cling more firmly to the notion of family continuity of farm occupancy through succession to the next generation, while the desire to pass on the business to the next generation has been eroded among the more radical households. Family succession, as a particular agricultural form of 'youth transition', provides a focus for the way family members give meaning to the farm business. Succession can serve as an orienting principle around which the relationship between household and business can be held together in symbolic as well as economic terms. If succession is ruled out, the farm comes to mean quite different things to family members.

Chapter 10 similarly demonstrates how economic restructuring and industrial change are stimulating changes in the ways households engage with wider economic processes and how they at the same time adjust internal work relations, often with a view to improving their flexibility. Here, economic recession in North East England has prompted the formation of new household business ventures. The case study in Chapter 10 highlights the ways that forming new firms brings with it changes in household tasks and changes in the make-up of the teams to carry them out.

Together the chapters in this section provide a range of examples of how household firms in different geographic, economic and social contexts are adapting to change. The chapters highlight the different ways households as social units relate to economic activities and the labour market and the ways these relationships are changing over time. In Chapter 8, the symbolic meanings within households associated with different forms of work are shifting. Agricultural work, for example, was commonly seen as part of the household's shared tasks and is increasingly becoming a specialised 'one-man show'. At the same time as women enter the labour market, so housework tasks increase in importance as a household 'joint venture', especially for members of the younger generation. In Chapter 9, agriculture among the 'traditional' households persists as a form of household-based production involving both man and wife. Here, maintaining the farm remains a crucial joint venture of the household, with a view to passing it on to the next generation. Among the 'radical' households, however, the farm is the point of departure for different kinds of separate economic activities. The radical households are much more willing to diversify their businesses and establish tourist enterprises, for example. For these households, the commitment to passing the farm on to the next generation is much weaker. Chapters 8 and 9 thus draw our attention to changes in households as a basis for agricultural production, partly in response to economic restructuring, partly in response to changes in lifestyle and the construction of identity. In turn, Chapter 10 explores the formation rather than fragmentation of household-based firms in response to economic restructuring.

The three chapters in this way illustrate the negotiations and renegotiations of relationships between household and work, involving marriage and gender relations, the symbolic aspects of different tasks and their economic outcomes. The chapters also highlight aspects of the flexibility of the household as a social and economic unit. Household and individuals' strategies may change to comply with the 'rules of the game', or these new rules may themselves come to be renegotiated within households. In renegotiating new roles and the division of labour, household members are often explicitly altering what the household is about - how its meanings are constructed by household members.

CHAPTER 9

'NATIONALISATION' OF RURAL HOUSEHOLDS? NEW TEAMS FOR OLD TASKS IN AGRICULTURAL HOUSEHOLDS

Agnete Wiborg

Introduction

This chapter discusses the changing role of the household in agricultural production in a rural locality in northern Norway characterised by economic restructuring and the reduction in traditional industries. Within primary industries, the household unit has been especially important with respect to resource management and production. Due to both external and internal influences, the position of the household in relation to agricultural work has experienced a transformation. The external influences arise from economic restructuring, while the internal influences concern the gendered division of work and the management of gender identity and changes in national agricultural policy. Agricultural work is now primarily one man's work, while housework is, at least at the symbolic level, a task where both husband and wife work together. This division of work is not only a question of finding instrumental solutions to practical and economic challenges, it also involves cultural codifications of different tasks.

During the last two or three decades, there have been profound changes in the economic base of rural areas. Restructuring and decline in traditional economic activity characterise the economic scene, and reflect changes in markets and in national policies. Primary industries - fishing, agriculture and forestry - no longer dominate economic and social relations. Local or regional natural resources have ceased to form part of a common economic base for the majority of households in rural areas in the way that they did a generation ago. New jobs and professions in the public sector, and other kinds of services are now represented at the local level. Processes inside the household are linked with changes in the symbolic and practical aspects of the gender-based division of work. What happens within the household is not merely a private concern, but reflects important social facts and cultural values. Through the evaluations and choices they make, household members both influence, and are influenced by, these changing structures in the labour market.

In the household the primary aim is not making money, but rather creating a way of life. Working life and home life are interrelated and the budgeting of time is equally as important as the financial budget of the household (Wadel, 1983). These concerns affect the decisions made in the household. Cultural values influence the rights and duties that are part of the relations between household members (Gullestad, 1984). This is the way that the practical and symbolic aspects of households become interrelated. The household is an arena where management of gender identity is a central issue. Today these cultural values are changing, and they are being renegotiated both in the national public arena, and at the local level within households.

Gender is a relational concept, so that what is considered male and female, man and woman, must be analysed in relation to each other. This has implications for the gender-based division of work in households and in the labour market. Work, like every other social activity, has an instrumental and a symbolic aspect. The instrumental aspect is related to achieving something, whether material or immaterial. On the other hand, work is connected to the cultural values and ideology of identity; gender, class and lifestyle (Wallman, 1979). Tasks are codified according to gender relations and prestige. These aspects are often combined: tasks associated with women tend to carry less prestige than tasks associated with men. The economic outcome of a household's decision making is often a result of discussions or understandings related to non-economic issues concerning the social and cultural aspects of family and household.

Rather than trying to define the household as a social unit, it can be useful to look at the household in terms of tasks and teams (Rudie, 1969/70; Yanagisako, 1979; Grønhaug, 1974). The household links with those aspects of family life to do with economy, work and dwelling. In this chapter, changes in the teams for performing the tasks of farmwork and housework will be used to illustrate how households, as social units, are changing both in terms of organisation as well as at the symbolic level.

The local setting

The study is based on interviews with some 25 households related to agriculture located in the small municipality of Sandvik, a rural locality in northern Norway. Households working in agricultural production are a heterogenous group in terms of farm size, the kind of agricultural production undertaken, how long they have been in agricultural production, and the level of economic output from the farm. They range from households where the farm provides the major income and workload for the household, to households where agriculture provides only a marginal output and where the symbolic aspects of maintaining the farm are as important as the economic aspects. This said, agriculture in Norway has always been small-scale, and the majority of agricultural households supplement their income with off-farm work.

Sandvik is a sparsely populated municipality with a gradually declining population. The economy was traditionally based on a combination of small-scale agriculture, fishing and forestry with supplementary wage work in mining, construction work and shipping. Now the labour market is characterised by a decline in agriculture and the loss of jobs from the traditional male dominated secondary industries. A deteriorating local labour market and high dependency on the public sector now characterise Sandvik's economic base, reflecting its integration into the national economy. The registered gross unemployment rate is high, and is actually equal to the number of those involved in agriculture. Although the area cannot be taken as representative of rural areas in general, the situation in Sandvik certainly illustrates many aspects of economic restructuring processes that are to be found in other rural areas.

It was in the late 1960s that the transformation of the primary industries of Sandvik began, with increased mechanisation, specialisation and capitalisation of agriculture. Fishing as an economic activity gradually disappeared. The result was that farms began to concentrate on a single type of production, farm units became bigger and investment in buildings and technology increased. Many small farms disappeared in the process. To illustrate: in 1970 almost half of the population was involved in agriculture, while by 1990 the proportion had declined to less than a fifth. There were, for example 106 farms which kept an average of less than five cows in 1972. In 1992, a mere 19 dairy farms remained, all of them having between 8 and 20 cows. We find the same pattern on goat farms.

These changes in agriculture took place in response to shifts in national agricultural policy, which now stresses more efficient and profitable production. Back in the 1970s, agricultural policy was favourable to those who wanted to start up in agriculture, encouraging many young households to take over farms (Almås, 1993). Now the economic situation is more strained and agricultural activities in Sandvik are gradually being marginalised on the economic scene, both in terms of numbers of agricultural households and as a profitable economic activity.

Farm work: from household work to one man's work

Taking the household as a point of departure, economic restructuring can be described by looking at changes in the internal division of labour and the relation between agricultural work and the household. Attention will here be focused on changes in tasks and teams in agricultural households connected to farmwork and housework, to illustrate the changing dynamics of the household.

Only a generation ago, the household was an important unit for production, and the farm depended, to a substantial extent, on family labour. Both men and women were involved in agricultural work. They had complementary roles in the household, and there was a clear division of labour between the sexes. Women were in charge of the animals, while men held responsibility for fields, buildings and equipment. Women combined the roles of being farmer, housewife and family caretaker (Larsen, 1980). Men combined jobs as fisherman, carpenter and /or construction worker. At times men had to travel to work elsewhere to earn the necessary cash income, and women then took sole charge of the farm.

This organisation of agricultural work has been substantially altered over recent decades. As farms have become bigger and more specialised, agricultural work has become predominantly men's responsibility. In legal and economic terms, the farmer is usually the man. Technology and farm size in Sandvik have made it possible for one man on his own to perform the daily farmwork. This process whereby men take over the main responsibility for farmwork and where women loose their central position in agriculture, can be described as a masculinisation of agriculture (Almås and Haugen, 1988). In one way, women are excluded, but at the same time, women withdraw voluntarily from agricultural production. We will return to this point. This masculinisation also implies a gradual disembedding of agricultural work from the household in the sense that the household has reduced its importance as a production unit in agriculture. The process can be analysed in both practical and economic terms.

Two important aspects of this process are the introduction of new technology, and an increased economic importance of agriculture. Both are closely connected to a cultural evaluation of work. In an industrialised society, men's work is often related to a certain level of technological competence which gives prestige. Agricultural work gradually changed its gender coding as it became disengaged from manual work, and instead associated with technological competence and skills (Thorsen, 1986). Feeding the animals and milking had traditionally been women's work, but the introduction of the milking machine changed this division of labour. A man could now perform this task without endangering his masculinity. As one woman remarked: 'My father never went into the cowshed before we got the milking machine.' The same recodification of tasks took place with the introduction of new kinds of technology in harvesting, fodder storage and hay making. The introduction of new technology is related to the fact that agricultural work became more important economically and therefore gave greater prestige.

The introduction of new machinery and technology made women's work on the farm superfluous in many respects. Many male farmers in Sandvik today take over the responsibility for the animals from their mothers or mothers-in-law, illustrating changes in the gender coding of this task. The result was that women withdrew from, or lost, their important role in agricultural production. Technological change not only made women superfluous to the agricultural labour force, but also functioned as a barrier for women who wanted to go into farming. One aspect of this barrier is practical: it takes time to learn to use new technology. The other aspect is symbolic: the association between men, technology and masculinity. The tractor represents the core technology on farms, and is also a primary symbol of masculinity (Brandth, 1993).

During harvest time, farmers in Sandvik need extra help, but this requires driving a tractor. Since many women in this area do not know how to drive a tractor, their position in this role is weakened. 'Farm work, especially driving the tractor, that's men's work,' as one farmer said. Some men explained that driving a tractor requires a lot of practice, indicating that it is no task for women. Yet at the same time men admire women who can drive a tractor. There are a few women who know how to drive a tractor, but, with a few exceptions, they do not do it on a regular basis. Therefore it is usually a male relative or a neighbour that helps during harvest.

Both men and women are ambivalent about women tractor drivers, because of the connection between tractors and masculine identity. Men may feel threatened by women entering their domain (Brandth, 1993). A female tractor driver inspires many comments and is in part considered as 'matter out of place', a problematic category (Douglas, 1966). There are other kinds of technology - milking machines for example - which are not connected with masculine identity in the same way. The milking machine is related to what was formerly considered a female task, nor is it so public, powerful and technically complicated as a tractor in the field.

Some women, especially among those of the younger generation, are not interested in participating in farmwork at all, except for giving a hand now and then. The majority have paid jobs in the public sector. They do not feel the obligation to participate in farmwork to the extent that their mothers did. Technological incompetence is used to protect themselves against this extra work load. As a nurse (40) says:

> I do *not* want to learn how to use the milking machine, because I have enough to do with my own work. If I learn how to use a milking machine it is too easy for him to ask me to help him with the milking. I do not want to learn to drive the tractor either. The fields are steep, and I am a bit nervous. The farm is his work, but I can keep him company in the cowshed just for fun.

With a more than full-time job and three children, this respondent feels that she has more than enough to do. She uses her incompetence as a protection against being drawn into the farm work. Instead a teenager in the village is called upon if they need someone to step in and take over the milking and feeding of the animals. The woman is drawing a clear line between his and her work and responsibility, illustrating a distinct separation between their respective modes of generating income. Farmwork is being disembedded from the household as a joint economic activity.

Technological change is not the only barrier against women participating in agricultural work. The changing agrarian economy does not provide incentives for women to work in agriculture either. With the introduction of milk quotas, farmers can no longer earn more from milk production by increasing the output of milk, but only by reducing costs and delivering milk of high quality which commands a better price. These changes have put many farmers in a difficult economic situation, because they cannot meet outlays and investment using extra labour inputs in agriculture. Households have not found alternative ways of employing women in farm production which could provide profit. This, combined with a shift in agricultural policy from production based support to non-production based support, reduces the economic gain from extra labour input. Many farmers and their wives argue that it is more profitable for the household if the wife gets an off-farm job, rather than using her labour power on the farm. Some women regret this situation:

> When we took over the farm, we hoped that both of us could work on the farm. If it were possible economically, I would like to work on the farm and stay at home with the children, but it is not. I

work in the kitchen of a nursing home for elderly people. We invested a lot in the farm when we started, and the income from it turned out to be lower than we expected.

The usual adaptation among younger and middle-aged households is that women take work in the public sector. The income from wage work is a necessary supplement for the household as economic security against expected and unexpected expenditures, and decreasing or fluctuating income from agricultural production. In a few households, the wife's income even exceeds the husband's net income from agricultural work. Especially on farms which have undertaken a lot of investment, the household depends on a full-time job outside the farm. Without the wife's income the farm could not survive economically, as in the case of Sarah and Robert. Sarah tells how:

> When we took over the farm, we had to invest in a new barn and build a house. In our business plan, we assumed that it would be sufficient if I worked part-time as teacher. I also wanted to have time to spend together with our three children. But then there were changes in the tax system, and reductions in milk quotas and economic support. The result was a substantial reduction in our income, and our domestic economy could not bear that, so I had to work even more than full-time to meet the expenses of the family and the farm. I still work more than full-time. Because I work so much, Robert has to take some of the housework and look after the children. Robert's parents also live on the farm, and they have helped a lot by looking after the children as well.

This case also illustrates that teams for performing different tasks like housework and child care, had to be changed in order to handle the household's economic situation, a point I will return to. It illustrates too how household flexibility and combination of sources of income can function as a buffer in the household economy and in performing household tasks.

Many women who used to work on the farm ten years ago, have gradually entered the local labour market and reduced their activity in agricultural work. They now work in the post office, the bank, public offices or health services. The expansion of the welfare state provided many new job opportunities in the 1970s and 1980s. One of the reasons that women go into the labour market is that the household needs more income, due to reduced income from agriculture, and aspirations for higher living standards. Now their children are grown up and do not need the same attention as small children and women want to have their own jobs and to get out of the house to meet other people. For many women the work place has turned into an important social arena and meeting place. While working outside the farm, women also acquire an independent position as an employee with a separate salary, compared to working on the farm in a subordinate position as part of a team where it is the husband who, in many contexts, is considered the primary farmer. Many women, especially the young, stress the importance of maintaining an independent position as a wage worker in the labour market. As one woman (35) says: 'Here we ask; are you working or are you *only* at home?' Having paid work is part of being a respected adult person, which also implies being able to be economically independent, at least symbolically, so that wage work and the work place are important factors in the construction of young women's social identity.

Only one generation ago, agriculture was highly labour-intensive and not only the wife, but also children and grandparents where involved as a team in agricultural production. Agriculture was a way of life that affected all household members. Men supplemented the household's economy from other sources. Today agriculture is a capitalised and specialised enterprise. The team has been reduced, and agriculture has turned into a 'one-*man*-show' both symbolically and practically. Many men see themselves as working alone on the farm. For women, being married to a farmer does not imply duties connected with farm work as it did a generation ago. Women can now to a greater extent choose what kind of position they will have in relation to the farm. In Sandvik many women have become the farmer's wife rather than a farming woman. The farm, and agricultural work are, in part, being disembedded from the household.

Housework: from women's work to household work.

Housework and wage earning are connected to different spheres: the private and the public. In the organisation of people's everyday life, however, housework and wage work are closely interrelated. We will therefore now examine changes in the organisation of housework as a further aspect of economic restructuring. As with agricultural work, the changes involve new teams combined with the altered gender coding of tasks.

Housework and child care has traditionally been considered a woman's domain. But nowadays the ideology of gender equality makes it less legitimate to claim that certain tasks and duties are either men's or women's work, especially when it comes to domestic tasks within the household. Young women implicitly refer to this ideology when they say that they expect their husbands to participate in housework and child care to some degree, especially if they work full-time outside the farm. This kind of argument, and negotiation between spouses over the division of tasks, is the same as for young urban households, and can be connected to ideals of equality, which are taken seriously in Norway (Gullestad, 1986). Men's participation in housework and child care is to a large extent considered an obligation to be a good father and husband, at least among younger couples. Young women feel proud if they have husbands who participate. Men who do not participate in housework, are considered 'traditional' in contrast to the more 'modern' who do.

Men also feel the obligation to participate in housework, even if they do not always fulfil it in practice. One farmer (43), who represents the attitude and situation of many, says of his participation in house work:

> I must be honest, it is no use wriggling out of it. It has been 90 per

cent on the wife and 10 per cent on me. Now she is working full-time, so I do a little bit more, but there is always work to be done on the farm.

Previously his wife had stayed at home and had taken full responsibility for the housework. In addition she also participated in farm work. Over the last year she has been working in a nursery school. This has influenced the division of work inside the household. She started working outside the farm mainly because she wanted to get out of the house, but also to supplement the household's income. Her husband now feels the obligation to participate in housework, although he admits that he does not do much.

In other households, men have taken over some of the domestic responsibilities because the wife has to participate more than full-time in the labour market in order to bring in sufficient income for the household. Farmers whose wives work full-time outside the farm, emphasise that they need to take their share at home. One farmer says:

Men have now entered the kitchen, especially among the younger generation. It is just fair that we do it, because the women have to work outside the farm due to the economic situation. When my wife comes home from the office, I have usually prepared the dinner. When the children were smaller, I spent more time together with them than my wife. I also do some cleaning, but I do not do it properly according to my wife.

Sharing and equality are considered as ideals, and justify the division of tasks between spouses. But even if men participate in housework, women often have the ultimate responsibility and set the standards for housework. In some households this leads to tensions between spouses. She feels that the cleanliness and tidiness of the house reflects her identity, and feels uncomfortable in what she considers a messy, and not particularly clean, house. But due to the household's time budget, there is no time left for extra housework, so she says that she has to put up with it.

A generation ago, men did not participate in housework or child care at all. Now some of the young men change nappies, clean the house and cook meals. The gender-based division of labour is not as explicit as it was, and the ideological context has changed, but there is still a gendered division of labour both within the household and in the labour market in Sandvik. Housework and child care are considered women's responsibility, although many men participate in this work. The local labour market also reflects the kinds of work that is considered men's and women's work. In the households men cook meals, take care of the children, clean the house, but only within their own house and family. They can perform the tasks as a father and husband in the private context of the household, but they do not want to perform these tasks as wage workers in a public context. An example of this is that the home for elderly people has tried to hire men, but without success. Traditionally housework and child care was women's work. Today teams for these tasks include men, at least symbolically, and partly also in practice.

Changes in teams and tasks.

In this chapter attention has been drawn to cultural and symbolic aspects of the internal organisation of work in farm households in response to agricultural and local labour market changes. These changes reflect the integration of rural localities into the national economy. During recent decades many aspects of the rural household as a social unit have changed in Sandvik. Farmwork has been transformed from household based production where the wife played an important part, into a job mostly performed by one man alone. Traditionally farming was way of life and a lifestyle for the whole household. Now the man can manage the farmwork on his own with help from a friend or relative during peak periods. The majority of farmers' wives are only marginally involved in agricultural production. This change is not only related to economic and practical circumstances, but also to the cultural codification of different tasks. Women now work to a large extent in the local labour market in the public sector, though also in private services. Work is an important meeting place for women, and having a paid job is an important part of being an adult.

When women are working outside the home, housework takes up a new position. Housework has, to a certain degree, changed from being an exclusively female task to work that men and women do together. Sharing housework is considered a moral obligation in marriage or partnership, especially by young women. In rural households husband and wife no longer work as a team for farm work, but rather in relation to housework and in the symbolic production of the household and marriage as a moral community. These changes in tasks and teams in agricultural households are consequences of changes in relations between spouses, in the household's relation to economic activities, and in gender identity and gender coding of different tasks in a context of economic restructuring and changing agricultural policies. The expanded public sector has made it possible for many women to get paid work. Today, the household economy in municipalities like Sandvik has become much more dependent on national policy making, on the public sector and on the welfare state. At the same time, national gender ideologies of men's participation in housework and women's participation in the labour market continues to prevail in the locality. It is in this sense that rural households might be said to have been 'nationalised'.

CHAPTER 10

ECONOMIC RESTRUCTURING, ENVIRONMENTAL CONSCIOUSNESS AND FARM FAMILY SUCCESSION IN BRITAIN

Neil Ward and Philip Lowe

Introduction

This chapter examines the changing aspirations of farm households in rural Britain, focusing upon two aspects of contemporary farming - the phenomenon of farm succession, whereby the farm is passed on within the farm family from one generation to the next, and the changing environmental sensibilities among farm households. Almost all farm businesses in Britain can be described as 'family farms' in the sense that the principals of the business are related by kinship or marriage, and business ownership is combined with managerial control (Gasson *et al.*, 1988; Gasson and Errington, 1993). An important element in the ethos of family farming is continuity of occupation through succession. Once it is agreed that a younger member of a farm family will take over the business from their parents, succession typically emerges as a framing principle around which medium and long-term planning of the business takes place, often crucially affecting the way the family views the business. As Symes points out, a commitment to family succession 'can imbue a sense of confidence and security and thus help to preserve harmony within the household' (1990, p.280).

Economic restructuring has dramatically altered the context for agriculture in Britain since the 1970s. Farming's profitability has been squeezed, as has its economic power within an increasingly oligopolistic food system. Public policy has shifted in emphasis from state support for a productivist and expansionist agriculture to the reduction of subsidised commodity prices towards world-market levels and the introduction of supply controls to tackle over-production. In this changing context, the desire to maintain family control and pass on an economically secure farm business to the next generation seems to be being eroded. For example, Harrison (1975) found that three-quarters of English farmers he surveyed in the late 1960s were planning to pass on their businesses to their heirs. These results can be compared with those of a series of studies carried out by researchers at University College London during the mid-1980s in five different farming regions (see Marsden *et al.*, 1989; 1992). When surveyed farmers were asked whether it was expected that the farm would be passed on to the next generation in the family, 66 percent of those who felt able to respond one way or the other said yes. The proportion was only 55 per cent in the study area where agriculture was under the greatest economic pressure, but was 77 per cent in the most agriculturally prosperous of the five study areas. Related surveys in 1991 found that only 58 per cent of farms were being managed with a succession to the next generation planned for (Ward and Lowe, 1994). These findings would appear to suggest that the falling profitability of some parts of the agricultural sector since the late 1960s, but more particularly since the mid-1980s, has gradually undermined confidence in the industry, and the proportion of farms where succession is planned is diminishing. Indeed, a survey of 26,000 UK farm businesses in 1991 found that almost a half (48 per cent) of respondents had no nominated successor for their farm (National Westminster Bank, 1992).

Succession and family farming

The dynamics of family enterprises stem from the interplay of household and business - production is organised through kinship and property and labour are combined. The unity of kin group and work group creates at least dual roles for each member and patterns a division of labour and inequalities of ownership and control based on gender and age relations (Whatmore, 1991). A commitment to succession helps to create certainty and common purpose in the running of a farm, and so helps farm families in coping with the contradictions that can arise between the family and the business, between the short and the long-term, and between individual and collective goals. These contradictions have been explored by Harriet Friedmann (1986) who has argued that,

> the unity of property and labour in simple commodity production is contradictory in capitalist societies because it internalises within one person or family the structured conflict between property owners and labourers, who are usually related as employers and employees (Friedmann, 1986, p.53).

Succession is thus more than simply a social or biological *fact*, where the business is either passed on to the next generation or is not. It is also a goal whereby farm families seek to integrate, over the long-term, the management of a business and of the family assets. Succession links together the key decisions and negotiations during the family life cycle with the strategic decisions about the development of the business. It is a goal through which farm families manage the fissiparous pressures upon them. The reciprocal obligations it expresses help to bind family members together, within and across the generations, as they seek to accommodate the family life cycle to the vagaries of the business-cycle and overcome the contradictions between property and labour.

It is mainly as a key instrumental value rather than necessarily as a deeply-rooted intrinsic value that we would see succession in the British context. Symes (1990) draws the contrast with continental Europe where 'concepts of family obligation and social status still serve as guiding principles for systems of land transfer' (p.285), while in Britain, 'the strength of these values is being undermined by more material considerations' (p.286) with land and improved farm buildings becoming commodified sources of financial investment, rather than a source of prestige and status, or even a means of production. But that having been said, planning for a succession remains an important influence on farm business management for farm families in Britain. A commitment to continuing in farming provides the farm family with an hermetic view of the future, with succession sometimes providing the key driving force of business change. This point was well-illustrated by some of the farmers interviewed during recent surveys who explained to us that the only reason that they were continuing to farm was because they had successors who were keen to take over the business. As one farmer in Bedfordshire put it, 'my son is very keen to take over the business, and if he was not, I would be out of it tomorrow.' Another farmer in Buckinghamshire felt the same way. He explained, 'There was money in [farming] when I first started, but there's not a hope in hell for anyone now. I've got two sons who are very keen to farm. If it was just me, I would be out and investing my money.'

As an instrumental value, commitment to succession may be eroded by economic or social change. One common explanation for the apparent decline in the proportion of farms with a succession planned is that the falling profitability of agriculture makes the prospects of taking over a farm business a less attractive proposition for the children of farmers. This claim can be empirically examined using the data from the University College London studies in the mid-1980s (Marsden *et al.*, 1989; 1992) to assess the link between the economic trajectory of each farm business and the farm family's commitment to succession. The 'economic status' of each farm in the sample of 423 businesses was established, concentrating on strictly agricultural enterprises. Farms were allocated to one of three categories based on answers received to a set of questions relating to: the profitability of the farm business at the time of interview; how this had changed since 1970; and the farmers' expectations of profitability over the next few years. The three categories were: i) *'Accumulators'* - businesses that provided their occupiers with a steady and often increasing profit since 1970, frequently in association with a growth in business size; ii) *'Survivors'* - businesses that generally made a profit but where their ability to support the family could not be automatically assumed; iii) *'Marginals'* - businesses where profitability had been falling steadily in real terms.

While the patterns of viability varied across the five localities, in total 35 per cent of businesses were classed as accumulators, 41 per cent were survivors and 24 per cent were marginals. Table 10.1 shows that two-thirds of farms in the 'accumulator' category were planning for a succession, whereas the proportion dropped to 55 per cent of 'survivors' and only 35 per cent of 'marginals'. At the same time, the proportion of 'accumulators' where succession had definitely been ruled out was under 20 per cent, rising to 27 per cent of 'survivors' and 52 per cent of 'marginals',

Table 10.1 Economic status categories and family succession

	Accumulators		Survivors		Marginals		Total
Succession							
Yes	95	(66%)	94	(55%)	35	(35%)	224
No	27	(19%)	46	(27%)	51	(52%)	124
Don't know	23	(16%)	32	(19%)	13	(13%)	68
Total	145	(100%)	172	(100%)	99	(100%)	416

Source: Ward and Lowe (1994)

suggesting a strong relationship between economic viability and the commitment to succession.

An alternative explanation relates to social change in rural areas. As new rural residents have moved, often from large towns and cities, into the deep countryside beyond small towns and larger villages, so farm families find themselves with neighbours with quite different values and lifestyles. The effects of this on the aspirations of farmers' children can only be guessed at, but it is plausible that they have, in greater numbers, embraced the career aspirations of their new peers and rejected the more traditional family farming ethic of carrying on the family business. It is possible that this may have been compounded by the greater economic integration of farm families through multiple job-holding. In any case, more generally, national cultural change has also eroded the distinctiveness of occupational communities.

Succession and environmental consciousness in agriculture

Recent studies have suggested that processes of succession on family farms can be linked to changes in the intensity with which environmental resources are managed. For example, Marsden and Munton (1991) have shown how the formal entry of a successor into the farm business can provide the opportunities for radical land management and landscape changes, most commonly involving intensification of land use and the removal of landscape features. Also, Potter and Lobley point out that

> the running down of a farm business in old age is more likely to take place where the elderly farmer is working alone on the farm and lacks the incentive to maintain capital assets and lay the grounds for the future expansion which a younger successor or heir is likely to provide (Potter and Lobley, 1992, p.60).

They conclude there has to be a good case for regarding elderly farmers (especially those without successors) as potentially important managers of the rural environment. However, it would be an over-simplification to equate farms without successors as inherently more 'environmentally friendly', and those with successors as less so. For example, our research on farm pollution control has shown that livestock farmers without successors are much less likely to want to invest in capital equipment to improve effluent management and reduce the risk of water pollution (Ward and Lowe, 1994). It is to this issue of the challenge to livestock farms posed by recent water pollution regulations that we now turn in order to explore the changing relations between farming households and businesses in a rapidly changing countryside.

For dairy farmers in particular, the pollution of rivers and streams with effluents such as cattle slurry, silage effluent and yard and parlour washings emerged as a problem in Britain in the 1980s when the annual number of reported farm pollution incidents more than doubled. The rising profile of the farm pollution problem took place in the context of social change in the countryside. New people moved to rural areas bringing new values about how the countryside should be managed and a greater willingness to 'blow the whistle' on farmers (Ward et al., 1995).

Devon, a county in the south-west of England, is an area where rural social change has been particularly marked. The non-agricultural middle classes moved into smaller villages and the deep countryside during the 1980s, a trend sometimes facilitated by farmers themselves who converted redundant farm buildings for residential purposes. The social fabric of once small agricultural villages has been dramatically changed, many farmers now having new neighbours with quite different perceptions of the function of the countryside. Of 60 dairy farmers we surveyed in Devon in 1991, for example, 10 had experienced direct pressure to change their farming practices from neighbours and local people. More generally, there is a perception among farmers that social change in the countryside is diminishing their autonomy. Middle-class newcomers are often viewed by farmers as the harbingers of new values and procedures by which farming will increasingly be judged by society at large. It is against this background of social change in the countryside, that our analysis of the shifting values in family farming, and especially the way succession is viewed, is set.

At a superficial level, the survey in Devon revealed a link between family succession and investment in pollution control equipment among the farm households, with investment in pollution control much more likely to take place on dairy farms where a succession to the next generation was planned for. On over two-thirds of the farms where a succession was expected, there had been some investment in pollution control facilities during the 1980s. Similarly, on almost two-thirds of farms where succession had been ruled out, no such investment had taken place.

However, whether farmers have simply invested in pollution control equipment or not is a poor indicator of how sound their environmental management practices might be. Both farmers and the Ministry of Agriculture, Fisheries and Food see investing in equipment as a sign that the problem is being addressed, but this is far from the view of National Rivers Authority pollution officers responsible for pollution regulation. Effluent storage facilities are prone to failure and have to be responsibly managed and regularly maintained. In addition, decisions about the timing of slurry spreading can be crucial in reducing pollution risk. Sound effluent management is integral to routine good farming practice if pollution risks to water are to be properly addressed. Simply installing the equipment is not enough on its own. Given this, the ways farmers understand and perceive the nature of the pollution threat to local water courses posed by the effluents from their farms can be crucial in preventing pollution.

Farmers' representations and understandings of the pollution problem were explored in our survey. The problem of agricultural pollution was viewed by different farmers in different ways, but with some consistent patterns. For analytical purposes, three categories were established, including two contrasting positions, and a large, middle-ground group. (For a fuller discussion, see Ward and Lowe, 1994)

Group A (the 'sceptical farmers') adopted the stance of 'what pollution problem?' and contained 10 farmers (17 per cent of the sample). These farmers felt that the pollution issue had been exaggerated and that regulation had 'gone too far' in restricting what they could do. All in the group felt that agricultural pollution was far less of a problem than industrial pollution, and suspected that farmers were being more strictly regulated because they were 'easy targets'. Six farmers in the group questioned whether farm effluents were 'serious' pollutants at all.

Group B (the 'ambivalent farmers') contained 37 farmers (62 per cent) who readily acknowledged that pollution from farm effluents was a problem and that measures had to be taken to solve it. Critically, however, they saw pollution as a problem *for* farming, rather than as a problem *of* farming. Pollution regulations had to be adhered to if only because it was unacceptable to break the law. These farmers tended not to question the *need* for action to curb pollution, although they were keen to distinguish between 'accidents' and the much more serious 'deliberate' pollution incidents, where, it was stressed, the full force of the law should be brought to bear.

Group C (the 'radical farmers') saw pollution as reprehensible. These 13 farmers (22 per cent) accepted the need for regulation to address farm pollution problems, describing pollution regulations as 'a good thing' that would help to 'put agriculture's house in order'. Most were emphatic that regulations must be adhered to and that the adoption of improved effluent management practices was for the good of the industry. It is, these farmers broadly felt, the responsibility of the individual farmer to ensure that pollution is adequately prevented.

Comparing the characteristics of the 'radicals' and 'sceptics', representing the two extremes in terms of how the pollution problem is perceived, we find the 'radicals' were mainly a group of younger farmers occupying larger farms. More than two thirds of the 'radicals' were under 50 years of age, and one third younger than 40. A strong pattern emerged around succession too. The extent to which farm families were committed to family continuity tended to decline as we move through the three groups. Of the 'sceptics', 8 out of 10 were planning for a family succession in the future, compared with fewer than two thirds of the 'ambivalent' farmers and under half of the 'radicals'. Indeed 5 of the 13 'radicals' had definitely ruled out succession. This lack of commitment to succession amongst the 'radicals' may reflect a wider rejection of the more 'traditional' views and agrarian values of the family farm, and is despite the fact that all but 2 of the radicals were from farming backgrounds themselves. What might account for the fact that the succession motive was so weak amongst this group in comparison with the others ?

The 'radicals' tended to have more complex land occupancy or tenurial relations. Only 4 were typical family owner-occupied dairy farms, the others being rented from private or institutional landlords, or managed as non-family partnerships, farming companies or under share farming arrangements. By comparison, for all 10 of the 'sceptics', farms were family owner-occupied, with the farm family much more closely and simply bound to the day-to-day management of the business.

The 'radicals' were also more likely to embrace diversification as a farm survival strategy. Five had taken steps to diversify during the 1980s, and 3 had established enterprises associated with countryside recreation or tourism. It was often the women that had the main responsibility for the tourist enterprises while the men concentrated their efforts on farm work. Willingness to diversify was much less apparent among the 'sceptics', with only one farm household involved in non-agricultural activities.

The reluctance to do anything other than farm to produce food was underlined by one 'sceptical' farmer who, when asked if he had any plans to diversify the business, replied 'Good God, no. It's too good a farm to do that.' His view was that establishing a non-agricultural enterprise was something that people on 'poorer quality' farms were forced to do in order to survive in business. Diversification, according to most of the 'sceptics', was understood as a diversion from the serious business of farming to produce food.

By drawing comparisons between these two 'extreme' groups (Figure 10.1), we can begin to see how a farmer's situation and values might influence the way in which pollution problems are perceived. The approaches of the two groups can be described as 'traditional' and 'modern'. The 'sceptics', who felt that farm pollution was being over-emphasised and was not a serious problem, could be said to show characteristics of a 'traditional' approach rooted in the ethos of family farming. They saw themselves as a special group in society, set apart from everyone else. Family farming dominated their lives and they argued that farming was 'all we know'. Thus, they tended to be more locked into a agricultural way of thinking and were much less likely to diversify their farm businesses. The group as a whole tended to have *reactive* as opposed to pro-active strategies. Changes on the farm during the 1980s were more likely to be agricultural, and made in response to changing economic or family circumstances. These farmers were more likely to feel embattled because of farming's poor economic fortunes, and added to this, environmental and pollution regulations were seen as another part of society's 'attack' on farmers. However, notions of family continuity remained strong among this group and were linked to dynastic notions of land ownership and farm improvement. They tended to belong to local farming families and had close relatives farming in Devon. It is possible that this reinforced their inward looking and 'agro-centric' view of the world.

On the other hand, the 13 'radicals', who saw farm pollution as reprehensible, could be said to show characteristics of a more 'modern' (some may even argue a 'post-modern') approach. They tended to have a broader, outward-looking view rather than a more agro-centric set of values. This could be because of their more extensive social and economic links beyond farming, not only through their diversification activities, which often involved welcoming members of the public on to their farms, but also through socialising outside the local farming community. For example, 4 of the 'radicals' were active in local sports clubs. These farmers, in enjoying wider links beyond farming, were in turn reflecting views about farming's environmental problems held by that wider society. Perhaps as a result of these different types of social network, they did not tend to see the farming community as a special group set apart from everyone else.

With regard to their own farms, these farmers with a more 'modern' approach tended to be non-risk averse and more flexible. They viewed themselves more as rural entrepreneurs or 'businessmen' and changes in the farm business were often pro-active, with these farmers more readily establishing non-agricultural enterprises on their farms, for example. At the same time, the 'radicals' were losing the dynastic sense of family continuity, and on several farms succession to the next generation had definitely been ruled out.

Figure 10.1 Characteristics of two 'extreme' groups of farmers, 'sceptics' and 'radicals'

Group A	Group C
'Sceptics'	'Radicals'
'Business as usual'	Playing to 'new rules of the game'
Farm pollution not as bad as industry	Farm pollution just as bad as industry
Farm wastes as a 'natural' substance	Farm wastes as potentially highly polluting
Regulations as 'unfair attack on farmers'	Regulations essential to 'put farming's house in order'
Older	Younger
Committed to family continuity	Not committed to family continuity
Reactive strategies	Pro-active strategies
More densely stocked	Less densely stocked
Unwilling to diversify	Willing to diversify
Farmers as a special group in rural society	Farmers as 'rural entrepreneurs'
Technical-fix storage solutions	Waste management solutions
Oriented to the conservation of physical capital	Oriented to the conservation natural capital

Source: Ward and Lowe (1994)

Conclusions

In explaining why fewer farmers seem to be planning the future of their businesses with succession in mind, two different explanatory models can be discerned. The first sees falling economic returns as the key determining factor, while the second sees social change in the countryside as impacting upon the values and aspirations of farm families. The analysis here suggests a more complex reality combining aspects of the two. Declining economic fortunes in farming can be seen to have been compounded by social change in the countryside, but economic change also effects social change *in* farming. Social change is not exogenous to farming, for farm households form an integral part of rural society. It is, therefore, a dialectic between the economic and the social which contributes to the transformation of agrarian values and fosters an openness to new types of values (surrounding the environment, for example). Through an examination of the construction of environmental values and understandings of pollution, we can begin to see how agrarian ideology and culture might be being challenged and reshaped within a changing rural society. New groups with different perspectives on rural environmental management are establishing themselves in the heart of localities once dominated by the farming way of life. At the same time, and in part as a result of such rural social change, regulatory policy has required that farmers incorporate a greater concern for reducing environmental risks into their routine farming practices. Complex sets of influences are thus bearing down on how farmers understand pollution, what counts as 'good farming' and their own farming strategies. One important outcome of this changing context is a reassessment of commitment to family continuity of farm occupancy.

This is not to say, however, that as new groups move to rural areas, so the values of the farming community simply become subordinated and disappear. Rather, the contacts between farmers and their new neighbours provide differential conditions and opportunities for farmers and farm families to position themselves within a rural society in which agriculture is no longer politically, economically and culturally dominant. In the process, commitment to family succession in farming is becoming less relevant for many farm families.

CHAPTER 11

SURVIVAL AND FLEXIBILITY IN THE URBAN SMALL BUSINESS HOUSEHOLD

Jane Wheelock

Local economic development policy and small business livelihoods

What is the economic character of the small business household? This chapter argues that economic behaviour and the values on which it is based must be seen in a household and family, rather than an individual context. It shows that when lives are related to livelihoods, a family economic unit and its distinctive work strategy are crucial to small business viability in the market. The chapter therefore explores the inter-relations between the formal market activities of self-employed men and women, and the formal and informal work activities of their households, families and friends.

It is now generally recognised that household and family members make an important contribution to rural businesses, particularly on Europe's periphery (Cécora, 1993). In Britain too, studies have shown that both farming households, and hoteliers located in remote rural areas, may be dependent on a family economic unit for the success of their business and the survival of the household (Whatmore, 1991; Lowe, 1988). The study reported on here was undertaken in a peripheral urban locality (Wearside) in North East England.[1] It demonstrates the importance of the household for the form of competitiveness taken by small businesses in urban local economies, and confirms the need to investigate family and reciprocally based relations in order to understand the impact of economic change.

Chapter 4 has already shown how economic restructuring has involved an increase in the significance of small businesses and self-employment. Although peripheral British regional economies started from a lower base, the rate of increase of small businesses since the start of the 1980s has been substantial (Mason, 1991). Successive governments have insisted that Britain and its regions need a market-based, enterprise culture to ensure regional economic development and international competitiveness (Michie, 1992). They have hailed the increase in the numbers of small businesses as evidence that this is being achieved. In addition, these New Right governments have seen changes in individual values as an important key to indigenous growth and to reversing economic decline. As British and other European governments have sought to roll back the frontiers of the state and to emphasise the role that markets play, it becomes the citizen's own responsibility to respond to opportunities and incentives. This requires a change in the attitudes of individuals (Keat and Abercrombie, 1991).

The chapter argues that New Right policies have placed too much store by the individual small business person. Starting from the entrepreneurial individual, as most small business researchers do, hides significant issues from view if local economic regeneration based on small business growth is the objective. Three interrelated and important policy issues can all best be answered by an analysis at the level of the small business household. Thus, the small firm and the enterprise culture have been promoted as important contributors to workforce flexibility, yet there has not been any specification of what this flexibility consists in, apart from the high birth and death rates of small businesses. Evidence from the Wearside study indicates that an important element of this flexibility derives from the distinctive work strategy of the small business household. What of the contribution that small businesses make to economic growth and regeneration? This question can only be answered if we consider the processes that ensure the social reproduction of the small business household alongside the maintenance and growth of the business. Lastly, it becomes apparent that the value system of the small business household is not based on responding to economic incentives alone, but that it is the satisfactions of being able to integrate the personal, the family and the public aspects of a predominantly domestic lifestyle that counterbalances the inherent self-exploitation of the small business family.

A model of flexibility

The Wearside study posited that economic activities are embedded in social life (Granovetter, 1985). Taped interviews were undertaken with the families of 24 small businesses set up during the 1980s, the 'decade of enterprise' (Daly, 1990; 1991). As might be expected in a regional and local economy subject to substantial de-industrialisation - and indicated in Chapter 4 - many of those interviewed had no prior experience of self-employment, and a number had previously been unemployed or out of the job market due to sickness or family responsibilities. In seeking to relate household work strategies and small businesses, it was important for the research design that female as well as male headed businesses should considered. In the event, eight female and eight male headed businesses were interviewed, together with seven husband and wife teams and one family partnership.

The research hypothesis was that small businesses and the self-employed would be likely to make use of the labour of other household and family members in addition to that of the proprietors themselves, and that this might provide the business with an important element of flexibility. But members of a household do not just have one work role. Any household unit combines work performed to earn income, and unpaid work done domestically. In the entrepreneurial household, it is therefore possible that three work roles are being fulfilled: a full-time or part-time job in the formal economy, work in the business, and unpaid work in the complementary

Survival and flexibility in the urban small business household 159

economy - using the terms introduced in Chapter 1. Individual households need to combine work for self consumption with work for income, taking account of the fact that the work they do in the social economy is unpaid. Given the predominance of labour as a factor of production within small-scale enterprise, flexibility in the use of household and family labour may provide a key to understanding the overall flexibility of such enterprises.

It became apparent that work for the business unit and work for the family unit were indeed closely interrelated in the small business household. This provided the basis for developing a model of the internal flexibility of the small business. Atkinson's (1985) model of flexibility for the large firm distinguishes functional and numerical flexibility in core and peripheral work forces respectively. It is the interrelation between the monetarily rewarded aspects of the family's work (business and employment) and its unpaid work (domestic and caring roles) that provides the basis for a small business model of flexibility (for details, see Wheelock, 1992b). Functional flexibility within the business work role is obtained when those working within the business, including family members, have a flexible set of skills to offer, and vary what they contribute according to the needs of the business. Numerical flexibility derives from the fact that the business is able to make use of work from three sources (see Figure 11.1). The business owner can draw on individuals from his or her own nuclear household unit, in other words from the domestic sector, s/he can turn to the wider social economy and draw on family or friends through the voluntary sector or s/he can go to the formal economy. In fact, many of the individuals who are originally found through the family and friendship networks of the social economy, subsequently get paid for their work contribution to the enterprise, and therefore become part of the formal economy.

Inevitably, the flexibility available to the business proprietor through the household is dependent on who undertakes the enabling domestic, caring and income earning roles. Neither the business nor the household can survive if these tasks are not performed. Members of the household are freed, or enabled, to contribute to the work of the business depending on the functional and numerical flexibility available for domestic and caring roles. Functional flexibility occurs when members of the household itself vary the domestic or caring roles that they take on. Numerical flexibility involves either calling on family or friends from outside the household in an unpaid capacity from the voluntary sector, or paying individuals in the formal or the irregular economies. It may also be important for members of the household to bring in income from employment, if the income from the business is inadequate to support its members.

The case study of Kate and Stuart illustrates many of these features. It also shows how the business household is located at the meeting point of the complementary and the formal economies, where private family roles and public business roles are integrated. Kate was employed as a hairdresser at one of the town centre salons when she began contemplating setting up in business on her own:

> I was really fed up with where I was working and it was a case of
> if I didn't go to do mobile hairdressing, I would have been packing

hairdressing in altogether so I just thought I'd give it a try and it was the best thing I ever did.

When Kate started her business, she and her husband had just moved house, so he had plenty to do even though he was temporarily laid off from the shipyards:

> We were laid off so at the time it was advantageous because we were doing work on the house, but there was the case of what we were going to do, and Kate says 'well, you know, we'll go for the business', and I said 'fair enough if you want to go for it, go for it', cause we didn't know whether it would take off, and fortunately it did.

The resultant change in domestic arrangements suited both of them:

> Whenever Kate was out it was a case of when I was working on the house. I mean she wasn't getting in my way and I wasn't getting in hers type of thing,

but in addition, Stuart could answer the telephone when she was out, arranging appointments with clients. At first clients did not believe that a man could undertake such a job, and were reluctant to explain that they wanted a blue rinse or a perm, but Stuart soon convinced them of his competence. From a security point of view, having her husband acting as her receptionist was very helpful.

> I've never advertised. And really, Stuart didn't want us to, because you never know where you are going really, and well a young girl going to a house on her own where you've never been before is very dodgy.

Indeed the telephone was one of the major ways in which business impinged on their private life. On the one hand, as Kate said:

> That's my lifeline to the business you know...at first you wanted the phone to ring so you're just diving for it.

Yet at the same time she found it one of the biggest difficulties of being in business:

> Really, learning to accept that it's just all business, isn't it, like you never really switch off from it...you're settling down to watch the telly but you make sure you've got the diary next to the phone and you've got the phone there.

She and her husband found that they had to adjust to the changes:

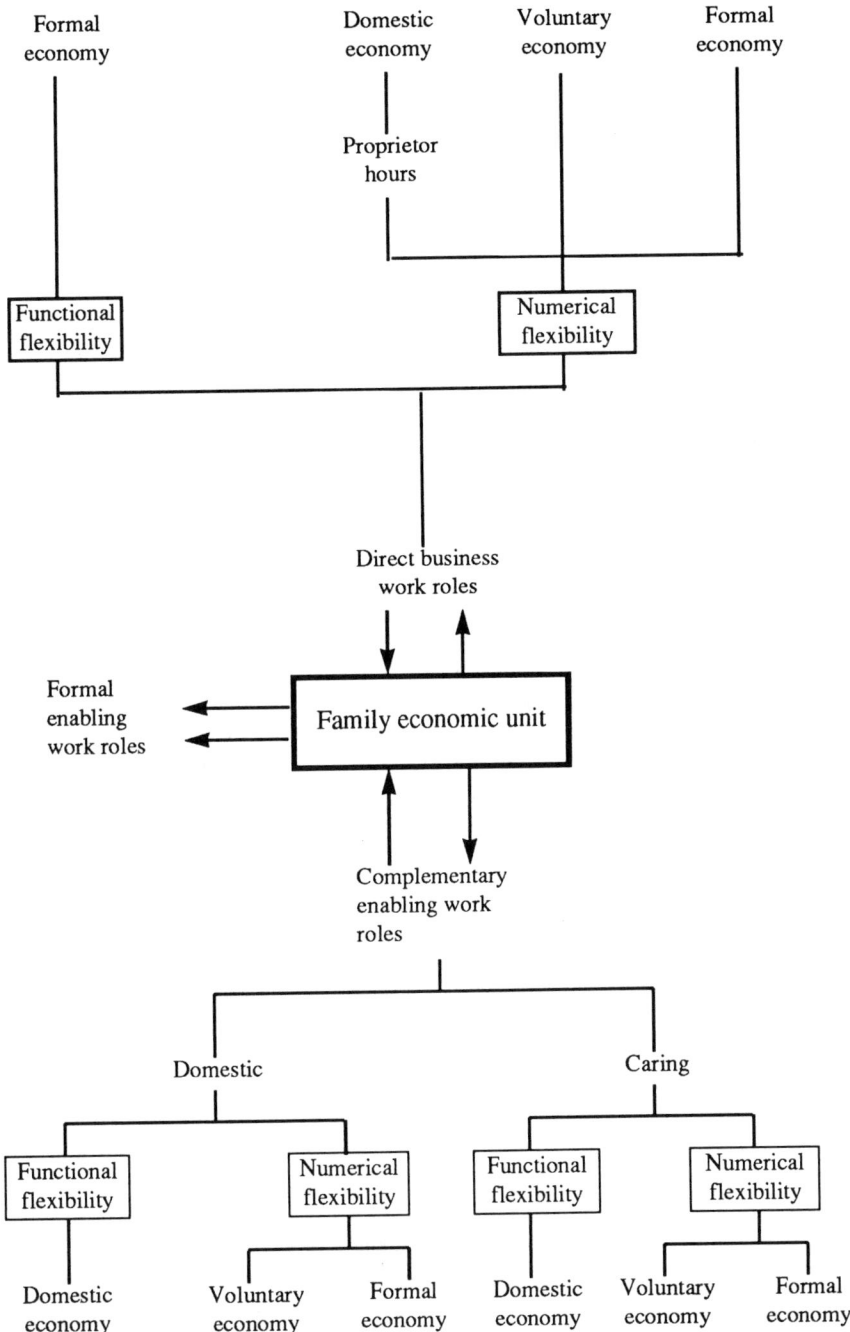

Figure 11.1 Flexibility in the family economic unit
Source: Wheelock 1992b

That took some getting used to didn't it?...It definitely changes your life like doesn't it? It definitely takes a while to settle into it ...(Stuart) And plus it was like - you're used to your privacy.

Kate and Stuart decided to buy an answerphone so that they could ensure time for themselves when they wanted it, In common with others though, they had hesitations about how far clients were prepared to use the technology. There were other problems associated with Kate's unsociable hours. As Kate said:

[In the salon] I was always home for 6 o'clock, whereas mobile, I mean that's part and parcel of it, the convenience of having their hair done at their time. So you would be lucky if I was home for 8 o'clock and by the time you've had your tea and washed up that's the night over...it all completely overtook us didn't it?
[Stuart] And she was coming in like shattered, take it out on me and I was saying 'Right well, that's it type of thing...you tell them you're cutting back' ...in the end we just had to knock it on the head...In fact we laughed at ourselves.

They also bought a dishwasher, something that they could afford once Kate was self-employed, which contributed to solving the problems.

At the time of interview Stuart had been made redundant from the shipyards, but had obtained a new job almost immediately. Kate was expecting their first baby. She spent a number of months on sick-leave, followed by maternity leave. She shed her clients and closed her business during this time. By the time of the follow-up phone call, she had returned to self-employment two afternoons a week, and her newly retired mother was looking after the baby.

The costs and benefits of flexibility for the small business household

The research showed business households using a wide range of strategies to ensure flexibility in the performance both of direct business tasks and of indirect enabling work, as the case study illustrates. Family and business needs were generally integrated with each other in these entrepreneurial families, many of whom were adopting a distinctly domesticated, or household oriented set of values (see Pahl and Wallace, 1985). Family involvement in the business project meant a particularly intense form of domestic value system which integrated private family roles and public business roles. The heart of the satisfactions of running a small business were found in this integration. Yet business owners and their families emphasised the very long hours that they worked (confirmed for example in Rainbird's (1991) Warwick study amongst others). Often exploitative hours were justified by the view that at least they were working that hard for themselves rather than for an employer.

New Right governments in Britain and elsewhere have seen the material rewards for business ownership as critically important, concerning themselves with creating a system of incentives that will ensure profits. The domestic orientation of the value system that came across so consistently from the Wearside study indicates that economically rational responses to market incentives may not play as important a part as policy makers and academic economists have argued (Young, 1991). Even modest income rewards were comparatively rare for the entrepreneurial families in the sample. Seven families were actually worse off than they had been, with four having about the same income level. Only five families saw themselves as distinctly better off as a result of being in business, with a further six marginally so. Even when looking at this group, it is worth realising that some households were on state benefits beforehand, so that income levels were still not high. A number of the business families were entitled to draw state benefits, including family credit, free school meals or prescription charges and housing benefit. It is not surprising that for a number of businesses, a further enabling income coming in to the house was essential.

While Marx talks in terms of the restlessness of the circulation process of capital to ensure that 'Mr Moneybags' the capitalist can accumulate, the small business proprietor (and household members) must work ceaselessly to obtain an often meagre financial reward. Why then are families prepared to do this? Essentially, what came across from the interviews was that the rewards derive from the way of life. A demanding way of life, but one which was intrinsically satisfying for most families, despite its problems and pressures in terms of hours of work or uncertain financial rewards. This came across as a way of life integrating family and business satisfactions and values. Personal satisfaction was gained from being in control of doing a good job, providing a quality service, with the hope of economic rewards, but with the reality of sheer survival as a base line. Largely, however, motivations are not individually based, but derived from reciprocally based domestic values within the household. In 1980s urban Sunderland then, we find an example of a Weberian hybrid industrial organisation, with values deriving both from the human needs of *Haushalten* and from business based capital accounting and *Erweben*.

Conclusions: surviving economic change

Wearside small businesses constitute an urban example of an in-between industrial organisation at the heart of a deindustrialised peripheral local economy. How does the flexible household business fit in with the macro-models of economic change identified in Chapter 1? And at a micro-level, how is the small business household responding to economic changes identified in Part II? In addition to answering these questions, the associated policy conclusions indicate a need to modify the methodological individualism of some economists.

It is clear that the flexibility of Wearside small businesses does not fit in with the industrial district model of macro-level flexibility that was introduced in Chapter 1. The networks of Wearside business households link business, household, family and friends, but do not involve links with other business, except on a very occasional basis. These networks do not facilitate innovative growth. Rather, they can be understood as a response to the effects of economic restructuring on a peripheral labour market. They involve a return to old ways of working - long hours, with low rewards under insecure conditions. In her study of nineteenth century Edinburgh, Stana Nenadic (1990) was examining family strategies for small firm creation and survival, and argued that 'family strategies for generating income went hand-in-hand with business strategies' (p.25). Helen Rainbird (1991) interprets the self-employment of the Warwick sample that she studied as a form of disguised wage labour, on the grounds that the majority were earning only a subsistence living.

The survival of these Wearside small business households, then, is survival at the margin between the formal and the informal or complementary economy, based as it is on the flexibility of the household economic unit and the intensification of its labour. The study showed the family-based small business confined to the periphery of competition, persisting only where the corporation cannot make an adequate profit. Many of the businesses interviewed were operating at the margin of profit, and beyond the production possibility frontier. Few relied on any form of innovation to survive. Their functioning relied on the value produced by labour. The business contributed to keeping the household in work - it was 'a cyclical escape from unemployment' (Linder, 1983).

The economic historian Forman-Peck (1985) describes small business growth as the chaff of economic recession, rather than the seed corn of revival. The Sunderland business households do indeed seem to provide an example of small firm growth as a symptom of economic decline. Storey and Johnson (1987) see this as a transfer of employment from uncompetitive large-scale enterprise, rather than any appreciable increase in overall employment. Economic restructuring then, calls forth what might best be called a 'culture of survival' in households who move towards partial or complete reliance on incomes deriving from small business.

The evidence from this chapter indicates that this culture of survival is quite distinct from the enterprise culture of those concerned to cut back on state involvement. Certainly in Britain, governments have orchestrated an ideology in support, which emphasises qualities like individualism, independence, self-help and anti-collectivism (Burrows, 1991). Yes, the business people interviewed on Wearside saw themselves as autonomous, but it was an autonomy which would have collapsed immediately were it based upon the individualism trumpeted by politicians of the enterprise culture, or assumed by economists who see 'rational economic men' operating in the market-place. These Wearside businesses survived (and in a few cases, prospered) thanks in large part to cooperative, reciprocal values operating at the level of the household.

The predominant stream of thought in economics follows Adam Smith in seeing the 'propensity to truck, barter and exchange' as a basic economic motivation, with the conflicting interests of self-seeking individuals harmonised though the market mechanism. Karl Polanyi (1946), and other economic anthropologists have proposed that reciprocity - the obligation to give, receive and return - as an alternative way of integrating the inherent opposition between self and other. Politicians of the New Right have followed economists in starting from the individual, rather than from the household and the family. True, the new household economists who follow Gary Becker (1965) do not see the economic actor as a Robinson Crusoe alone on his island, when they seek to understand economic behaviour. However, they persist in positing that individual household members are economic maximisers, rather than behaving reciprocally.

This is simply not the case for the hybrid organisation that the Wearside small business comprises, where the household acts as a collective worker by linking family and business life cycles and where reciprocal values provide the rewards of a household-based way of life. Yet this is also a source of exploitation thanks to the fusion between economic and affective relationships (see Roberts and Holroyd, 1992), with the likelihood that several household members will be working long hours to sustain the business. It is possible that in North East England, the importance of the complementary economy for the small firm transforms the disadvantages of location in a peripheral region into the means for its survival. It is a survival which relies on a flexibility based on cooperative, reciprocal relations within the household to overcome the destabilising effect of low wage competition in a region in economic decline.

Notes

1. With thanks to the Economic and Social Research Council, whose grant (award no. R000 23 2524) made the research possible, and to the Sunderland business families who were will to be interviewed.

SECTION C

SHIFTING YOUTH TRANSITIONS AND IDENTITIES[1]

Robert Hollands

Generation is a crucial element in understanding the shifting relationship between households, work and social change. Young people's changing labour market position, increased dependency on the family home, and their quest for new identities in the consumption and community spheres, are symptomatic of the effects of global economic restructuring and modernisation. Yet, at the same time, youthful responses to these processes are also prescriptive in signalling future trends and social possibilities. This is particularly the case with respect to changing gender roles and identities, not to mention the younger generation's role in the creation of new patterns of employment, in changing household boundaries and on leisure lifestyles.

Young adults' transitions and identities today are incomprehensible if we do not take account of the impact of economic change. The decline of manufacturing and rise of service-based employment, changes in the gender composition of the workforce, new production regimes and 'flexible' employment practices, and attempts to make education and training more attuned to the 'needs' of industry, all have their influence. Generation has been a key variable in the institutionalisation of these changes, and it is young people who have often felt the effects of restructuring most directly, as they experience higher than average levels of unemployment or become experimental fodder for training schemes. Gender has also been an important component in this process, with young women recently outperforming young men in the educational sphere and experiencing lower unemployment rates (Wilkinson, 1994).

Yet as some restructuring theorists argue (Massey, 1984), these global trends are highly differentiated in their effect on particular localities. For instance, regional unemployment levels in areas like North East England and northern Norway exceed national averages, and this is true for all age groups, including young people (*Regional Trends*, HMSO, 1993; *Regional Utveckling i Norden*, 1993). The relationship between economic restructuring, youth transitions, household relations, and the construction of inter-generational gender identities, becomes particularly important in the context of regions characterised by depressed youth labour markets. Traditionally, the socialisation of young people into 'appropriate' gender identities took place both within the family, as well as through the transition into a highly segmented labour market. The chapters in this section unravel the impact in urban Newcastle and rural 'Fjord' of the 'feminisation' of the labour-market and young women's increased involvement in education.

At the same time, it is important to note how the effects of restructuring can be influenced by national policies and state intervention. It is interesting to contrast Britain and Norway in this regard. Due to Norway's stronger commitment to the relocation of public service employment to the periphery, unemployment in Norland is only 4 per cent higher than the national average, while in the unregulated UK, the North East unemployment rate is 35 percent higher than the country as a whole. Significant differences in education, training, social security and housing policy between the two countries also affect young people's identities and opportunities. Young women's job prospects and quality of working life can be enhanced by the creation of full-time, reasonably well-paid public service jobs, a more likely prospect in Norway than in Britain, where 'breadwinning' women and their households are often left to cope on part-time poorly paid work (Bradley, 1989).

While most research continues to show a distinct gendered division of labour in the home, there are hints at a change of roles for a particular section of the young male and female youth population (Hollands, 1995). Young people of working age, regardless of gender, are increasingly identified in economic terms. They are either seen as an important source of additional income and/or as contributor to the domestic economy; or they can be viewed as an added drain on already depleted family resources. This is politicising male and female relations in the home at the very time when opportunities for young adults to establish their own households is limited by poor job prospects. What of young people's rights to independence and an autonomous living-space in the face of such pressures?

The chapters which follow show that there is a close connection between the institutionalisation of the delayed transitions for many young adults created through economic change, the role of community and the household on the one hand, and the increasing importance of new youth cultural forms and consumption identities on the other. Both chapters indicate that there are both continuities of social relations like class and gender, as well as changes and recompositions. The relationship between three institutional sites in particular: the economy, the household and young people's engagement in the cultural realm, are shown as the main pillars for understanding the shifting relations of gender and generation. The concept of modernity or modernisation is central here, including its impact on identity formation. Modernity refers to changes in the pace of contemporary life, the rapidly shifting nature of modern institutions: work, family, community. Young people play a particularly important role here, for - paradoxically - they often appear to be bearing the brunt of some of the dramatic changes being wrought, while also actively pushing this process forward. Young adults appear as victims who are used to redefine the economic landscape of contemporary capitalism, with its rhetoric of servicing and flexibility. Yet they are also actively involved in the consumption of global culture, new technologies and various 'risk cultures'. This section shows that the disruption of traditional communities based on agriculture (Chapter 13) and manufacturing (Chapter 12), has meant that the younger generation has to construct new definitions of *Gemeinschaft* in other spheres, like leisure and youth culture.

The importance of 'space' is crucial here, and although we do not wish to fall into a spurious distinction between urban and rural, there are some important national differences to consider when comparing the following two case studies. In the English case, extensive early urbanisation and rapid decline of occupational communities in the 1980s, has meant that cities and towns have increasingly become a site of identification for many young people (see Worpole, 1992). In Norway, support for local agricultural communities means that rural areas can continue to help provide young people with a sense of continuity and belonging, although the global availability of youth culture and the attraction of urban areas for many young people are increasingly influencing traditional identities and transitions. Finally, rapid change has meant that traditional gender identities have began to break down and fracture in the leisure and consumption sphere. While aspects of the historical legacy continue to influence young women's and men's experiences in the consumption field, they have also resulted in a much more diverse range of youth identities, styles and cultures characteristic of the current generation (see Hollands, 1995).

The chapters which follow explore young men and women's orientations to new forms of employment, their use of the household in the negotiation of work and leisure, and the growing importance of cultural consumption, community and leisure in the formation of contemporary youthful identities. That economic change may generate institutional disjunctures between household and economy is particularly apparent when we examine the contrasting gender responses that become apparent from the case studies.

The fragmentation of work identities arising from limited employment opportunities is common to both Fjord and Newcastle. It is unskilled young men who bear the brunt of the numerical flexibility brought about by high levels of unemployment in rural Norway, though in urban Newcastle, young women also suffer extensively. The problem for young men is however exacerbated by the contradiction between the traditional male provider role and insecure employment. Traditionally, young women are not so reliant upon work for their identity, and Magnussen argues that qualified young women in Norway, who see it as important to obtain work to establish their identity, are representatives of modernity. For young Norwegian women, service sector employment provides the opportunity for expressing a modified form of the traditional feminine identity - in the sphere of work, rather than in the domestic sphere, as her mother would have done it.

The research reported on in urban Britain (Chapter 12) and rural Norway (Chapter 13) shows both young men and young women seeking to confirm their identity in the leisure and consumption sphere. For many young men, this represents a continuity based on a modified form of the traditional male identity. This means transposing their fathers' male work identity derived from working in shipyards or mines in Newcastle, or from hunting and outdoor activities in Fjord, to asserting masculinity through leisure pursuits - the pub or club; and in Fjord, with the addition of outdoor leisure. Hollands shows some attempting to replicate masculinist and patriarchal forms in a new guise (e.g. 'new laddism', football culture), or even exaggerating them as forms of misogynist behaviours and attitudes. Yet he also finds evidence of a disavowal of traditional gender identities by some young men in terms of a rejection of masculine work and identity and an engagement with more androgynous subcultures, for example in dance and music.

However, for young Geordie women, their involvement in the consumption sphere constitutes a break with traditional social values, a break which is paradoxically financed through continuity in the traditional gender bargain within the household. Young women remain firmly part of their household team for undertaking domestic tasks, and in doing so absolve themselves from the requirement to make as large a financial contribution to board and lodging. The rather surprising outcome of this is that young women, who are likely to be paid even less than their brothers, actually spend a higher percentage of their income on nights out.

Young Norwegian women tend to make rather different choices. Magnussen points out that the rural moral community, as well as parental social morality, can limit their freedom. Their choice, in contrast, is generally to leave the parental household and the community. Young Norwegian women are rejecting their traditional domestic role as well. There is evidence in both Newcastle and 'Fjord' that young women may be taking advantage of an admittedly constrained labour market to gain personal and financial independence; to begin the process of constructing 'alternative careers' to marriage and domestic life in education or in the leisure sphere. It is also interesting to note that in both localities, faced with the fragmentation of economic life, leisure provides a new form of social solidarity, moulding both community and regional identity.

There is the suggestion in both chapters that the symbolic construction of adult identity through the consumption sphere may also provide a substitute for the decreasing availability of that other, more practical aspect of the transition to adulthood - setting up an independent household. For setting up house requires the ability to support oneself financially, and present day labour market conditions in both Norway and Britain preclude this possibility for many young people. The nature of the boundaries around households are changing, as young people find themselves blocked in the transition between household of origin and new household formation. Indeed, Hollands goes on to suggest a fundamental uncoupling of going to the pub as a rite of passage to adulthood. Rather, night-life has now become a ritual continuing through a long, unspecified period of post-adolescence. In Britain, this enforced dependency of young people on their household of origin is reinforced by the benefit system. In Norway, the individual insurance based system allows more possibility for joint flexibility in the labour market in new young households.

How far are we setting up a set of social disjunctures based on a generation of Peter Pans whose ability to grow up is limited because they cannot achieve the adult status derived from full economic independence? If households of origin in Norway and Britain continue to provide an economic buffer for the next generation, does this not simply reinforce shorter-term horizons for young adults, who do not gain the experience of responsibility for their own household? The prospects for the future are made more bleak by the difficulties that may arise from contrasting gender experiences. For young women's identities appear to be more nurtured by the economic changes that are taking place, and they seem to be flourishing better than their partners and brothers. Young men are perhaps the real losers in their limited ability to adapt to the changing rules of the big game of economic restructuring. Young women have different expectations from their mothers in a number of respects; their brothers are still tending to model themselves on fathers, when the means of fulfilling their provider role is no longer available. It is unclear where these disjunctures will lead in terms of the sustainability of a new generation of households. At present the evidence would seem to point to the need for both young men and young women to be flexible when they form new households. But not only do new households require flexible partnered workers at home and in the labour-market, who can complement each other's insecure contracts, they may also need regular support from state benefits as well as support from other households, through parents and relatives.

Notes

1. The term youth is hampered not simply by its ideological dimensions and certain bio-political assumptions, but by a failure to define its limits in terms of age. Delayed transitions into work and marriage, high and persistent youth unemployment, the effect of the 'baby-boomer' culture, and increased numbers of young people going into education, have all contributed to the idea of 'post-adolescence' (a lengthening of the youthful phase) and the use of the term 'young adults' here.

CHAPTER 12

FROM SHIPYARDS TO NIGHTCLUBS: THE RESTRUCTURING OF YOUNG GEORDIE WORK, HOME AND CONSUMPTION IDENTITIES[1]

Robert Hollands

'Extraordinary though it may seem, Tyneside is not now famous for its manufacturing industries, but for its shopping malls, night-clubs and flashy cocktail bars' (Robinson, 1988).

Introduction

This chapter sets out to examine the impact of economic restructuring on young peoples' cultures and transitions in work, the home and consumption in North East England. It seeks to answer a number of important questions. How has economic change influenced young adults' transitions into, and orientations towards work, home and the local community? What role does the domestic household play in the coping strategies adopted to deal with their financial situation, and how does it contribute to the construction of gender identity? How are the consumption patterns and cultures of young people at leisure predicated on work and domestic life, and in what ways are they transcending them? What do these changes mean for regional identities?

The crux of the argument presented here is that there has been a significant shift in the basis for youth transitions and local cultural identity. Economic restructuring is one key ingredient here; the other concerns the increasingly important role that cities play in relation to economic change, cultural consumption and the experience of modernity (Giddens, 1990). The decline in manufacturing and shift towards service-based employment, changing production regimes organised around ideas of flexibility, an increase in women workers, and the global and spatial reorganisation of capital (Harvey, 1989; Bagguley, 1990) have all had an impact on young adults' identities and transitions. This has affected young people's opportunities and orientations towards work, and, combined with shifting household relations, has influenced consumption patterns and created a variety of different youth lifestyles.

Modernity refers to our contemporary experience of the social world as akin to being on a merry-go-round: intensely pleasurable at times, but moving so fast that it makes it difficult to know where to get off. The city reflects this mixed feeling of wonder and joy, anonymity and freedom on the one hand; danger, vice and disorder on the other. Paradoxically, the city is home to both the expression of regional identities and feelings of security and belonging, as well as being a primary site for the consumption of more global images, not to mention various 'risk' cultures central to many aspects of youthfulness (Beck, 1992).

The chapter shows a weakening of traditional sites of identity formation for young adults, represented by delayed transitions into self-fulfilling work and a lack of opportunity to set up autonomous households. This contrasts with the growing importance of youth cultural activity to constructing a sense of self, centring around the phenomenon of 'going out'[2]. There is a selective reinterpretation of the previous male occupational culture, as well as the creative adoption of new lifestyles. These changes in economic, domestic and cultural life are slowly leading to a questioning of traditional gender relations and roles, and providing the basis for a new sense of regional affiliation.

The empirical material used to support the argument is drawn from an ethnographic study of young adults' cultural experiences of urban city space and night life in the city of Newcastle Upon Tyne (Hollands, 1995).[3] The cohort was derived from a random sample of post-coded addresses obtained from the City Council, and quota sampling was used to match the characteristics of this group to 1991 census data. In-depth, semi-structured interviews were conducted with thirty local women and men between the ages of 16-31 (average age 25) at their homes or at the university, while participant observation methods were employed to analyse leisure patterns and their use of the city.

Young adults and the meaning of post-industrial work

Sixty years ago the backbone of the North East economy was coal, shipbuilding and heavy industry, and as late as 1971 manufacturing and work in the primary industries still accounted for 40 per cent of employment in the area (Robinson, 1988). A strong white, patriarchal and masculine occupational identity - one of the original meanings of the term 'Geordie' is pit man or miner - spilled over into the wider local culture, influencing the structure of home life, leisure and community.

The Tyneside economy of the 1990s is almost unrecognisable in light of this earlier history. Only 17 per cent of local people now work in manufacturing, while over 70 per cent are employed in the service sector, with many of these new jobs being part-time and filled by women (Tyneside TEC, 1993). Women's employment has risen over the last decade and they now make up nearly half of the labour force, while male jobs have declined dramatically, resulting in higher than average unemployment rates on Tyneside in comparison to both regional and national levels (Robinson, 1994; see also Chapter 4).

The impact of these economic changes on young adults' identities and transitions is complex. Clearly one result concerns opportunities for employment. Census figures for Newcastle in 1991 show that just over half of 16-29 year olds are in either full- or part-time work, nearly 15 per cent are classed as unemployed and just over 16 per cent are students (see Table 12.1). The true extent of unemployment amongst this group is masked partly by 16-17 years olds' ineligibility to claim income support, but also because a significantly high percentage of young women are classed as 'other inactive'.

In the study sample, young women who were economically active were currently working in clerical, caring (nursing), shop work and sales occupations. Previous jobs held since leaving school were also located within a narrow band of what might be referred to as traditional women's work. Over half of those economically active were working part-time. A number relied on student grants, others on state benefit, meaning that the average weekly income for the young women in the sample was £70, with £105 a week for those in employment. So, despite the fact that there has been some increase in employment opportunities for young women in Newcastle - something which arguably may result in higher levels of sociability and self-esteem (Wilkinson, 1994) - most females are still limited to work in a narrow range of part-time, low paid servicing jobs, characterised by poor promotion prospects, a lack of training and low status (Robinson, 1988; Stubbs and Wheelock, 1990). This paradox is represented well in the following statement from one of our respondents who worked in a travel agency:

Sue (L19)   Em, I love working with the public, because we're in reception, working with the public, it's alright being under pressure 'cos everybody helps together, all the girls, it's really good fun. Just basically all the holidays, it's good working with it, it's exciting you know, booking people on holidays. I would like to be doing the same job, but more em, responsibility, you know, be taking over some part of the holidays rather than being an assistant. There is only one manager, whereas you could have like a supervisor, or something, moving up like you say.

Young men's occupational choices and possibilities, while not quite so narrow, were also hampered by higher overall unemployment levels and the dramatic decline in traditional forms of manual labour. Clerical and distributive jobs in the civil service, portering and management employment in the hotel and leisure field, sales assistant in the food industry, painting and decorating and bar work were the main occupations currently engaged in. Again, part-time work, and reliance on student grants or unemployment benefit meant that the average weekly income for young men was £102, with waged workers having £144. Over half of the males in employment stated that they would prefer to be doing a different job in five years time. When asked whether they liked their current work, Doug's is one typical response:

Table 12.1 Economic position of young adults (16-29) in Newcastle

	All (sample)	(Census)	Males (sample)	(Census)	Females (sample)	(Census)
Employed (total)	56.7	51.0	60.0	51.9	53.4	50.1
(Full-time)	40.0	43.5	53.3	48.4	26.7	38.8
(Part-time)	16.7	7.5	6.7	3.5	26.7	11.3
Self-employed	-	2.6	-	3.8	-	1.3
Scheme	-	3.3	-	4.2	-	2.3
Unemployed	18.3	14.7	20.0	20.0	13.3	9.7
Eco active	74.7	71.6	80.0	80.0	67.7	63.4
Student	23.3	16.4	20.0	17.6	26.7	15.2
Sick/retired and other inactive	2.0	12.0	-	2.3	6.6	21.4
Eco inactive	25.3	28.4	20.0	20.0	33.3	36.6

Source: 1991 Population Census for Tyne and Wear

Doug (L31)   No. The main reason, boredom. There is no variation in the work. It is a typical desk job. The kind of work, dealing with child benefit, is not really something that holds a great deal of interest for me.

While there was some indication that a small section of young men continued to prefer manual work (Hollands, 1994), most of the male sample expressed a strong desire for more challenging professional jobs. Young women were also committed to having a career and improving their position economically, mentioning work like research, management and personnel and self-employment. But can the regional economy deliver jobs of this nature in sufficient numbers or provide the necessary training and education for local young adults to move into such careers? At the moment, it is clear from the sample that post-industrial servicing jobs are not socially rewarding enough for many young Geordies. Nor, as the next section shows, do they provide the financial means for ensuring independent living arrangements and separate households.

Home, sweet, home? Negotiating work and consumption

Household relations and organisation are crucial in understanding how families and individuals cope with and construct their identities as social and economic change occur. The household comprises a central mechanism for constructing gender identities for young adults. Its importance both as an economic buffer and as a source of conflict should not be underestimated. As we shall see, young people's leisure and consumption practices and expenditure patterns can only be made sense of in the context of the domestic economy.

Young adults' job prospects and income had a significant knock on effect on their opportunities to move out of the family household. Only 13 per cent of the sample lived on their own, with only one individual owning their own flat. Fifty per cent lived with their parent(s), while the remaining 37 per cent either shared with friends or partners. Marriage rates amongst young adults on Tyneside also support this pattern of delayed transitions into separate households (see Table 12.2). Fluctuations in marriage rates of course reflect changing values in society, by failing to capture increases in cohabitation. It is nevertheless interesting that the decline in marriage rates parallels the dwindling job prospects for young adults in the area. According to census figures from the last 30 years, marriage rates for all ages groups (between 15-29) have fallen by almost half, with the largest percentage drop amongst the 20-24 year olds (from 42.2 per cent being married in 1961 compared to only 12.9 per cent in 1991).

There have been recent suggestions of a decline in the moral respectability of the institution of marriage and fatherhood, particularly amongst young northern working-class men (Dennis and Erdos, 1992). In contrast, our research revealed a relatively high regard amongst young men for their future responsibilities towards partners and children, though this commitment was most likely to revolve around traditional

Table 12.2 Marriage Rates (%) by age and sex in Newcastle

	All Persons (ages)			Males (ages)			Females (ages)		
	(15-19)	(20-24)	(25-29)	(15-19)	(20-24)	(25-29)	(15-19)	(20-24)	(25-29)
1961	3.0	42.2	75.0	0.1	30.0	68.0	5.0	54.0	82.0
1971	4.8	40.0	71.3	2.4	31.4	65.0	7.3	50.0	78.0
1981	2.6	31.0	63.6	1.3	23.0	58.0	4.0	38.0	69.0
1991	0.9	12.9	42.4	0.4	9.0	37.0	1.4	17.0	47.0

Source: Population Census

notions of being the 'breadwinner' and 'protector'. The vast majority of local men spoke about future relationships primarily in financial terms; whether they would be able to afford them.

Delayed transitions into marriage and autonomous households, then, appear as the main coping mechanisms young adults on Tyneside have to deal with their less than satisfactory financial position. This of course, has implications for households of origin. On the whole, it seems that parental households are exceedingly generous in accommodating young adult family members, even though they sometimes make an increased monetary and domestic burden (Allatt and Yeandle, 1992). Our study shows that there are important differences with respect to the economic power of young men and young women in the household, and differential expectations of the domestic duties each will perform.

Previous research suggests that young women deal with their subordinate economic position at least partly through their adaptation to particular household arrangements (Griffin, 1985; Wallace, 1987; Hollands, 1990). In line with this, to be able to cope financially, the majority of young females in our sample required a shared living space involving partners, parents, lodgers, students and friends. Just over a half lived in a shared household or with a partner, while 40 per cent lived with parents. Only one women - in full-time employment - lived on her own. This type of household arrangement involved a cost for young women concerned. The price was generally paid in kind, in the form of domestic labour. Over a quarter of young women in our sample said that they themselves were primarily responsible for the housework, and 80 per cent said it was either themselves or it was shared. This contrasts with other research on young people at home, which has found that even young women appear to do very little (Hudson and Jenkins, 1989). Those young women in our sample who stated that they did very little domestic labour they were primarily drawn from the group who lived at home with their parents.

It was young women with children who suffered most from the burden of domestic labour. Local research has shown that leisure for women in this age grouping is nearly halved due to the time consuming nature of child care (Blackie, 1993). The interviews we had with women with children were threaded through with references to a lack of time, the difficulty of work, getting babysitters and the need for a break from their children. Jan makes a typical remark about the unequal gender division of household duties:

RT   Who is primarily responsible for doing the housework in your household?

Jan (L29)   Em, me I suppose. Because I mean, things like the hoovering I never do, but it's the only thing I don't do. I do all the washing, all the cooking, all the decorating, even like the DIY things, which should be a man's job. I wouldn't trust him to do it, I do that meself.

Many of the young men interviewed also chose to stay at home. While a higher percentage of men (20 per cent) could afford to live on their own compared to women, a higher percentage also stopped with parents (50 per cent), with only 20 per cent sharing accommodation. A number of the employed young men who lived in the parental home offset any domestic labour obligations by paying keep or board. Overall, a mere 13 per cent of men stated that they were primarily responsible for domestic tasks, while nearly half said it was someone else, usually their mother. Compare what Carl has to say with Jan's comments:

Carl (L18)   My mum, she virtually does all the housework, I do very little around the house...I really do absolutely nothing, it is quite embarrassing really, I've never done my own ironing or washing. Well from time to time I keep my own room tidy and my things tidy, but I have a meal put in front of me every evening, and eat it and walk off afterwards.

It is nevertheless interesting to find 40 per cent stating that the domestic work in their household was shared, involving both themselves and fathers and brothers:

RH   Who's primarily responsible for doing housework in your household?

Decker (L19)   It's mostly...I don't know actually, that's an interesting question cos...sometimes it's me mam if she's got a week off and she's got this thing about tidying the house up cos like lately me brother and me have has a lot of friends around and stuff. Or it could be me dad and stuff or it could be me brother and that if, if someone's not well. I would say shared (...) I mean I come home yesterday and me dad's in the front room with the CD player on doin' the ironin' and that, like in the front room and I was like, woo...oh god, its weird man, I expected him to have curlers in and stuff, you know (...) I'm always usually going to do the shoppin' and stuff cos I'm a big strong lad and carry the bags and stuff (laughs).

Even though he jokes about his own and his father's contribution (an ex-shipyard worker, now unemployed), Decker is also convinced that the system works and is largely a fair one. While there still may be some gender segmentation within this more flexible domestic labour situation, it is clear that there are some examples of changing individual and family forms (Wheelock, 1990).

To sum up, while young women have made some economic advances, these are not sufficient to offer them either an independent household, or relief from doing much of the domestic work. At most, those living at home with parents may merely be able to leave the domestic burden with another female member of the household. Young men, thanks to their stronger financial position, appear able to use their economic and social position to mostly avoid doing housework, although there are some examples of changing domestic arrangements. Yet the gender relations played out here, while important, remain confined to the private sphere, and household identities remain largely hidden. The interesting issue is the way in which these shifting economic and domestic relations are nevertheless beginning to impact on young adults' identity formation in the more public sphere of leisure and consumption.

From shipyards to nightclubs: youth cultural identification in the post-industrial city

In an atmosphere of declining occupational and community based identities, and a rise in more global images and icons, the city is an ideal place for young people to reconcile tradition and change, and literally re-create themselves (Redhead, 1993; O'Connor and Wynne, nd). The growing importance of the city as a site of social identity is also connected to a set of additional factors. First, it is a public space, in the sense that going out is a visible display of identity. Second, urban regeneration, in terms of leisure, public entertainment and the redevelopment of clubs and pubs, occurred in the same time-frame as the region experienced its most rapid economic decline. And finally, this new consumption space did not discriminate against the local population by age, class or gender criteria, so that many young adults were able to appropriate sections of the city by claiming them as their own (Shields, 1991).

The combination of extended transitions with shifts in the sites where young people construct their identities, has had several significant and contradictory effects. One of the most important ones has been that the meaning and social context of going out has begun to be transformed from a simple 'rite of passage' to adulthood, towards a more permanent 'socialising ritual' for many young adults (Sande, 1995b). Involvement in youth cultures and night-life rituals have become a more central and stable aspect of identity formation, creating a space for activities, attitudes and behaviours which are neither youthful nor adult, but somewhere in-between. This can both reflect, and stand in for the loss of traditional identities, and can allow young people to step outside of established roles and social expectations. There has also been an increased fragmentation of youth identities and cultures in the contemporary period around issues of class, gender, race, sexuality, politics and consumption lifestyles (Featherstone, 1987). The ritualisation of nights out has become, if you like, young adults' attempt to construct a modern equivalent of 'community', or more correctly, communities.

This movement from rites to rituals signals an underlying change in the meaning and function of going out. Locally, nights out were historically much more closely tied to growing up and adulthood. Traditional rites revolved around introduction to alcohol, courtship and marriage and integration into the community through the local pub. Drinking and going out in the North East was also embedded in a wider cultural apprenticeship based around masculinity and women's subordination in the home. Young men in particular were introduced to alcohol in a community setting by fathers or relatives, and learnt to appreciate the taste of ale while acquiring the capacity to hold their drink (Gofton, 1983). Their induction into the pub paralleled their transition into manual work and manhood generally. Hence the traditional image of the hard-working, hard-drinking Geordie man. Women's subordinate role within this masculine occupational culture meant that they were largely limited to the private and domestic sphere, with the pub being primarily a male preserve. While there is evidence that some women did occupy some public spaces, their motivations were largely understood within the confines of domestic or sexual discourses (Common, 1951; McConville, 1983).

The significance, meaning and wider social context surrounding youth cultures and going out has changed dramatically in the contemporary period (Gofton 1986; 1990). Certain aspects of the historical legacy survive, and young people still initially enter into night-life activities as a form of initiation into adulthood, but the social and economic conditions to make the wider transition are no longer secure. The uncoupling of these processes has meant that going out can be engaged in for its own sake, and need not be viewed as an element of growing up. The result is that youth cultural activity has increasingly become an important and more permanent site of identity formation in its own right, and is utilised by many young adults as a form of expressing their regional identity, rather than a marker signifying adulthood.

One response to delayed transitions and the shift towards consumption, is the attempt by young adults to reinvent what it means to be a Geordie. For many youngsters, regional identity now has less to do with work and industrial production; more to do with consumption in the city. Yet the forms through which some young locals express themselves on a night out, while contemporary, may attempt to reproduce elements of a mythical collective past (Colls and Lancaster, 1992). If young adults can never be Geordies in any true occupational sense, they can reconstruct such an identity through a selective borrowing of historical images and traits, combined with present day experiences and realities in other spheres. Indeed, young adults recognise the attempts of others to rejuvenate elements of the industrial archetype through the image of the Geordie 'hard man':[4]

Carl (L18)   I seem to think it's a bit personified by some of the lads' drinking in the city centre, this stereotypical Geordie bloke, Geordie town, where you have to be hard, you have to drink twenty pints, you have to have a curry, hit a policeman, then go on the pull afterwards, you know.

In one sense elements of this reconstruction continue to affect the style and pattern of nights out for many young men, despite the fact that for the majority it is largely a stylistic ritual. The so-called 'hard lads' may be a minority response, but the symbolic aspects of male Geordie culture extend far beyond the stereotype, despite an increased diversity in male identity. At the same time, many misconceptions and much of the hype surrounding violence in the city, confuses often playful adoptions of some of these symbols with an undying commitment to masculine values and anti-social behaviour.

Shifts in the meaning and social context of going out have also changed fundamentally because of the dramatic increase of women in the city (Wilson, 1991). Young women in Newcastle go out more frequently, would feel worse if restricted, and spend a higher percentage of their income on nights out than their male counterparts (Hollands, 1995). Despite the persistence of historical and contemporary barriers in employment, the domestic household and leisure (Blackie, 1993), women have made significant leaps forward in re-forming their own identities in the city. They have played a central role in promoting the socialising aspect of going out. While young women continue to be influenced by domestic and sexual ideologies, female solidarity in dance and drug cultures (Henderson, 1993) and 'ladies only' nights out are two examples of this changing context. Take the case of Meryl:

Meryl (L19)   ...'Cos I've got a big circle of friends. Sometimes all the girls will go out, like tonight its a girl's birthday, so there'll be ten girls going out... On Thursday I always go out with girlfriends.

RT   When you go out on girls' nights out, do you ever meet up with blokes, or do you really stick together?

Meryl   Stick together.

Important changes are taking place with respect to young women's attitudes and cultures. While elements of this shift may be partly related to their movement into the labour market and delayed transitions into marriage, it is in the arena of consumption and sexuality that young women have fought for and obtained a degree of freedom. Many have discovered that it is both possible and viable to maintain female friendship relations as well as engage in courtship, and in certain circumstances they are consciously choosing to have same-sex nights out, where they can enjoy the companionship and solidarity of other women. The assertion of women's sexuality, as a force in its own right, has also begun to challenge traditional notions of subordination and domesticity (McRobbie, 1993).

In fact, the loosening of traditional roles generally has resulted in an increased differentiation amongst young adults and created the conditions for a proliferation of more specific youth cultures. Many young people are utilising extended transitions to explore the possibilities of alternative identities around not only gender (Wilkinson, 1994), but also sexual orientation (Whittle, 1994), involvement in social movements and student subcultures, not to mention a range of music, drug and dance-based cultures (Newcombe, 1991; Merchant and MacDonald, 1994; Coffield and Gofton, 1994; Henderson, 1993; Thornton, 1995). While elements of these cultures cross over into orientations towards work, education, and politics, one of the main shifts has been a move away from some of the more traditional and localised attitudes and behaviours, towards the consumption of more global images and styles.

Conclusion

The phenomenon of going out is becoming a more central element in the production of contemporary youth identities, rather than simply a frivolous enjoyment. It is clear that while jobs and the desire for employment continue to be an important and significant element of young people's experiences in the locality, neither traditional nor so-called post-industrial work appear to provide young Tynesiders with a viable identity and sense of the future. Similarly, high levels of unemployment, low pay, and poor career prospects mean that many young adults in the region get by and cope through a reliance on and negotiation with the domestic household. Poor economic prospects, delayed transitions into marriage and declining occupational communities, have meant that the search for a modern Geordie identity has largely taken place in what were once marginal spaces in the sphere of consumption and city and urban life. It is here, rather than at home or in work, that identities are being forged and ritualised, and where future possibilities need consideration.

To fully comprehend the nature of generation, locality and identity, requires bringing together economic, domestic and cultural perspectives. The restructuring perspective provides a useful social and historical context for understanding economic change in a particular locality. On its own however, it can lead towards an economic determinism which ignores the role of the domestic household and the experience of modernity and consumption as important in the formation of identities (Savage and Warde, 1993; see also Chapter 1). Post-modernist theories, on the other hand, often substitute a kind of cultural or global media-based determinism to explain contemporary youth cultures (Redhead, 1993). In doing so, they tend to miss the significance of economic and household relations, and ignore the continuing impact class, gender, race and local cultures play in structuring young adults' identities and experiences. This chapter has argued that it is important to combine studying youth cultures, styles, and experiences of consumption (Hall and Jefferson, 1976; Hebdige, 1979) within the context of economic restructuring and household responses (Banks et al, 1992). This approach helps to illuminate and bridge some of the gaps in our knowledge of the combined effect of capitalism, place, culture and generation.

Finally, what of the future of regional identities, particularly for young people, in the context of global economic capitalism and the sharpening of the cultural consequences of modernity? Urban youth cultures open up the debate about post-industrial cities, raising questions of what we want them to be like, how should they be used, and by whom (Worpole, 1992; Lovatt, 1994; Landry and Bianchini, 1995). If Colls and Lancaster (1992) are right when they suggest that who Geordies are depends on who they imagine themselves to be, then it is crucial to listen to and understand the rapidly changing life-world of the next generation. The future identity of Tyneside may depend on what we hear.

Notes

1. A revised and lengthened version of this chapter appears in *The Berkeley Journal of Sociology,* Vol 41, 1997. I would like to thank the Berkeley Journal of Sociology Collective for their kind permission to reproduce a version of that paper here. Finally a special thanks to Allan Sande, Helen Carr, Rob MacDonald, Mo O'Toole and Jane Wheelock, who all commented on or contributed to this paper in some way.

2. 'Going out', for the purpose of the research, is defined as attending a bar/pub, club or music venue in city centre in the evening. While night-life does not subsume the expression of all youth cultural activity, it is nonetheless a highly significant social and spacial element.

3. I would like to acknowledge the financial assistance of the ESRC for its funding of 'Youth Cultures and the Use of Urban City Spaces' (reference number R00 23 4622), and to thank Ros Taylor, the project research associate, for her assistance in the research. The key to the taped interviewes is as follows: RH- Robert Hollands; RT- Ros Taylor, ...pause; (...) material edited out. The names of all respondents have been changed to protect their identities. Interviewee names are followed by an L for local, and a number for age, so that Sue (L19) is a 19-year-old local woman.

4. A weekend newspaper article when covering the death of Viv Graham, a notable Newcastle 'hard man' who made a living out of his physical prowess, first as a bouncer and then as an 'enforcer' who was paid protection money to keep a number of pubs and clubs orderly in the city, appeared to suggest that this line of work was becoming an 'alternative' career in the area. The assertion was that Tyneside gyms had never been so full of young men pumping iron (*The Independent* 13.3.94). Additional research conducted by the principal researcher (Young and Hollands, 1994) into drug use and 'harm reduction' policy in the North has revealed that steroid rather than heroin users are the main beneficiaries of some needle exchange programmes in the region. The expression of masculinity in leisure, sport (including football supporters), criminality and as an 'alternative' employment career, in the context of the decline of manual/physical work, deserves additional study.

CHAPTER 13

MARGINALISED YOUNG MEN AND SUCCESSFUL YOUNG WOMEN? RURAL YOUNG PEOPLE ENTERING ADULTHOOD[1]

Tone Magnussen

Introduction

Today, young people find themselves on their way to adulthood in a rapidly changing world where modernity, individualism and restructuring predominate. The consequences of these structural changes affect young men and women entering the local labour market. Traditional male jobs based on informal on-the-job-training such as construction, engineering and crafts, are disappearing. While young men with a more or less complete vocational training background seem to lose out in the competition for fewer jobs, young women with higher education tend to be the winners in the local labour market (Fylling 1994, Magnussen 1995).

Achieving status as an adult is a transitional process which involves two central aspects; the practical setting up of a household, and the symbolic construction of an adult identity. The contruction of a household is one of the rites of passage in the transition from youth to adulthood. The household is a social unit that encompasses certain key activities, such as housekeeping, budgeting, production, child care and cooking (Gullestad 1984). Setting up a household is a process which involves working towards attaining status as an adult, and describes aspects of economy, work and housing related to the family. Young people's attachment to the parental home is changing. In the early post-war period, the main tendency was for young people to move away from home at a progressively earlier age. Over the last decade this trend has changed, with young adults staying longer in the parental home (SSB 1992). Economic restructuring, rising unemployment and new patterns of employment have led to delayed youth transitions into the labour market and out of the family household.

Attaining identity as an adult is another crucial aspect of the transition into adulthood. Modern society is characterised by freedom of choice and individualism; people are seen as free to create themselves and their own lives. Modernity may in this sense be considered as a condition in which people are forced to make active choices about who they want to be and how they want to live (Giddens, 1991). People are responsible for constructing themselves as individuals; they are responsible for, and free to construct, their own identities. In a modern context, there is a multitude of alternative ways in which social identities are constructed and identity management is a crucial part of an individual's struggle to create a self.

The empirical material in this chapter is based on a study of young adults and their adjustment to rural communities and labour markets during the transition from school to work or further education. The study took place in Fjord[2], a rural community in northern Norway. A combination of semi-structured interviews and participant observation was used to collect information from 25 young women and men aged 20-30. We here discuss the impact of economic change on young adults in terms of labour market adjustment, and how young men and young women experience and cope with this situation in different ways. Do changing global and national conditions lead to new and different transitions into adulthood and, if so, how do they impact on gender relations? What does this changed framework mean for gender identities? Has there been a shift in the basis for construction of identity?

The economy of Fjord has traditionally been based on primary industries and local natural resources. Two or three decades ago, traditional industry consisted of a combination of farming and fishing. Today, the transition from primary industries to service employment is striking. The rise of the Norwegian welfare state, and especially the growth in public services during the 1970s, created new jobs in rural areas. Within the new state and municipal institutions, new kinds of jobs were established locally. At the same time, improved means of transportation made it possible to continue living in rural areas while commuting to work elsewhere. The development of public transport systems integrated the rural areas into larger regional contexts, including larger and more varied labour markets. The strong ties between work, local resources and local community, were loosened (Foss, Halvorsen and Vatne, 1994). Schools, nursing homes and local administration created new jobs and a demand for new professions. Most of these jobs, whether unskilled or professional, are held by women. Structural changes in the local economy have created a new and more difficult challenge for young adults trying to enter the labour market. Decline in the traditional resource-based industries and rise in service employment have restructured the labour market and have led to fewer jobs. Unemployment rates are rising[3].

These marked structural changes in the local economy are connected to more general trends in the labour market characterised by disappearing recruitment positions and stronger demands for formal training. A move towards a more polarised labour market is noticeable. On the one hand, there are knowledge-based and information-intensive occupations with high wages and good working conditions. On the other hand there is a labour market consisting of routine, unskilled work; jobs that are often temporary, with low wages, and poor working conditions (Foss 1993; Lash, 1994). In recent years, national unemployment rates have grown. Young adults under the age of 25 represent 18 per cent of the national labour force, but 40 percent of the unemployed were under 25 years old (1992 figures). Compared to Great Britain, there are a higher proportion of young people among the unemployed in Norway (Hammer

1994).

Rising unemployment in cities and central core areas have consequences for rural areas; growth in central areas is crucial for rural mobility. When the economy in central areas is on the decline, they become less attractive as places to live and work. In considering migration, young adults would then rather choose to stay in the rural community (Seierstad, 1992). The Norwegian welfare system assures everyone a minimum level of economic provision. This is a key condition in the choice of this kind of strategy. Unemployment benefits and other forms of social security create a secure economic situation for the unemployed, regardless of where they might choose to live. When economic life is fragmented and individualised, it becomes more important to experience continuity and belonging. As the structural base of the community is being weakened by social change, it is replaced by symbolic expressions of belonging (Cohen, 1985).

Let us now take a closer look at young men and women in Fjord and their experiences of and adjustments to the local labour market. The typical stories of John, Julie and other young adults will be used as a framework for describing coping strategies regarding work, financial situation and leisure[4].

Young men choosing a traditional working career

John is 24 and unemployed. Four years ago he finished his vocational training consisting of a number of basic courses, but with no further training beyond these courses. He was unable to get an apprenticeship contract. He applied for many jobs in engineering workshops all over the region, but did not manage to get a permanent position. In subsequent years John had several short-lived jobs as a mechanic and in construction. In-between whiles he was unemployed and receiving unemployment benefits. Some of his jobs were ordinary, short-term jobs, others were offered by the state employment service through special work programmes. During his periods of unemployment, John took part in work on the farm owned by his parents. He has never had a permanent job, though most of the time he has had work and income. As John sees the situation in the local labour market:

> There are a lot of temporary jobs in Fjord. I know a lot of people, and have had some offers. I could have got a job as a carpenter if I'd gone in for it. But there is nothing permanent. Getting a permanent job is almost impossible, but there is always something to do.

Like most of the other young men interviewed, John has chosen the traditional working career for rural young men. Some years back, it would have been possible to enter the local labour market as a semi-skilled worker, with some small businesses in mechanics and construction providing on-the-job training. Now these firms have closed down as a consequence of economic restructuring. In rural areas young men still utilise practical skills as mechanics or craftsmen applied to farm maintainance. These skills may lead to short-term jobs inside the community, but outside the community there are no jobs where this competence is applicable. Leaving the community to enter the labour market in a nearby town is no longer a real alternative for John or other young men in his situation.

The economic situation amongst youth has become a main reason for a prolonged stay in the parental household. To set up one's own household requires a certain amount of economic support, through wage income or other sources, and includes the transition from being provided for, to being the provider. As entrance into the labour market has become more problematic, this has consequences for the transition into adulthood. The story of Ivar shows how the form of this transition has changed.

After leaving school, Ivar (now 21 years old) wanted to get a job, but could not find one. He lived with his parents in Fjord while waiting to complete his military service. After the first year of his military service, he went back to his parents. Back home he attended a variety of training courses offered by the state employment service, but he remains unemployed. Unemployment benefits are his only source of income, and this does not allow Ivar to be financially independent. He therefore remains living in the parental home, where he is subsidised by his parents. Ivar is not satisfied with this situation:

> It's just not right that they are providing for me. Actually, I should buy my own food and pay rent to my parents, but I can't afford that, not with the unemployment benefit. Some of the money I have to use for clothes and things like that. Cigarettes and such like I pay for myself. Everything I use for myself I pay for, it's just the food...

The Fjord empirical study found that most young, single men are unemployed, with no clear future plans, living on a low income. Unemployment benefit or social security is their only source of income. They often keep on living in their parents' household. None consider this an ideal situation, but for the time being, they regard it as the only solution. Shortage of money is the main reason for the prolonged stay in the parental household. These young men have not succeeded in establishing the financial independence that is a precondition for setting up of a household, as the example of Ivan makes clear. They have been unable to take any steps towards an independent household, and are still members of their household of origin.

When work no longer serves as the main arena for constructing, showing and confirming masculine identity, young men have to seek other arenas. Leisure activities have an important function in including and creating a sense of togetherness among young people. Among young men, hunting, fishing and other forms of outdoor life are especially important, as well as car maintenance. These are traditional masculine activities, in Fjord and in other rural communities. Weekend activities such as parties, nights at the pub and cars seem to have a special importance. The local pub on a Friday night is a popular meeting place where everyone congregates. Young people come from school in the nearby town, from work in the community, and from their life as the unemployed. In the pub young people can have a chat with old friends, get information about what has happened, make plans for the rest of the weekend, or just drop by and feel a sense of togetherness. Shortage of money does not exclude anyone from this arena. Even with a low income based on unemployment benefits, you can afford a Friday night at the pub, because this is the only event of the week that is considered important. One young man puts it like this:

> Living in the countryside is not very expensive. You are not tempted in the same way as in other places. You make your arrangements according to the pub opening hours. You know that you can go to the pub Friday night. You get drunk Friday night, and you know that it's only once a week. Most young people can afford that. They don't have much to spend their money on.

Young women making modern choices

Julie represents a contrast to John and other young men's choice of a traditional working career. She is a young woman who has made plans for her working life, plans which make her typically modern. Julie is 26, and works in the local administration. By training she is an accountant, and, having finished four years of higher education at the advanced commercial college, she got a job in a bank. She lived for some years in the nearby town, but was quite strongly attached to Fjord and the place where she grew up. She spent most of her weekends in Fjord, visiting family and friends and involving herself in different leisure activities. Julie married a man from Fjord, and they both started to look for jobs in the area.

Julie had done some careful planning in line with her education, her work and where she wanted to settle down. While women in Julie's mother's generation entered the labour market motivated by wanting a wage and the social contact, Julie has different and more specific expectations of work. For her, being employed and having a job is of great importance of her identity, and it is in this sense Julie is a modern young woman. Individualism characterises modernity; individuals are more free to create their own lives by choosing between different norms of behaviour and courses of action. Julie's choices and plans concerning work can be understood in this frame of reference. The job represents a chance to fulfil the need to express herself in her work, and to combine these self-creating demands with the basic need of earning money. Like other young people, Julie has subjective demands of the job, demands pertaining to the job content and communicative aspects of work.

Another young woman expresses her expectations of education and work like this:

> I want to get some formal education. These days, you have to, in case you end up on your own. Marrying, and then suddenly being on your own. With no education and a child to support. It's better to start by getting an education, and then build a family, having children and a house of your own.

We found that young women more often want to be able to identify themselves with their work, involve themselves, and experience confirmation of their own competence through their work. They want to interpret their job in terms of personal development and self-experience. Julie's professional background represents a competence which she can transfer from job to job, and gives her a privileged position in the labour market, which functions as a 'golden passport' to the local, regional and national labour market.

Different work opportunities make for different starting points in setting up a household. In contrast to Ivar and other young men, very few young, single women have chosen to stay in Fjord, partly due to the fact that young women are more controlled by the local moral community than young men. Rural communities are often considered 'transparent'; places where private life is visible to a certain degree. It then becomes important for young women to control where they are seen, by whom they are seen, who they are seen with, and in what situation. It is only by controlling the information available to others that they are able to manage their reputation, and protect their respectability. As one of the young, single women put it:

> No one can spread a rumour about me, because I'm watching myself. I know what behaviour leads to rumours. So I watch myself, and keep out of that.

Small wonder that young single women find the community less attractive in this stage of life! It is even less appealing to continue staying in their parents' household, because this often leads to social control and to undertaking an extensive part of the domestic work. Young women who stay in the family household become more involved in domestic chores, often because they want to relieve their mothers from this work, whereas their brothers are usually exempt from this kind of work. The leisure activities of young women are also different. Young women tend to spend more time in private clubs, voluntary organisations and at the local cafe, than young men do. They make more active use of the local public arenas, and are engaged in more organised leisure activities than young men.

The struggles of young men versus the success of young women

What is then the impact of economic restructuring on rural young people's transition into adulthood? The empirical findings are unambigious: labour market changes have generally made it more difficult to start a working career and obtain financial independence. Traditional jobs based on practical skills are disappearing, and new demands for more formal qualifications now characterise the modern labour market. Young women can go on making traditional choices in a modern way by doing some careful planning in their choice of education, and get a job in teaching, nursing or care activities. Young men making traditional choices do not get the same returns, for their traditional labour market has disappeared.

This means delayed transitions both into the labour market, and out of the family household. One aspect of achieving status as an adult - setting up your own household - may therefore be denied; the symbolic construction of an adult identity may still be possible. But rapid economic change and new demands for more formal qualifications have made it difficult to get paid work, so that work loses its significance as a source of identity. In particular, this is the case for young men who are then forced to reinvent themselves elsewhere, creating themselves as adult persons in relation to alternative fields. It is in their leisure activities that young men can find this identity.

The amount of time people spend on leisure activities varies according to work and household commitments. Young, single people spend more time engaging in leisure activities compared to young families. This is particularily the case among young people in Fjord, where some spend most of their time outside the household, in the company of their friends, while others stay with their families. Participation in voluntary organisations varies, but there is a tendency for most adults to take part in organised leisure activities. In Fjord, there are a lot of voluntary organisations: gardening, local history, youth clubs, sports associations, choirs, music bands, football teams and different humanitarian and religious organisations. Young people do not find these activities especially attractive, and tend to be more interested in non-organised activities such as informal meetings over a cup of coffee at the local cafe or attending parties at the weekends.

Young men in Fjord emphasise traditional masculine activities such as outdoor life, hunting, car maintenance and heavy drinking. These activities have clear parallels with young working-class men in urban England, and their strategies for maintaining masculine identity (Hollands, 1995). In times of large-scale unemployment, where they experience great difficulties gaining access to the labour market, it is of vital importance for these young men to maintain the symbolic aspects connected to their fathers' working-class jobs. Today, it is going out at the weekends, and not the hard life in mining and manufacturing industries, that are important arenas for showing and confirming masculinity, strength and toughness. In the rural Norwegian context, these symbolic aspects are being expressed in rather different ways. The masculine aspects of rural culture characterised by fishing, hunting, outdoor life and cars become important arenas for creating and confirming male identity. Indeed Åsbrenn (1989) claims that it is boys more than girls who have been socialised into rural life, and who have learned to appreciate the typical rural way of life.

Another way of describing the experience of young adults who choose to live in rural communities, is to turn to the theories about modernisation mentioned at the start of the chapter. In times of increasing individuality, social disintegration and disembedding between people and places (Giddens, 1991), young adults face new challenges. In a world of change, the wish for wholeness and continuity is strong. This is probably a particularly strong wish among young men who have experienced being refused admission into the labour market, and being shut out from what traditionally has been a source of identity: working life. They want to go back to what they know, to the activities and arenas where they manage and cope. In rural areas they can rely on competencies which cannot be used outside the local arena. Such competencies include the practical skills connected with fishing, hunting and outdoor life. The local community becomes a place of retreat when life outside is too difficult to manage. To use the words of Eriksen, our study confirmed that among these young men there is an 'emphasis of local distinctive character because they feel that they are losing themselves, so to speak, in times of rapid social and cultural change' (Eriksen, 1993).

In a situation where there is occupational specialisation and differentiation of jobs, and the economic life of the community is fragmented, the non-economic life represented by leisure activities is becoming more important for bringing people together to create a sense of local identity and community (Magnussen, 1993; Wiborg, 1993; 1995). Societal changes represented in modern culture have forced individuals to create themselves and their own lives by choosing between norms and courses of action. The non-economic arenas connected to different leisure activities represent important possibilities for construction of identity. The empirical findings reported on here show that the consequences of the changed framework for job possibilities are quite different, depending upon gender and qualifications. While Julie and other young, well-educated women are able to choose among a variety of jobs, John represents the young unskilled men whose traditional labour market is disappearing, due to economic restructuring. Changes in the labour market have led to delayed transitions into a working carreer and financial independence; central preconditions for the setting up of a household. They also lead to gender differences in the construction of identity. Young women from rural areas are more likely to be able to draw on work for their identity, and to have left their household of origin. Rural young men tend to remain in the parental household, and to turn to leisure to constuct an identity which substitutes for the traditional male work based identity.

Notes

1. This chapter is based on research funded by The Norwegian Research Council, programme for rural development which has been published in *Fri for arbeid*, Report 8/95, Nordland Research Institute, Bodø. Thanks to Danielle Galbraith, Even Hødahl, Åge Mariussen and Agnete Wiborg for helpful and encouraging comments.

2. Fjord is a small, sparsely populated municipality in the northern part of Norway. From more than 2,000 inhabitants in 1950, the population had fallen to 1,000 by 1994. The age structure has also changed: the average age is high with many elderly people and few children.

3. In 1994, the unemployment rate in Fjord was close to 20 per cent while the rate for the county of Nordland was 10 per cent.

4. To preserve informants' anonymity John and Julie are partially fictitious persons. Names and details are changed and 'types' are constructed by combining common traits of several persons.

CONCLUSIONS

CHANGING ECONOMIES, CHANGING HOUSEHOLDS

Jane Wheelock and Åge Mariussen

Summing up

The empirical material presented in this book has been drawn from a variety of locations in two northern European countries, England and Norway. This difference brings out contrasts between national level regulations:

- the 'market-led' approach to industrial restructuring versus a corporatist, Scandinavian approach. These differences are brought out in Part II
- different welfare systems, as analysed in Chapter 3
- differing regulation of agriculture

In the context of these national level differences, we return to the questions raised in the Introduction, concerning the relation between household, work and economic change.

The book has discussed how the big, macro-level changes in an economy affect the smaller micro-level ways that people make a living in households. Throughout, we have argued that the household is a flexible institution. Inside the household, tasks are handled by teams. People respond to change by establishing new teams to handle old tasks, and by changing the tasks they take upon themselves, for as some new tasks are accepted, old tasks may be rejected or lost.

The empirical chapters of the book (in Part III) show the household as an institution within which people deliver flexibility by adapting to economic restructuring in ways which enable them to take initiatives and be creative.

This 'flexibility' of the household does not, however, mean that the agenda of the household is wide open, as in the rational choice model. In such a model, economic behaviour is determined by perfectly rational actors, who seek new solutions to market-based change, solutions which are quite independent of the past. These economic actors make instantaneous responses to changing circumstances. In contrast, institutionalists emphasise the way in which institutions create and reinforce habits of action and thought. Action guided by institutions follows procedures, habits, ways of doing things and norms which are not ordinarily reflected upon in the way that the rational action model presumes. It is the institutional model which is confirmed by the wide variety of case studies presented in Part III.

But just what paths of institutional transformation do households follow in the contrasting restructuring environments of Britain and Norway? How far does household *adaptation* on the one hand, and *enabling* on the other actually go? In Chapter 2, we argued that households survive on the basis of inputs from three circuits: purchased goods and services from the market circuit, services and goods from the state circuit and unpriced goods and services from the domestic circuit, usually produced within the household itself. The cloverleaf diagram (Figure 2.1) shows the household forming the link between production, reproduction and consumption as its different members participate in the market, state and domestic production circuits that make up the whole economy. Institutions regulate the intersections between these three circuits. By looking at institutional transformations, we also address the household as socialising girls and boys into gender and occupational roles as men and women.

We can use the empirical outcomes of this institutional regulation to highlight the successes and failures of the New Right theory of the relation between the household and the formal economy. This theory assumes that the outcome of different actors' strategies in the three circuits is a set of spontaneous, optimal intersections between domestic and market circuits. These spontaneous adaptations, so it is claimed, mean that policy makers are free to continue with deregulating the economy, drastically cutting back on the redistributive state circuit, because the household circuit is adaptable enough to cushion fluctuations and changes in the market circuit.

This theory comes from the New Right in various guises, but all insist that the family and family values can provide a solution to the problems generated by an increasingly deregulated and turbulent economy. In its most radical version, deregulation of the economy and the abolition of the welfare state strengthens the family as an institution, with values based on self-help making it more independent. Households organised by strong families, based on strong family values and with property and resources make it possible to survive in insecure business environments and labour markets. On this basis it becomes possible to radically reduce, or even to dispose altogether of the redistributive circuit of the state.

In a world organised by these principles, we are left with only two circuits: the domestic and the market. In this situation, what are the mechanisms by which a strong family organising a flexible household can provide a solution to the problem of order? In *Beyond Left and Right* (Giddens, 1994a), Anthony Giddens analyses the actor strategies giving rise to strong domestic institutions, with his concept of 'reflexive life policies'. Through a reflective life policy, argues Giddens, it is possible to define a life strategy where different resources are gradually accumulated in the domestic circle throughout a lifetime, resources which make it possible for the household to sustain itself in the chill conditions of a post-welfare state world.

So, is it true that households which are both stronger and more flexible are being

Conclusions: changing economies, changing households 197

constructed in our late modern world? The cloverleaf diagram illustrates the crucial socio-economic role of the household in providing different kinds of labour to the economy. With economic change, there are shifts within and between each production circuit. In conditions of simple, well-organised, industrial modernity, the traditional, strong family institution was taken for granted. It was based on gender identities which were formed by socialisation, and embedded in the work habits of the time. Fundamental to the changes that go on at both the macro-level of the economy and the micro-level of the household are the values incorporated in male and female work circuits in all three circuits. The shift to a post-industrial economy has had far-reaching effects on the gender meanings of work. Can a strong family based household institution really be reconstructed, in response to the kinds of wide-ranging economic change exemplified in either the Mo, Scandinavian style restructuring or the Wearside Anglo-American type?

The empirical material presented in Part III, shows a rather different picture. In the Introduction, it was suggested that one could expect to find two types of household institutional transformation which could create positive relations between household and economic change. One would be represented by the development of linkages between households and production - between the domestic and the market circuits - where household strategies would *enable* economic change to take place. Enabling households of this kind would make a direct contribution to macro-economic change through their involvement in business and production activity for the market. Alternatively, there would be households which *adapt* in the face of economic turbulence, sustaining the needs of household members in ways which prevent social disintegration. But less optimistically, a third type of household institutional transformation can be posited, where economic change generates disjunctions between the household and the economy: where we can see the household disintegrating. This last type of household institutional transformation is unlikely to provide a solution to the problem of order. If we now turn to the empirical material presented in Part III we can see how far the New Right model holds up.

Institutional comparisons: empirical analysis

Let us start with the already established households that have apparently been able to adapt to unemployment of the male provider. Section A looked at Norwegian and British households *adapting* to redundancy and prospectively long periods of economic inactivity for their menfolk, and at Norwegian households where both men and women might be facing periods of temporary employment interspersed with unpredictable periods of unemployment. On the positive side, and in line with the New Right model, long periods of economic inactivity for men has given rise to greater flexibility in gender roles, as Sande and Wheelock show in their chapters. In terms of the cloverleaf diagram, as men are pushed out of participation in the market circuit, women may take on the provider role, dropping some of their activities in the household circuit, which are then taken up by their spouses. The astonishing capacity of households to adapt through increased flexibility and changing gender roles is also documented in the chapters by Stone and Mariussen, in their analysis of restructuring in Mo and Wearside.

As the Introduction and Part I argued, gender definitions are institutionally determined through habit and tradition. Whilst it is evident that economic change has induced changes in gendered work practices, rigidities are also apparent. The households of Section A are affected by the decline in the total work package that society makes available to them. The unpaid work package remains the same, but the paid work package has declined. Problems arise at the level of the household with the distribution of this smaller work package between household members because of the rigidities in gender work roles. If women continue to undertake the same or nearly the same amount of work in the domestic circuit, and are also working in the market circuit, their workload will tend to increase. If men are either only intermittently involved, or not involved at all, in work in the market circuit, and do not take up all the work in the domestic sector, they will have a smaller total work package.

The most limited redistribution of the work package inside the household is apparent where industrial restructuring has led to a movement away from the standard, Fordist labour contract, as shown in the chapter by Karlsen. In terms of institutitionally based insights, this is unsurprising, since the intermittent and temporary nature of the changes in work patterns are not so capable of influencing the deeply ingrained gender-coded work roles of women and men. What we have then - inside the household - is a situation where women will tend to be overworked, while men will be underworked.

The studies in Section A show that changes in gender roles can be taken positively in that men gain the possibility of taking satisfaction and pleasure in being fathers, grandfathers, or carers; in taking on the more nurturing role in the household which is traditionally associated with women. Women too, gain from the satisfactions derived from being in paid work. So it is not simply gender-based work roles that are changing, but also the associated sets of male and female value systems.

The negative sides of these changes in values is that many of the men in the households looked at in Section A are at the same time losing the provider role traditionally associated with male identity. In some cases, the dignity of the household as a financially independent unit is preserved by the woman becoming the provider. Whilst women may tend to bear a greater burden in terms of work, in terms of identity, they have more opportunities for enhancing this than their menfolk.

It is possible for the state circuit to influence the flexibility and adaptiveness of household gender work roles. The chapters in Section A show households where women take on a partial breadwinning role, with the state circuit providing additional household income in the form of benefits. The state here assists households to make compromise adaptations. It is ironical that such household compromises are less likely to be adopted under the family based means tested British system than under the individually based insurance system of Norway. In Britain, calls for moves to cut back on the state circuit, and to increase targeting on needy households, will, under slack labour market conditions, mitigate against household flexibility because they tend to drive the whole household out of the labour market along with the individual household member who has already suffered job loss, illustrating the difficulties with a means tested benefit system raised by Michael Hill in Chapter 3.

It is when we turn to the group who are in transition between households, the young people on the verge of forming their own households who are looked at in Section C, that the negative aspects of the impact of economic change become even more apparent. For here we find the whole transition into adulthood affected by radical changes in the insitututional environment, amounting to its destruction in certain contexts. Lack of paid work impacts particularly severely on the young, and high rates of youth unemployment are familiar features of most European countries. The *adapting* path possible for the households in Section A are not open to the young. In the first place the insecurity of flexible work means that young people cannot readily set up autonomous households. In line with the New Right view, young people are turning to their household of origin, by remaining financially dependent for longer. But this does not lead to long-term planning and preparation for a future of independence predicted by that model. For young men in particular, the inability to form their identity through work in the shipyards in the way that their fathers did, leads to seeking that identity through nightclubs instead (Hollands). We find a similar pattern of young men not able to follow the example set by their fathers in rural Norway (Magnussen).

Thus two cases, under different national level conditions, indicate that there is not - at least from a two-generational perspective - a broad movement in the direction of a long-term reflexive life policy based on a strong domestic sphere capable of handling economic turbulence, as Giddens would have it. What we see here is a process of institutional *disintegration*. The norms into which boys were socialised in the working-class families they grew up in, no longer correspond to the actual situation that results from economic restructuring. They are prepared for a labour market which no longer exists. The answer found by many in this situation is far from any kind of reflexive life policy leading towards new masculine identities. On the contrary, young men reinterpret their masculinity through 'the nightclub option'. 'The nightclub' becomes the orthodox defence of a masculinity which no longer carries the image of success in working life.

Young women, in contrast to their brothers and boyfriends, are more able to adapt. In the first place, the jobs that are available in an expanding service economy are jobs which are traditionally defined as women's work. Women are taking an increasing proportion of the available jobs, and deindustrialisation speeds up that process. In addition, young women are more prepared to integrate themselves in the domestic circuit. If they contribute to domestic work, parents are less likely to expect them to make a financial contribution to the household they live in, and this may supplement low female wages. Young women do not face the same ambiguities in taking this path as young men, who are faced with contradictions between male identity and housework. Young women's greater flexibility is also reflected in longer-term planning, as when young Norwegian women undertake education more willingly than young men.

So, the gender imbalances visible amongst the established households of Section A as they adapt to economic change, are even more marked amongst young people.

The scene would appear to be set for greater discrepancies between the overall work load of the next generation, with future mothers continuing to shoulder a double burden, and a transformation of gender identities in which future fathers are the real losers. There is a disjuncture between the identity that young men are refashioning for themselves through consumption, and their role as providers. This may also prove a problem for young women. Changes at the level of the macro-economy are laying the seeds of social *disintegration* at the level of the household.

Such a conclusion must be seen in the context of the scope of variation amongst the cases presented. It is possible that other institutional conditions may lay the basis for paths of development where economic destabilisation is indeed compensated by a strengthening of the domestic sphere. However, at the very least, our cases show that this is not a universal result. When there is a transition from a fairly well-regulated rural or industrial economy, to a deregulated, service based one, institutional disintegration appears the likely result.

It is when we turn to the households in Section B, those which depend in some degree on household-based production in farming or in small businesses, that we appear to find the New Right ideal family. Different members are involved in a household-based economic enterprise. They respond with *enabling* flexible work strategies as market and labour market opportunities open and close, combining different forms of labour market and work in the business as the market circuit dictates. In doing so, women and men may also be quite flexible about who does what work in the domestic circuit: certainly, some changes in gender codings are visible. Men whose work on the farm or in business ties them to the home, with wives who are working - often in the state circuit - may prepare the evening meal or look after young children at the same time. In the cases analysed in Section C, we find evidence of households' capacity to enable economic activity, which, in a differentiated economy, could not have been sustained. Integrated into a household, the small business not only survives, it may even bloom, as in the case of more successful family farms.

Blooming family firms are long term, intergenerational family projects, whose strategy is determined by family decisions and family values. However, this coin has two sides to it. When we look closer, there is not as close a correspondence with either the New Right or the post-Left ideal as this first glance suggests. For the reality is that people in such production based households are often either working very long - and frequently unsocial - hours, or, like the unemployed households of Section A, their business does not provide them with enough work. Overwork and underwork succeed each other. Incomes can be very low indeed.

The market opportunities which these *enabling* households take up on are usually either in low-tech, highly competitive service areas like window cleaning, or, in the case of farming, based on historically high levels of subsidy. The household ideal of the New Right is that entrepreneurial behaviour provides monetary rewards for those who take this path, a path which encourages independence. Indeed, in terms of values, it would seem that even those new to being in business, are imbued with the kind of ideals that sustain this institutional context. People value the independence of their way of life, but far from being rewarded, they are instead confronted with whether they and their household can afford to maintain the way of life that incorporates such values.

Theoretical implications

This book has dealt with the interrelations between household, work and economic change from the perspective of institutional theory. We started by quoting Dahrendorf's position: that growing flexiblity is destroying social cohesion (Dahrendorf, 1995). By discussing the household in terms of the relation between social integration and economic change, we have found that the household is indeed important to the way people cope with change, as well as to the way they contribute to the economy. Contrary to the position of 'simple modernists', we find that the economic significance of the household is increasing, the outcome of growing flexibility.

However, we have pointed out that we are not returning to some kind of 'premodernity' where people can do without the state redistributive circle thanks to a strengthened domestic sphere. We have found little to resemble the reconstruction of the traditional, strong and flexible household in the localities we have studied. A programme promoting 'reflexive life policies' to enhance the capacity of the household is unlikely to solve the basic problem which Parsons discussed in relation to the state and welfare: the need to reconcile the tensions between sustaining human needs and an uncontrolled and uncontrollable market system which is designed to maximise a means, not an end (Parsons, 1947). As shown in subsections IIIA and IIIB, households do adjust and adapt. However, this adjustment and adaptation has limits. Our data highlights processes where modern households, institutionally differentiated from the economy, are facing new conditions. From the data presented in these sections, no phoenix arises from the ashes of the modern household. The strong, traditional household is not reflexively reconstructed under these conditions. Individual reflexivity does not solve the growing problems of social disintegration facing modern households. Instead, tensions are created.

Again, this conclusion must be seen as lying within the scope of our data. Other paths of development cannot be excluded. All the same, the significance of the nation state level, in providing social policy conditions and regulation which make better solutions feasible is clear. What is needed is an increased *collective* reflexivity, with policies which address the increasingly difficult problem of order. This collective reflexivity implies emphasis on policies where the state supports the capacity of the household to adapt and cope with economic change. Such support needs to be informed by research into the significance of the domestic sphere to economic change and social integration. In this book, central themes of such a research programme have been discussed.

But before indicating some policy areas where practical initiatives might be taken, let us make some concluding comments on a central question in this discussion: gender.

Adam Smith asserted that social harmony is ensured as the outcome of individuals pursuing their own self-interest in a market context. In Parson's vision of modern society, everything is also seen to be in harmony. One important source of this harmony was the fit between socialisation in the family and work in the formal economy. The modern family household produced men who were socialised to enter work in modern, formalised businesses. This world was morally integrated, although with some minor exceptions, identified as deviance. But what is described in this book is not deviance, it is increasing tension between different institutional principles.

Simple modern industrial society has disintegrated into something which no longer holds together. In line with Smith and his orthodox economics followers, the New Right hopes that the market will provide the solution. But can it?

One source of tensions is gender identities. As demonstrated in Part III, economic change creates a new set of winners and losers in the games where the masculinity and femininity of work are defined. Gender roles change as households adapt to economic restructuring. Women advance and gain stronger positions, men lose power, albeit in a generally incremental way. The game continues to follow the same gender rules, but with different sets of winners and losers. This creates strains and tensions; for example women are overworked - and underpaid - while young men have trouble in handling their inheritance, their fathers masculinity. Contemporary processes of disintegration are closely connected to the disjunction between gender definitions, as they are institutionalised in households affected by economic change, and by the opportunities of the new service economies.

Paradoxically, one answer to this disjuncture may be yet further shift towards the new gender identities, where both men and women are better fitted to share the changing burdens of working life inside and outside the household. These new gender identities have so far not emerged on any broad basis. The reasons for this may run deep. Gender identities seem to be a case of 'habitus' dispositions. The image of the father and mother, and the logic of household practices are so deeply engraved in people, that the reflexive adaptations which people make to handle the new situations cannot reach those dispositions.

In the days of simple modernity, working-class households contributed to the economy by socialising working-class kids into dedicated workers, motivated for the kind of life which mining, shipbuilding and other demanding production industries offered. One aspect of this socialisation was the boy's admiration for his father, the male identity and 'habitus' his father represented, where the values of the successful worker were imaged. Today, this culture is breaking down in industrial areas experiencing restructuring. The new, flexible labour market is more compatible with the aspirations and values of young women, socialised by their mothers to a 'service' disposition, while young men - socialised into job opportunities long gone - become lost souls.

In the Anglo-American model of restructuring policies, as analysed in Part II, this breakdown of working-class culture was celebrated as an important breakthrough in rendering the labour market more flexible, an important precondition for the new sources of growth: inward investments, and small indigenous businesses. Cultural transformation thus becomes necessary, and beneficial, to the economy. However, it is not beneficial for social integration. Today, there is a disjuncture between socialisation in the household and the work roles men are offered, which is not so pronounced for women. The final outcome of this process of institutional transformation remains to be seen. What will be the long-term effects of the 'nightclub' strategy of traditional male orthodoxy?

An alternative to these cultural conflicts of deindustrialization is apparent in the Norwegian model. Here, restructuring was not posed as contradictory to the values of the old order. On the contrary, industrial transformation has been carried out through compromises with (older) union traditions and values. This has not prevented any kind of 'nightclub' process in Norway. In the chapter by Magnussen, a 'nightclub' strategy among young rural Norwegians living in an economy where their father's job is gone, is described. Empirical material not included here, indicates that the 'nightclub' option most certainly was open in Mo as well (Sande, 1995).

Gender identity seems to be an area of 'habitus', which escapes reflexive institutional transformation to a considerable extent. The rules of the game of man and woman are determined by relating, not only to contemporary actors, but to a large extent to the father and mother. It may not be a government policy option to redefine gender. However, throughout this book we have found evidence that government policies have an influence on economic change. If gender is habitus, shaped by long term logics in work practice, then there is a long-term link between economic policy, work and gender. Government policies and regulations establish paths which - in the long run - do bring about change. Often, however, this is in unpredicted and undesired directions. Evidence pointing in this direction is given in the chapters by Stone and Mariussen, where interconnections between economic restructuring and changing gender roles in the labour market of Mo and Wearside are documented. The interrelation between policy and regulation in agriculture, and gender in rural households, is illustrated in Part IIIB. Government policy has significant long-term effects on the way the household is organised - and on the way gender is defined.

However, government economic policy is decided by the large games of global market competition and national economic development, not by gender or household considerations. Instead, gender and household effects are unintended by-products. Perhaps this is inevitable. After all, policy makers are usually not able to consider more than one policy objective at a time. Give them two, and they get caught in all kinds of trouble.

But if gender transformation is an unintended long-term by-product of government policies, there is a strong indication that governments should at the very least be aware of this. And what is more, this awareness needs to open up the agenda for policies to compensate for, or prevent, negative effects.

What governments can do is to take the normative conflicts generated by industrial restructuring more seriously, and facilitate the gender changes that some households are already making, by ensuring that the paid work package is more evenly distributed between people in households. The Scandinavian model of corporatist restructuring does not solve these problems, but at least it tries to avoid humiliating fathers in front of their sons.

Policy implications

In the empirical chapters of this book, we have described processes of institutional transformation where some gain, while others lose. There are 'reflexivity winners' in the new games linking economic change and householding; there are certainly also 'reflexivity losers'. Some may cope, and develop sustainable households capable of handling more liberal, market winds. However, others cannot, because they are caught in institutionalised paths of development which prevent the leap to the 'reflexive life policies' implied by the New Right programme. A New Right programme of strong families as the institutional basis for a flexible and deregulated economy must therefore be rejected as a universal solution, since it cannot prevent social disintegration. It is not possible to do without the state redistributive circuit, at least not for modern households facing government policies and global economic forces making for labour market flexibility.

Having said that, however, we also must add another empirically based observation: under certain conditions, the household can provide important preconditions for sustaining human needs and human flourishing. Only some of these conditions may be within the scope of policy makers.

Note that it is not only those men who plan their lives from the perspective of 'the nightclub' who are 'reflexivity losers'. Policy makers too, may have short perspectives. In our discussion of the relation between the domestic circuit and the state redistributive circuit there is one remarkable paradox. In the British case, where the state acknowledges the household's economic significance, through means testing total household resources as the basis for social support, this very acknowledgement leads to adaptations which are destructive of households. In the Scandinavian case, in contrast, people seeking social benefits are regarded as individuals by the government. The result of this perspective is a system which is more supportive to householding.

We would like to see the strengthening of the household as a major policy objective. There are several ways in which policy makers could strengthen households. In the first place, they could stop punishing people who establish households, through means testing and taxes. One simple way to stop punishing households would be to stop using people's household situations as an excuse to increase taxes or reduce their social funding. The next step would be to establish incentives for householding in the tax and welfare systems. Household flexibility is a fundamental resource to economies faced with adapting to national and global restructuring. Pressure on households is reflected in statistics showing the problems with forming and maintaining households: delayed youth transitions, later marriage, fewer children, rising divorce rates, extended 'retirement'. It is a fundamental mistake to endanger the life of the goose that lays the golden eggs.

Households are currently often expected to pick up the final tab when it comes to economic change. Household members are left to redistribute work - whether labour market or household - between themselves as best they may. As a further step forward, a policy programme which invests in households by actively redistributing work in line with the needs of households as institututions which have to negotiate and compromise between individual members is required. Policies to redistribute employment, we would argue, are a 'feasible capitalist' solution, not just to the unemployment of some households or household members, but also to the overwork that others have to contend with, including female household members or households reliant on small businesses for their livelihood. Certain types of household are already tentatively moving towards dividing work more equally. The positive side of this process is the advance of women on the labour market. The dark side is the double workload which this may entail, particularly if deregulation is also removing the cushion provided by the state circuit.

It is now increasingly recognised that unemployment is the principal means of exclusion which severs people from recognition as active partners in economic endeavour, and from non-material as well as material resources. The right to work turns each citizen from being an individual part of a political community into an active participant in social life, as Polanyi recognised (Polanyi, 1946). Women, who started their political struggle for the vote at the start of this century, want to share the right to employment equally with men as we move to the next. But why should they avoid economic exclusion at the expense of the overwork of combining being active out in the labour market with work inside the household?

At the same time, overemployment in terms of long hours can actually prevent men from participating in the work and rewards of household life - involvement in householding, caring for children, for the old, the sick and the infirm. Social exclusion needs to be seen in a wider context, and one which pays proper attention to differences in its gender construction. For men have a right to share the unpaid work of caring and nurturing inside the household, from which their employment can currently exclude them. And if men are encouraged to exercise this right, of course it helps women to exercise the right to employment without overwork. Redistribution of employment therefore provides a precondition for a redistribution of unpaid work between women and men. Such redistribution can be achieved with policies to shorten the working week.

We are then, calling for a policy programme to feminise Keynsianism. The restructuring of economies that has gone on since the oil crisis of the 1970s has raised fundamental questions about the meaning of full employment and has led to a questioning of the role of the welfare structures used to complement Keynsian policies. Consideration of the effects of policy at the household level provides an opportunity - long overdue - to redefine full-employment as full-work. Full work combines a much shorter working week for men and women with recognition that both may want to take part in caring and householding. If the outcome is less gender segregation in paid and unpaid work, it becomes possible to review the role of the state circuit as a provider of care, without immediately overburdening women.

A full work perspective on economic restructuring requires a flexible system of social security. We need to look very carefully at how social insurance and means testing can be modified to suit part-time and flexible work in a way that does not disadvantage women or men, the young, children or the old, yet which at the same time serves the needs of a labour market that takes employees rights seriously. The individualised social security system of Norway allows households more flexibility in the negotiations between household members. Some form of basic income or citizen's income would be likely to achieve the same ends.

Such a policy programme will empower household members and enable them to make less restrained choices: to become flexible in the context of the household's own agenda. A feminised Keynsianism of full work would not force household change in the stark and uncompromising ways that unmediated economic change does; it would provide the circumstances to facilitate change for those households who want it. It would encourage human flourishing. A well considered set of policies could work *with* contemporary economic change to realise a promise of more radical reinterpretations of gender than we have seen so far, without overburdening some or driving others into idleness. Household flexibility is a resource to be nurtured, not exploited or squandered.

BIBLIOGRAPHY

Aglietta, M. (1979) *A Theory of Capitalist Regulation*, London: New Left Books.

Alexander, J. C. (1982) *Theoretical Logic in Sociology*, Berkeley, Los Angeles: University of California Press.

Allatt, P. and Yeandle, S. (1992) *Youth Unemployment and the Family*, London: Routledge.

Almås, R. (1990) 'Backwards into the 1990s: a critique of neo-liberal agricultural policies'. In R. Almås and N. With (eds) *Rural Futures in an International World*, Trondheim: Centre for Rural Research.

Almås, R. (1993) 'Farm policies and farmer strategies: The case of Norway'. In R. Almås (ed) *Norways Gift to Europe - Fifteen Selected Articles on Rural Persistence and Change*, Report No. 2, Trondheim: Centre for Rural Research.

Almås, R. and Haugen, M. (1988) *Norwegian Gender Roles in Transition. The Masculinization Hypothesis in the Past, Present and in the Future*, Rural Research Paper No. 1: University of Trondheim.

Almås, R. and Ward, N. (1994) 'The Norwegian agro-food system: problems and prospects'. In *Restructuring the Agro-Food System: Global Processes and National Responses*, Trondheim: Centre for Rural Research.

Almås, R. and With, N. (eds) (1990) *Rural Futures in an International World*, Trondheim: Centre for Rural Research.

Amin, A. and Thrift, N. (eds) (1994a) *Globalization, Institutions and Regional Development in Europe*, Oxford: Oxford University Press.

Amin, A. and Thrift, N. (1994b 20-22 March) *Institutional issues for European regions: from markets and plans to powers of association*, Paper presented at Fourth General Conference of the European Science Foundations RURE Programme, Rome.

Andersen, O. J. (1996) 'Omstilling mellom kontinuitet og oppbrudd: erfaringer fra fisjonsprosesser i tidligere Norsk Jernverk og Bygg-gruppa i Moelven - konsernet' [Restructuring between continuity and disembedding: Experiences from fission processes in Norse Ironworks and Moelven] in Mariussen, Å, Karlsen, A. and Andersen O.J. (eds) Oslo: Norwegian University Press.

Anderson, M., Bechhofer, F. and Gershuny, J. (eds) (1994) *The Social and Political Economy of the Household*, Oxford: Oxford University Press.

Armstrong, P., Glyn, G. and Harrison, J. (1991) *Capitalism Since 1945*, Oxford: Basil Blackwell.

Åsbrenn, K. (1989) 'Uttynningssamfunnet. Det demografisk uttynnede - men ikke avfolkede utkantsamfunn [The thinned out community. The demographic thinned out - but not depopulated periphiral community]', *Tidsskrift for Samfunnsforsking*, 4/1989: 509-519.

Asheim, B. (1990) 'Innovation diffusion and small firms'. In Ciciotti, Alderman and Thwaites (eds) *Technological Change in a Spatial Context*, Springer-Verlag.

Asheim, B. (1992) 'Flexible specialisation, industrial districts and small firms: a critical appraisal'. In H. Ernste and V. Meier (eds) *Regional Development and Contemporary Industrial Response*, London, New York: Belhaven Press.

Atkinson, A. B. (1993) *Beveridge, the National Minimum, and its Future in a European Context*, Welfare State Programme Discussion Paper, No. 85, London: London School of Economics.

Atkinson, J. S. (1984) *Flexibility, Uncertainty and Manpower Management*, No. 89, Falmer, Sussex: Institute of Manpower Studies.

Atkinson, J. S. (1985) 'The changing corporation'. In D. Clutterbuck (ed) *New Patterns of Work*, Aldershot: Gower.

Bagguley, P. (1990) *Restructuring: Place, Class and Gender*, London: Sage.

Bagnasco, A. (1981) 'Labour market, class structure and regional formations in Italy', *International Journal of Urban and Regional Research*, 5(1): 40-4.

Banks, M., Bates, I., Breakwell, G., Bynnes, J., Emler, N., Jamieson, L. and Roberts, K. (eds) (1992) *Careers and Identities*, Milton Keynes: Open University Press.

Beatty, C. and Fothergill, S. (1996) 'Labour market adjustment in areas of chronic industrial decline: the case of the UK coalfields', *Regional Studies*, 30 (7 November): 627-40.

Bechhofer, F. and Elliott, B. (1981) *Comparative Studies of an Uneasy Stratum*, London: Macmillan.

Bechhofer, F. and Elliot, B. (1986) 'Persistence and change: the petite bourgeoisie in industrial society'. In J. Curran, J. Stanworth and D. Watkins (eds) *The Survival of the Small Firm, Vol. I The Economics of Survival and Entrepreneurship,* Aldershot; Gower.

Beck, U. (1992) *Risk Society: Towards a New Modernity,* London: Sage.

Beck, U. (1994) 'The reinventing of politics: towards a theory of reflexive modernization'. In A. Beck, A. Giddens and S. Lash (eds) *Reflexive Modernization, Politics, Tradition and Aesthetics in the Modern Society Order,* Cambridge, Oxford: Polity Press.

Beck, U., Giddens, A. and Lash, S. (eds) (1994) *Reflexive Modernisation: Politics, Tradition and Aesthetics in the Modern Social Order,* Cambridge, Oxford: Polity Press.

Becker, G. (1965) 'A theory of the allocation of time'. Reprinted in A. M. Amsden (ed) (1980) *The Economics of Women and Work,* Harmondsworth, Penguin.

Becker, G. S. (1981) *The Treatise of the Family,* Cambridge, Mass.: Harvard University Press.

Behrman, J. R. (1990) 'Peeking into the black box of economic models of the household'. In B. L. Rogers and N. P. Schlossman (eds) *Intra-household Resource Allocation,* Tokyo: United Nations University Press.

Ben-Porath, Y. (1980) 'The F-connection: families, friends, and firms and the organisation of change', *Population and Development Review,* Vol. 6: 1-30.

Berg, P. O. (1965) *Ringvirkniger av ny Storindustri: Utvikling i Naeringsliv og Bosetting i Årdal og Mo i Rana siden 1949 [Spin-offs of Large Scale Industry: Industrial and Population Development in the Regions of Årdal and Mo i Rana since 1946],* Oslo: Distriktenes Utbyggingsfond.

Berger, P., Berger, B. and Kellner, H. (1974) *The Homeless Maid,* New York: Vintage Books.

Blackie, J. (1993) *Women's Leisure Experiences and Their Use of Public Leisure Provision in Newcastle Upon Tyne,* unpublished MA dissertation, Leeds Metropolitan University.

Bourdieu, P. (1992) *The Logic of Practice,* Cambridge, Oxford: Polity Press.

Bradley, H. (1989) *Men's Work, Women's Work,* Cambridge, Oxford: Polity Press.

Brandth, B. (1993) 'Kvinner er ikke lenger hva de var [Women are not what they used to be]'. In B. Brandth and E. Verstad (eds) *Kvinneliv i Landbruket [Women's*

Lives in Agriculture] Oslo: Landbruksforlaget.

Braverman, H. (1974) *Labour and Monopoly Capital,* New York: Monthly Review Press.

Briggs, L. (1994) *Meeting the challenge: Australian labour market trends and the income support system,* Paper presented at International Social Security Association research meeting, Vienna.

Brox, O. (1966) *Hva skjer i Nord-Norge? [What Happens in Northern Norway?],* Oslo: Pax Forlag.

Brox, O. (1986) *Nord-Norge - fra allmenning til koloni [Northern Norway - from Common Property to Colony],* Oslo: Pax.

Brusco, S. (1982) 'The Emilian model, productive decentralisation and social integration', *Cambridge Journal of Economics,* 6: 167-184.

Bryson, L. (1992) *Welfare and the State,* Basingstoke: Macmillan.

Bulmer, M. (1986) *Neighbours: the Work of Philip Abrams,* Cambridge: Cambridge University Press.

Burrows, R. (ed) (1991) *Deciphering the Enterprise Culture,* London: Routledge.

Cambridge Econometrics (1993) 'Regional economic prospects', *Regions,* (184): 16-22.

Caslin, T. (1987) 'De-industrialisation in the UK'. In H. Vane and T. Caslin (eds) *Current Controversies in Economics,* Oxford: Basil Blackwell.

Castles, S. and Miller, M. J. (1993) *The Age of Migration,* Basingstoke: Macmillan.

Cécora, J. (ed) (1993) *Economic Behaviour of Family Households in an International Context,* Bonn: Society for Agricultural Policy Research and Rural Society (FAA).

Chandler, A. D. (1977) *The Visible Hand: The Managerial Revolution in American Business,* Cambridge: Cambridge University Press.

Cheal, D. (1989) 'Strategies of resource management in household economies: moral economy or political economy'. In R. R. Wilk (ed) *The Household Economy: Reconsidering the Domestic Mode of Production,* Boulder: Westview.

Clasen, J. and Freeman, R. (eds) (1994) *Social Policy in Germany,* Hemel Hempstead: Harvester Wheatsheaf.

Close, P. and Collins, R. (eds) (1985) *Family and Economy in Modern Society*, London: Macmillan.

Coase, R. H. (1937) 'The nature of the firm', *Economics,* 4: 386-405.

Coenen, H. and Leisink, P. (eds) (1993) *Work and Citizenship in the New Europe*, Aldershot: Edward Elgar.

Coffield, F. and Gofton, L. (1994) *Drugs and Young People,* London: Institute for Public Policy Research.

Cohen, A. P. (1985) *The Symbolic Construction of Community,* London: Tavistock Publications.

Colls, R. and Lancaster, B. (1992) *Geordies: The Roots of Regionalism,* Edinburgh: Edinburgh University Press.

Common, J. (1951) *Kiddar's Luck,* London: Turnstile Press.

Crow, G. (1989) 'The use of the concept of "strategy" in recent sociological literature', *Sociology,* 23(1): 1-24.

Dahrendorf, R. (1995) 'Can we combine economic opportunity with civil society and political liberty?', *The Responsive Community,* 5(3, Summer): 13-39.

Daly, M. (1990) 'The 1980s - a decade of growth in enterprise: data on VAT registrations and deregistrations', *Employment Gazette,* November: 553-565.

Daly, M. (1991) 'The 1980s - a decade of growth in enterprise: self-employment data from the Labour Force Survey', *Employment Gazette,* March: 109-134.

Davidson, A. P. (1991) 'Rethinking household livelihood strategies', *Research in Rural Sociology and Development,* 5: 11-28.

Dennis, N. and Erdos, G. (1992) *Families Without Fathers,* London: Institute for Economic Affairs.

Doeringer, P. and Piore, M. J. (1971) *Internal Labour Markets and Manpower Analysis,* Lexington Mass.: D.C. Heath.

Douglas, M. (1975) *Implicit Meanings,* London and New York: Routledge.

Douglas, M. (1986) *How Institutions Think,* London: Routledge & Keegan, Paul.

Durkheim, E. (1968) *The Elementary Forms of the Religious Life,* London: George Allen and Unwin Ltd.

Edwards, R., Reich, M. and Weisskopf, T. (1985) *The Capitalist System,* Englewood Cliffs, N. J.: Prentice-Hall.

Eidheim, H. (1981) *Grand Bay. Lokalorganisasjon i en Vestindisk Landsby [Grand Bay. Local Organisation in a West Indian Village],* Occasional Paper No. 3: Institutt for Sosialantropologi, Universitetet i Oslo.

Ekins, P. and Max-Neef, M. (eds) (1992) *Real-life Economics: Understanding Wealth Creation,* London: Routledge.

Ellingsaether, A. L. (1995) *Gender, Work and Social Change,* Oslo: Institute for Social Research.

Eriksen, T. H. (1993) *Små Steder - Store Spoersmål, Innføring i Sosialantropologi [Small Places - Large Issues. Introduction to Social Anthropology],* Oslo: Norwegian University Press.

Esping-Andersen, G. (1990) *Three Worlds of Welfare Capitalism,* Cambridge: Polity Press.

Evans, A. (1991) 'Gender issues in rural household economics', *IDS Bulletin,* 22(1): 51-59.

Featherstone, M. (1987) 'Lifestyle and consumer culture', *Theory, Culture and Society,* 4(1): 55-70.

Field, F. (1989) *Losing Out: The Emergence of Britain's Underclass,* Oxford: Blackwell.

Fine, B. and Leopold, E. (1993) *The World of Consumption,* London: Routledge.

Flakstad, A. G. (1984) 'Kan endring innen kvinnearbeidet utløse strukturendringer? [Can change in women's work cause structural change?]'. In I. Rudie (ed) *Myk Start - Hard Landing [Soft Start - Hard Landing]* Oslo: Norwegian University Press.

Folbre, N. (1986) 'Hearts and spades: paradigms of household economics', *World Development,* 14(2): 245-55.

Folbre, N. (1994) *Who Pays for the Kids? Gender and the Structures of Constraint,* London: Routledge.

Foreman-Peck, J. (1985) 'Seed corn or chaff? New firm formation and the performance of the interwar economy', *Economic History Review*, 38(3): 402-22.

Foss, O. (1993) 'Norge har ikke noe sysselsettingsproblem! [Norway does not have any employment problem]'. In *Regionale Trender 2/93* Oslo: Institutt for By-og Regionforsking.

Foss, O., Halvorsen, K. and Vatne, E. (1994) *Lokalsamfunn og internasjonalisering [Local communities and internationalisation]*, No.1, Oslo: Norsk Institutt for By-og Regionforsking.

Friedmann, H. (1986) 'Family enterprises in agriculture: structural limits and political possibilities'. In G. Cox, P. Lowe and M. Winter (eds) *Agriculture, People and Policies* London: Allen and Unwin.

Fulsås, N. (1987) 'Household economy and capitalistic economy in Nordland, 1850-1950', *Journal of History*, Vol. 66, Part I: 28-52'.

Fylling, I. (1994) *Levekår og Livskvalitet i Nordland [Living Conditions and Life Quality in Nordland]*, NF-rapport No. 15/94: Nordland Research Institute, Bodø.

Galbraith, J. K. (1975) *Economics and the Public Purpose,* London: Andre Deutsch.

Gasson, R., Crow, G., Errington, A., Hutson, J., Marsden, T. and Winter, M. (1988) 'The farm as a family business: a review', *Journal of Agricultural Economics,* (39): 1-41.

Gasson, R. and Errington, A. (1993) *The Farm Family Business,* Wallingford: CAB International.

Gershuny, J. (1978) *After Industrial Society,* London: Macmillan.

Gershuny, J., Godwin, M. and Jones, S. (1994) 'The domestic labour revolution: a process of lagged adaptation'. In M. Anderson, F. Bechhofer and J. Gershuny (eds) *The Social and Political Economy of the Household*, Oxford: Oxford University Press.

Giddens, A. (1979) *Central Problems in Social Theory,* London: Macmillan Press.

Giddens, A. (1981) *A Contemporary Critique of Historical Materialism*, London: Macmillan.

Giddens, A. (1990) *The Consequences of Modernity,* Cambridge: Polity Press.

Giddens, A. (1991) *Modernity and Self-Identity. Self and Society in the Late Modern Age,* Cambridge, Oxford: Polity Press.

Giddens, A. (1994a) *Beyond Left and Right: The Future of Radical Politics*, Cambridge, Oxford: Polity Press.

Giddens, A. (1994b) 'Living in a post-traditional society'. In U. Beck, A. Giddens and S. Lash (eds) *Reflexive Modernisation. Politics, Tradition and Aesthetics in the Modern Social Order*, Cambridge, Oxford: Polity Press.

Gilbert, B. B. (1970) *British Social Policy 1914-39*, London: Batsford.

Glimstedt, H. (1993) *Mellan Teknik och Samhalle [Between Technology and Society]* Publications from the Historical Institution, Gothenburg: Gothenburg University.

Gofton, L. (1983, November 17) 'Real ale and real men', *New Society*, p. 271-273.

Gofton, L. (1986, December 20/27) 'Drink and the city', *New Society*, p. 502-504.

Gofton, L. (1990) 'On the town: drink and the "new lawlessness"', *Youth and Policy*, (29): 23-39.

Goody, J. (1958) *The Developmental Cycle in Domestic Groups*, Cambridge: Cambridge University Press.

Granovetter, M. (1985) 'Economic action and social structure: the problem of embeddedness', *Americal Journal of Sociology*, 91(3): 481 - 509.

Granovetter, M. (1992) 'Economic institutions as social constructions - a framework for analysis', *Acta Sociologica*, 35(1): 3-11.

Gregson, N. and Lowe, M. (1993) 'Renegotiating the domestic division of labour - a study of dual-career households in north-east and south-east England', *Sociological Review*, 41(3): 475-505.

Griffin, C. (1985) *Typical Girls?*, London: Routledge.

Grønhaug, R. (1974) *Micro-Macro Relations*, Paper series No. 7: Institute of Social Anthropology, University of Bergen.

Grønhaug, R. (1978) 'Scale as a variable in social analysis: fields and social organization in Herat, Northwest Afghanistan'. In F. Barth (eds) *Scale and Social Organization* Oslo: Norwegian University Press.

Gullestad, M. (1984) 'Sosialantropologiske perspektiver på familie og hushold. [Social anthropological perspectives on family and household]'. In I. Rudie (ed) *Myk Start, Hard Landing [Soft Start, Hard Landing]* Oslo: Universitetsforlaget.

Gullestad, M. (1985) *Kitchen Table Society,* Oslo: Universitetsforalget.

Gullestad, M. (1986) 'Equality and marital love.', *Social Analysis,* 19(August): 40-53.

Hall, S. and Jefferson, T. (1976) *Resistance Through Rituals,* London: Hutchinson.

Hallenstvedt, A. (1982) *Med Lov og Organisasjon. Organisering av Interesser og Markeder i Norsk Fiskerinaering [With Law and Organisation: Organising Interests and Markets in Norwegian Fisheries],* Tromsø, Oslo: Norwegian University Press.

Hammer, T. (1994) *Konsekvenser av arbeidsledighet fra ungdom til voksen alder [Consquences of unemployment for youth and adults],* No. 5/94: UNGforsk, Oslo.

Harris, O. (1981) 'Households as natural units'. In K. Young (ed) *Of Marriage and the Market: Women's Subordination in International Perspective* London: CSE Books.

Harrison, A. (1975) *Farmers and Farm Businesses in England,* Miscellaneous Study No. 62: University of Reading, Department of Agricultural Economics.

Harvey, D. (1989) *The Condition of Postmodernity,* Oxford: Basil Blackwell.

Hatland, A. (1984) *The Future of Norwegian Social Insurance,* Oslo: Universitetforlaget.

Hebdige, D. (1979) *Subculture,* London: Methuen.

Henderson, S. (1993) *Young Women, Sexuality and Recreational Drug Use,* Manchester: Lifeline.

Hernes, G. (ed) (1978) *Forhandlingsøkonomi og Blandingsadministrasjon [Negotiation Economy and Mixed Administration],* Oslo: Norwegian University Press.

Hill, M. (1990) *Social Security Policy in Britain,* Cheltenham: Edward Elgar.

Hill, M. (1996) *Social Policy: A Comparative Analysis,* Hemel Hempstead: Harvester Wheatsheaf.

Hills, J. (1993) *The Future of Welfare: A Guide to the Debate,* York: Joseph Rowntree Foundation.

Himmelweit, S. (1994 July 15-17) *The discovery of 'unpaid work': the social consequences of the expansion of 'work',* Paper presented at The Society for the Advancement of Socio-Economics Conference, Paris.

Hinde, K. (1994) 'Labour market experiences following plant closure: the case of Sunderland's shipyard workers', *Regional Studies*, 28(7): 713-24.

HMSO (1993) *Regional Trends*, No. 28: London.

Hobsbawm, E. (1994) *Age of Extremes: The Short Twentieth Century 1914-91*, London: Michael Joseph.

Hodgson, G. M. (1988) *Economics and Institutions: a Manifesto for a Modern Institutional Economics*, Oxford: Blackwell.

Hodgson, G. M. (1994) 'Some remarks on "economic imperialism" and international political economy', *Review of International Political Economy*, 1(Spring): 21-28.

Hollands, R. G. (1990) *The Long Transition: Culture, Class and Youth Training*, London: Macmillan.

Hollands, R. G. (1994) 'Back to the future? preparing young adults for the post-industrial Wearside economy'. In P. Garrahan and P. Stewart (eds) *Urban Change and Renewal: The Paradox of Place*, Aldershot: Avebury.

Hollands, R. G. (1995) *Friday Night, Saturday Night: Youth Cultural Identification in the Post-Industrial City*, Newcastle: Department of Social Policy, Newcastle University.

Holter, Ø. and Aarseth, H. (1993) *Menns Livssammenheng [Masculine Lifeworlds]*, Oslo: Gyldendal, adNotam.

Holton, R. J. and Turner, B. S. (1986) *Talcott Parsons on Economy and Society*, London, New York: Routledge.

Høydahl, E. (1992) *Med Mo i Rana som arena: ungdom i Rana som deltagere i et arbeidsmarked i endring [With Mo i Rana as an Arena: Young People in Rana who Take Part in a Labour Market in Change]*, University of Bergen: Institute of Geography.

Hudson, R. (1991) 'The North in the 1980s; new times or just more of the same?', *Area*, March: 17-26.

Hudson, S. and Jenkins, R. (1989) *Taking the Strain: Families, Unemployment and the Transition to Adulthood*, Milton Keynes: Open University Press.

Jacobsen, K. D. (1965) 'Loyalitet, nøytralitet og faglig uavhengighet i sentraladministrasjonen [Loyalty, neutrality and independence in the central administration]', *Tidsskrift for Samfunnsforsking*, 1: 231-248.

Jahoda, M. (1982) *Employment and Unemployment: A Social-psychological Analysis,* Cambridge: Cambridge University Press.

Kabeer, N. (1993 2 -5 June.) *Beyond the threshold: Why policy makers need to know about intra-household relations,* Paper presented at the International Conference on Feminist Perspectives on Economic Theory, Amsterdam.

Kaiser, A. and Hedin, M. (eds) (1995) *Nordic Energy Systems: Historical Perspectives and Current Issues,* Canton: Watson Publishing International.

Karlsen, A. (1996a) 'Fra hieraki til marked? [From Hierarchy to Market?]'. In Å. Mariussen, A. Karlsen and O. J. Andersen (eds) *Omstilling - fra Løsriving til ny Forankring [Restructuring - from Disembedding to Reembedding],* Oslo: Norwegian University Press.

Karlsen, A. (1996b) 'Mellom Masseprodusjon og Kundetilpasning [Between Mass Production and Customer Adaptation]'. In Å. Mariussen, A. Karlsen and O. J. Andersen (eds) *Omstilling - fra Løsriving til ny Forankring [Restructuring - from Disembedding to Reembedding]* Oslo: Norwegian University Press.

Keat, R. and Abercrombie, N. (eds) (1991) *Enterprise Culture,* London: Routledge.

Keesing, R. M. (1976) *Cultural Anthropology,* New York: Holt, Rinehart, Winston.

Keynes, J. M. (1936) *The General Theory of Employment, Interest and Money,* London: Macmillan.

Landry, C. and Bianchini, F. (1995) *The Creative City,* London: Demos in association with Comedia.

Larsen, S. (1980) 'Omsorgsbønder et tidsnyttingsperspektiv på yrkeskombinasjon, arbeidsdeling og sosial endring [The caretaker farmer: a time use perspective on combination of jobs, division of labour and social change]', *Tidsskrift for Samfunnsforskning,* 21: 283-296.

Lash, S. (1994) 'Reflexivity and its doubles: structure, aesthetics, community'. In U. Beck, A. Giddens and S. Lash (eds) *Reflexive Modernisation: Politics, Tradition and Aesthetics in the Modern Social Order* (pp. 111-173), Cambridge, Oxford: Polity Press.

Lie, M. (1994) 'Fleksibilitet: Et nytt arbeidsliv eller gammelt nytt? [Flexibility: A new working life or old news?]', *Sosiologisk Tidskrift [Journal of Sociology],* 4: 287-302.

Linder, M. (1983) 'Self employment as a cyclical escape from unemployment: a case study of the construction industry in the United States during the post-war period', *Research in the Sociology of Work*, 2: 271-4.

Löfgren, O. (1974) 'Family and household among Scandinavian peasants. An exploratory essay', *Ethnologica Scanidinavica*, (74): 17-52.

Lovatt, A. (1994 July 14) *Out of Order: Hyper-regulation in the City*, Paper presented at City Cultures, Lifestyles and Consumption Practices, University of Coimbra, Coimbra, Portugal.

Lowe, A. (1988) 'Small hotel survival - an inductive approach', *International Journal of Hospitality Management*, 7(3): 197-223.

Lustiger, H. and Salée, D. (eds) (1994) *Artful Practices: the Political Economy of Everyday Life*, Montreal: Black Rose.

Magnussen, T. (1993) *Når Fritida mi Blir Arbeidet Ditt [When my Leisure Time is your Work]*, NF-rapport No. 13/93: Nordlandsforsking, Bodø.

Magnussen, T. (1995) *Fri for Arbeid - om Unge Vaksne i Bygdesamfunn og Deira Handtering av Undersysselsetjing [Free from Work - Young Adults in Rural Communities and Their Management of Underemployment]*, NF-rapport No. 8/95: Nordlandsforsking, Bodø.

Mann, K. (1994) 'Watching the defectives: observers of the underclass in the USA, Britain and Australia', *Critical Social Policy*, 41(2): 79-99.

Manser, M. and Brown, M. (1979) 'Bargaining analyses of household decisions'. In C. Lloyd, E. Andrews and C. Gilroy (eds) *Women in the Labour Market.* New York: Columbia University Press.

Mariussen, Å., Karlsen, A. and Andersen, O. J. (eds) (1996) *Omstilling - fra Løsriving til ny Forankring [Restructuring - from Disembedding to Reembedding]*, Oslo: Norwegian University Press.

Marsden, T. and Munton, R. (1991) 'The farmed landscape and the occupancy change process', *Environment and Planning A*, 23: 663-676.

Marsden, T., Munton, R. and Ward, N. (1992) 'Incorporating social trajectories into uneven agrian development: farm businesses in upland and lowland Britain', *Sociologia Ruralis*, 32: 408-430.

Marsden, T., Munton, R., Whatmore, S. and Little, J. (1989) 'Strategies for coping in capitalist agriculture: an examination of the responses of farm families in British agriculture', *Geoforum*, 20: 1-14.

Martin, R. and Rowthorn, B. (eds) (1986) *The Geography of De-industrialisation*, London: Macmillan.

Mason, C. (1991) 'Spatial variations in enterprise: the geography of new firm formation'. In R. Burrows (ed) *Deciphering the Enterprise Culture* London: Routledge.

Massey, D. (1984) *Spatial Division of Labour*, London: Macmillian.

Mayer, A. J. (1975) 'The lower middle class as historical problem', *Journal of Modern History*, 47: 409-436.

McConville, B. (1983) *Women Under the Influence*, London: Virago Press.

McKee, L. and Bell, C. (1985) 'Marital and family relations in times of male unemployment'. In B. Roberts, R. Finnegan and D. Gallie (eds) *New Approaches to Economic Life: Economic Restructuring, Unemployment and the Social Division of Labour* Manchester: Manchester University Press.

McRobbie (1993) 'Shut up and dance: youth culture and changing modes of femininity', *Cultural Studies*, 7(3): 406-426.

Merchant, J. and MacDonald, R. (1994) 'Youth and the rave culture, ecstasy and health', *Youth and Policy*, (45): 16-38.

Messer, E. (1990) 'Intra-household allocation of resources: perspectives from anthropology'. In B. L. Rogers and Schlossman (eds) *Intra-household Resource Allocation*, Tokyo: United Nations University Press.

Michie, J. (1992) *The Economic Legacy 1979-1992*, London: Academic Press.

Milkman, R. and Townsley, E. (1994) 'Gender and the economy'. In Smelser and Swedberg (eds) *The Handbook of Economic Sociology* New York: Princeton University Press, Russell Sage Foundation.

Mincer, J. (1962) 'Labour force participation of married women'. Reprinted in A. M. Amsden (ed) (1980) *The Economics of Women and Work*, Harmondsworth: Penguin.

Mingione, E. (1985) 'Social reproduction of the surplus labour force'. In N. Redclift and E. Mingione (eds) *Beyond Employment: Gender Household and Subsistence*, Oxford: Basil Blackwell.

Mingione, E. (1991) *Fragmented Societies: A Sociology of Economic Life Beyond the Market Paradigm*, Oxford: Basil Blackwell.

Mommsen, W. J. (1989) *The Political and Social Theory of Max Weber*, Cambridge, Oxford: Polity Press.

Morris, L. (1985) 'Renegotiation of the domestic division of labour in the context of redundancy'. In B. Roberts, R. Finnegan and D. Gallie (eds) *New Approaches to Economic Life: Economic Restructuring, Unemployment and the Social Division of Labour*, Manchester: Manchester University Press.

Morris, L. (1990) *The Workings of the Household*, Cambridge, Oxford: Polity Press.

Muellbauer, J. and Murphy, A. (1991) 'Regional economic disparities: the role of housing'. In A. Bowen and K. Mayhew (eds) *Reducing Regional Inequalities* London: Kogan Page/NEDO.

Murray, C. (1984) *Losing Ground*, New York: Basic Books.

Murray, C. (1990) *The Emerging British Underclass*, London: IEA.

National Westminster Bank (1992) *NatWest National Farm Survey: Summary Report and Tables*, Coventry: National Westminster Bank Agricultural Office.

Naustdalslid, J. (1991) 'Bygdesamfunnet i norsk politikk: Fra makt til avmakt [The local community in Norwegian politics. From power to powerlessness]'. In *Åtte Perspektiver på Bygdeutvikling [Eight perspectives on Rural Development]* NVLF-publikasjon 3/91.

Nenadic, S. (1990) 'The life cycle of firms in late nineteenth century Britain'. In P. Jobert and M. Moss (eds) *The Birth and Death of Companies: a Historical Perspective*, Parthenon.

Netting, R. M. (1984) 'Introduction'. In R. M. Netting, R. R. Wilk and E. J. Arnould (eds) *Households. Comparative and Historical Studies of the Domestic Group* Berkeley, Los Angeles, London: University of California Press.

Netting, R. M., Wilk, R. R. and Arnould, E. J. (eds) (1984) *Households. Comparative and Historical Studies of the Domestic Group*, Berkeley, Los Angeles, London: University of California Press.

Newcombe, R. (1991) *Raving and Dance Drugs*, Liverpool: Rave Research Bureau.

NIERC (1992) *LEDU Monitoring and Evaluation Report*, Belfast: Northern Ireland Economic Research Centre.

Northern Region Strategy Team (1977) *Strategic Plan for The Northern Region, Vol 2, Economic Development Policies*, London: HMSO.

O'Connor, J. and Wynne, D. (nd) *From the Margins to the Centre: Cultural Production and Consumption in the Post-industrial City,* Working Papers in Popular Cultural Studies No. 7: Manchester Institute for Popular Culture.

O'Hara, P. A. (1995) 'Household labour, the family and macroeconomic stability in the US 1940s-1990s', *Review of Social Economy,* VIII(1): 89-120.

OECD (1991) *Agricultural Policies, Markets and Trade: Monitoring and Outlook,* Paris: OECD.

OECD (1994) *New Orientations for Social Policy,* Paris: OECD.

Ortner, S. B. and Whitehead, H. (1981) 'Introduction'. In *Sexual Meanings. The Cultural Construction of Gender and Sexuality* Cambridge: Cambridge University Press.

Pahl, J. (1989) *Money and Marriage,* London: Macmillan.

Pahl, R. E. (1984) *Divisions of Labour,* Oxford: Basil Blackwell.

Pahl, R. E. and Wallace, C. (1985) 'Household work strategies in economic recession'. In N. Redclift and E. Mingione (eds) *Beyond Employment: Gender, Household and Subsistence* Oxford: Basil Blackwell.

Parker, H. (1989) *Instead of the Dole,* London: Routledge.

Parker, H. (1993) 'Citizen's income'. In J. Berghman and B. Cantillon (eds) *The European Face of Social Security* Aldershot: Avebury.

Parsons, T. (1947) 'Introduction'. In M. Weber *The Theory of Social and Economic Organisation,* New York, London: Free Press, Macmillian.

Parsons, T. and Smelser, N. J. (1956) *Economy and Society: A Study in the Integration of Economic and Social Theory,* Glencoe, Il.: The Free Press.

Peck, F. (1990) 'Nissan in the North East: the multiplier effects', *Geography,* 75(4): 354-57.

Peck, F. and Stone, I. (1992) *New Inward Investment and the Northern Region Labour Market,* Sheffield: Research Series No. 6, Employment Department.

Peck, F. and Stone, I. (1993) 'Japanese inward investment in the North East of England: reassessing "Japanisation"', *Environment and Planning C Government and Policy,* Vol. 11: 55-67.

Piore, M. and Sabel, C. (1984) *The Second Industrial Divide*, Oxford: Basil Blackwell.

Pleck, J. H. (1979) *Men's family work: three perspectives and some new data*, The Family Co-ordinator, Oct. 481-488.

Polanyi, K. (1946) *Origins of our Time: the Great Transformation*, London: Victor Gollancz.

Pollak, R. (1985) 'A transaction cost approach to families and households', *Journal of Economic Literature*, XXIII(June): 581-608.

Pollert, A. (1988) 'Dismantling flexibility', *Capital and Class,* 34: 42-75.

Porter, M. E. (1992) *The Competitive Advantage of Nations*, London, Basingstoke: Macmillan.

Potter, C. and Lobley, M. (1992) 'Elderly farmers as countryside managers'. In A. Gilg (ed) *Restructuring the Countryside: Environmental Policy in Practice*, Aldershot: Avebury.

Rainbird, H. (1991) 'The self-employed: small entrepreneurs or disguised wage labourers?'. In A. Pollert (ed) *Farewell to Flexibility*, Oxford: Basil Blackwell.

Rainnie, A. and Kraithmann, D. (1992) 'Labour market change and organisation of work'. In N. Gilbert, R. Burrows and A. Pollert (eds) *Fordism and Flexibility, Divisions and Change*, New York: St. Martin's Press.

Redclift, N. and Mingione, E. (eds) (1985) *Beyond Employment: Gender Household and Subsistence*, Oxford: Basil Blackwell.

Redclift, N. and Whatmore, S. (1990) 'Households, consumption and livelihood: ideologies and issues in rural research'. In T. Marsden, P. Lowe and S. Whatmore (eds) *Rural Restructuring: Global Processes and Their Responses,* London: David Fulton Publishers.

Redhead, S. (ed) (1993) *Rave Off: Politics and Deviance in Contemporary Youth Culture*, Aldershot: Avebury.

Regional Utveckling i Norden (1993) Copenhagen: Nordic Council of Ministers.

Richardson, R. and Gentle, C. (1993) 'Tradeable services and the Northern economy', *Business Review North,* 5(2): 16-23.

Roberts, B., Finnegan, R. and Gallie, D. (eds) (1985) *New Approaches to Economic Life*, Manchester: Manchester University Press.

Roberts, I. and Holroyd, G. (1992) 'Small firms and family forms'. In N. Gilbert, R. Burrows and A. Pollert (eds) *Fordism and Flexibility: Divisions and Change*, London: Macmillan.

Roberts, P. (1991) 'Anthropological perspectives on the household', *IDS Bulletin*, 22(1): 60-64.

Robinson, F. (ed) (1988) *Post-Industrial Tyneside*, Newcastle: Newcastle City Libraries.

Robinson, F. (1994) 'Something old, something new? The great north in the 1990s'. In P. Garrahan and P. Stewart (eds) *Urban Change and Renewal: The Paradox of Place* Aldershot: Avebury.

Robinson, F. and Shaw, K. (1991) 'In search of the Great North', *Town and Country Planning*, October: 279-83.

Rogers, B. L. and Schlossman, N. P. (1990) *Intra-household Resource Allocation*, Tokyo: United Nations University Press.

Rowthorn, B. (1986) 'De-industrialisation in Britain'. In R. Martin and B. Rowthorn (eds)

Rudie, I. (1969/70) *Household Organization: Adaptive Process and Restrictive Form. A Viewpoint on Economic Change*, Folk.

Sabel, C. and Zeitlin, J. (eds) (n.d.) *Worlds of Possibility: Flexibility and Mass Production in Western Industrialization*, Unpublished manuscript.

Sainsbury, D. (1993) 'Dual welfare and sex segregation of access to social benefits: income maintenance policies in the UK, the US, the Netherlands and Sweden', *Journal of Social Policy*, 22(1): 69-98.

Sainsbury, D. (ed) (1994) *Gendering Welfare States*, London: Sage.

Sande, A. (1991) *Hjemmeliv under omsmelting [Domestic Life during Restructuring: A Study of Families, Household Work and Gender Roles During at Process of Industrial Restructuring]*, NF-Report No. 13/91 - 50: Nordland Research Institute, Bodø.

Sande, A. (1994) *The Family and the Social Division of Labour during Industrial Restructuring*, NF-Report No. 23/94: Nordland Research Institute, Bodø.

Sande, A. (1995a) 'Førr kunn eg aldri tenk meg å heng klea ut og det gjaer eg nå' [Before I didn't even think of washing the clothes, now I just get on with it]. Ottar. *Populeorvitenskaplig tidsskrift.* Nr. 205: 54-60.

Sande, A. (1995b) *The Liminal Phase in 'Rite of Passage' to Adulthood*, NF report no. 12/95. Nordland Research Istitute, Bødo.

Saugestad, S. (1984) 'Om likestilling i ekteskapet - ganle roller under endrede omstendheter' [About the equal sharing of household work in marriage - old roles under new conditions]. In I. Rudie (ed) *Soft Start - Hard Landing: Women's Living Conditions and Life Carriers* Universitetsforlaget.

Savage, M. and Warde, A. (1993) *Urban Sociology, Capitalism and Modernity*, London: Macmillan.

Scott, A. (1988) 'Flexible production systems and regional development: the rise of new industrial spaces in North America and Western Europe', *International Journal of Urban and Regional Research*, 12(2): 171-86.

Scott, J. C. (1976) *The Moral Economy of the Peasant*, Newhaven: Yale University Press.

Seierstad, S. (1985) *Kystsamfunn på Kå [Coastal Society on Social Security]*, Oslo: Norwegian University Press.

Seierstad, S. (1992) 'En teori om det rasjonerte arbeidsmarkedet og omstilling i distriktene [A theory about the rationed labour market and transformation in the rural areas]', *Tidsskrift for Samfunnsforsking*, 2: 253-270.

Seiz, J. A. (1991) 'The barginning approach and feminist methodology', *Review of Radical Political Economy*, 23(1 and 2): 22-29.

Sen, A. K. (1985) *Commodities and Capabilities, Lectures in Economics Vol 7*, Amsterdam, Oxford, New York: North Holland.

Sen, A. K. (1990) 'Gender and cooperative conflicts'. In I. Tinker (ed) *Persistent Inequalities: Women and World Development* Oxford: Oxford University Press.

Sengenberger, W. and Campbell, D. (eds) (1994) *Creating Economic Opportunities: The Role of Labour Standards in Industrial Restructuring*, Geneva: ILO.

Shanin, T. (1990) *Defining Peasants*, Oxford, Cambridge: Basil Blackwell.

Shields, R. (1991) *Places on the Margin: Alternative Geographies of Modernity*, London: Routledge.

Silverstone, R. and Hirsch, E. (1992) *Consuming Technologies: Media Information in Domestic Spaces,* London: Routledge.

Sinfield, A. (1978) 'Analysis in the social division of welfare', *Journal of Social Policy,* 7(2): 129-156.

Smelser, N. J. (1995 April 20-22) *Economics and sociology: limitations of each and promises of mutual aid,* Sociology and the Limits of Economics, Conference, University of Liverpool.

Smelser, N. J. and Swedberg, R. (eds) (1994) *The Handbook of Economic Sociology,* New York: Princeton University Press / Russell Sage Foundation.

Smith, J. and Wallerstein, E. (1992) *Creating and Transforming Households,* Paris: Cambridge University Press.

Smith, S. (1986) *Britain's Shadow Economy,* Oxford: Oxford University Press.

Solheim, J. H. and Holter, G. Ø. (1986) *Nordsjøliv og hjemmeliv [Offshore Working Life and Domestic Life],* No. 35/86, Oslo: Work Research Institute.

Stanfield, J. R. (1982) 'Towards a new value standard in economics', *Economic Forum,* 13(Fall): 67-85.

Stanfield, J. R. (1986) *The Economic Thought of Karl Polanyi: Lives and Livelihoods,* New York: St Martin's Press.

Stone, I. (1994a) 'The UK Economy'. In F. Somers (ed) *European Economies: A Comparative Study,* London: Pitman.

Stone, I. (1994b) 'Wearside in the "new" North East: longer-term perspectives on industrial restructuring'. In P. Garrahan and P. Stewart (eds) *Urban Change and Renewal: The Paradox of Place,* Aldershot: Avebury Press.

Stone, I. (1995) 'Symbolism and substance in the modernisation of a traditional industrial economy: the case of Wearside'. In R. Turner (ed) *The British Economy in Transition: From the Old to the New* London: Routledge.

Stone, I. and Peck, F. (1996) 'The foriegn-owned manufacturing sector in the UK peripheral regions: structure and performance', *Regional Studies,* 30(1): 55-68.

Stone, I. and Stevens, J. (1986) 'Employment on Wearside: trends and prospects', *Northern Economic Review,* (12): 39-56.

Storey, D. and Johnson, S. (1987) *Job Generation and Labour Market Change,* London: Macmillan.

Storper, M. and Scott, A. (1988) 'The geographical foundations and social regulation of flexible production systems'. In J. Welch and M. Dear (eds) *Territory and Social Reproduction* London: Allen & Unwin.

Stubbs, C. and Wheelock, J. (1990) *A Woman's Work in the Changing Local Economy,* Aldershot: Avebury.

Symes, D. (1990) 'Bridging the generations: succession and inheritance in a changing world', *Sociologia Ruralis,* 30: 280-291.

Thompson, E. P. (1971) 'The moral economy of the English crowd in the eighteenth century', *Past and Present,* 50(February): 76-136.

Thomsen, S. and Woolcock, S. (1993) *Direct Investment and European Integration; Competition Among Firms and Governments,* London: Pinter.

Thorsen, L. E. (1986) 'Work and gender. The sexual division of labour and farmers' attitudes to labour in central Norway, 1920-80', *Ethnologia Europaea,* XVI: 137-148.

Thornton, S. (1995) *Club Cultures,* Cambridge, Oxford: Polity Press.

Thue, L. (1995) 'Electricity rules: the formation and development of the Nordic electricity regimes'. In A. Kaijser and M. Hedin (eds) *Nordic Energy Systems Historical Perspectives and Current Issues,* Canton: Watson Publishing International.

Titmuss, R. M. (1968) *Commitment to Welfare,* London: Allen and Unwin.

Townsend, A. (1985/86) 'Part-time employment in the North', *Northern Economic Review,* 12: 2-15.

Townsend, A. R. and Champion, A. G. (1990) *Contemporary Britain: A Geographical Perspective,* London: Edward Arnold.

Tyne and Wear Research and Intelligence Unit (1994) *1991 Census Topic Report: Economic Activity and Employment,* Newcastle upon Tyne: TWRIU.

Tyneside Training and Enterprise Council (1993) *Training People ... Developing Business: Labour Market Report 1992-3,* Newcastle upon Tyne: TTEC.

Veblen, T. (1912) *The Theory of the Leisure Class,* London: Macmillan.

Wadel, C. (1979) 'The hidden work of everyday life'. In S. Wallman (ed) *The Social*

Anthropology of Work, A.S.A. Monograph 19, London: Academic Press.

Wadel, C. (1983) 'Dagligivet som forskingsfelt [Everyday life as a field of research]'. In C. Wadel, C. Strømsheim, G. Leira, A. Kalleberg and S. Daatland (eds) *Dagliglivets Organisering [The Organisation of Daily Life]*, Oslo, Bergen, Stavanger, Tromsø: Norwegian University Press.

Walker, R. and Parker, G. (eds) (1988) *Money Matters: Income Wealth and Financial Welfare*, London: Sage.

Wallace, C. (1987) *For Richer, For Poorer: Growing Up In and Out of Work*, London: Tavistock.

Waller, W. and Jennings, A. (1991) 'A feminist institutionalist reconsideration of Karl Polanyi', *Journal of Economic Issues,* vol. 25(no. 2): 485-497.

Wallerstein, I. and Smith, J. (1990) 'Households as an institution of the world-economy'. In J. Smith and I. Wallerstein (eds)

Wallman, S. (1979) 'Introduction'. In S. Wallman (ed) *The Social Anthropology of Work* A.S.A Monograph 19, London: Academic Press.

Wallman, S. (1984) *Eight London Households*, London and New York: Tavistock.

Wallman, S. (1986) 'The boundaries of the household'. In A. Cohen (ed) *Symbolising Boundaries* Manchester: Manchester University Press.

Ward, N. and Lowe, P. (1994) 'Shifting values in agriculture: the farm family and pollution regulation', *Journal of Rural Studies,* 10: 173-84.

Ward, N., Lowe, P., Seymour, S. and Clark, J. (1995) 'Rural restructuring and the regulation of farm pollution', *Environment and Planning A,* 27: 1193-1211.

Warde, A. (1990) 'Household work strategies and forms of labour: conceptual and empirical issues', *Work, Employment and Society,* 4(4): 495-515.

Waring, M. (1989) *If Women Counted: a new Feminist Economics*, London: Macmillan.

Weber, M. (1930) *The Protestant Ethic and the Spirit of Capitalism*, London: Unwin University Books.

Weber, M. (1947) *The Theory of Social and Economic Organization*, New York: Free Press.

Whatmore, S. (1991) *Farming Women: Gender, Work and Family Enterprise*, Basingstoke: Macmillan.

Whatmore, S., Lowe, P. and Marsden, T. (1991a) 'Artisan or entrepreneur? Refashioning rural production'. In S. Whatmore, P. Lowe and T. Marsden (eds) *Rural Enterprise, Shifting Perspectives on Small-Scale Production,* London: David Fulton Publishers.

Whatmore, S., Lowe, P. and Marsden, T. (eds) (1991b) *Rural Enterprise, Shifting Perspectives on Small-Scale Production*, London: David Fulton Publishers.

Wheelock, J. (1990) *Husbands at Home: the Domestic Economy in a Post-industrial Society,* London: Routledge.

Wheelock, J. (1992a) 'The flexibility of small business family work strategies'. In K. Caley, F. Chittenden, E. Chell and C. Mason (eds) *Small Enterprise Development: Policy and Practice in Action*, London: Paul Chapman Publishing.

Wheelock, J. (1992b) 'The household in the total economy'. In P. Ekins and M. Max-Neef (eds) *Real-life Economics: Understanding Wealth Creation*, London: Routledge.

Wheelock, J. (1994) 'Survival strategies for small business families in a peripheral local economy: a contribution to institutional value theory'. In H. Lustiger and D. Salée (eds) *Artful Practices: the Political Economy of Everyday Life,* Montreal: Black Rose.

Wheelock, J. (1996) 'People and households as economic agents'. In M. Macintosh (ed) *Economics and Changing Economies*, London: International Thomson Business Press.

Wheelock, J. and Oughton, E. (1996) 'The household as a focus for research', *Journal of Economic Issues,* XXX(1): 143-159.

Whittle, S. (ed) (1994) *The Margins of the City: Gay Men's Urban Lives*, Aldershot: Arena.

Wiborg, A. (1993) *Mozart, Beatles og Myllarguten. Amatørmusikklivet i Møte Med Kultursektoren [Mozart, Beatles and Myllarguten. Amateur Music Life Meets the Cultural Sector]*, NF-rapport No. 12/93: Nordlandsforsking, Bodø.

Wiborg, A. (1995) *Mellom Økonomisk Fornuft, Livsstil og Symboler [Between Economic Reason, Life Style and Symbols]*, NF-rapport No. 4/95: Nordlandsforsking, Bodø.

Wilk, R. R. (1989) 'Decision making and resource flows within the household: Beyond the black box'. In R. R. Wilk (ed) *The Household Economy: Reconsidering the Domestic Mode of Production*, Boulder: Westview.

Wilkinson, H. (1994) *No Turning Back: Generations and the Genderquake*, London: Demos.

Williamson, O. E. (1975) *Markets and Hierarchies*, New York: Free Press.

Williamson, O. E. (1987) 'The economics of organisation: the transaction cost approach', *American Journal of Sociology*, 87(3): 548-77.

Willis, P. (1977) *Learning to Labour: How Working Class Kids Get Working Class Jobs*, Westmead: Saxon House.

Wilson, E. (1991) *The Sphinx in the City*, London: Virago Press.

Wolf, D. L. (1991) 'Does father know best? A feminist critique of household strategy research', *Research in Rural Sociology and Development*, 5: 29-43.

Worpole, K. (1992) *Towns for People: Transforming Urban Life*, Buckinghamshire: Open University Press.

Yanganisako (1979) 'Family and household: the analysis of domestic groups', *Annuale Review of Anthropology*, 8: 161-205.

Yeandle, S. (1984) *Women's Working Lives*, London: Tavistock.

Young, C. and Hollands, R. (1994) 'How far has the northern region adopted a harm reduction approach to dealing with drug misuse?', *Youth and Policy*, (45): 53-58.

Young, D. I. (1991) *Enterprise Years: A Business Man in the Cabinet*, London: Headlines.

Zeitlin, J. (1994 July 15-17) *Why are there no industrial districts in UK?*, Paper presented at Sixth Annual International Conference on Socio-Economics, Paris.

INDEX

A
accumulation, capital 18, 19, 23, 26, 29, 50 ,86, 163
adaptation 20, 41, 49, 103, 118, 125, 128-9, 130, 141, 196, 199
adulthood 124, 182, 187, 199
agicultural policy 87, 133, 134, 139, 141, 147, 148, 195, 203
altruism 45
anthropology 16, 21-22, 40, 41, 164
Australia 59, 64
Austria 53

B
bargaining 45-6
barter 108
Belgium 57
Beveridge 53
breadwinner 21, 30, 62, 104, 106, 107, 114, 118, 121, 128, 178, 198
budgeting 44, 47, 117, 138, 187
bureaucracy 18,19

C
capital, human *see* human capital
career   121, 127, 131, 170, 177, 192
children 38, 42, 62, 108, 143, 149, 151, 179
child care 29, 32, 40, 113, 141, 179, 187, 205
class *see* working-class
coalmining *see* mining
commodification/commoditisation 26, 38, 46
commodity production 38, 148
Common Agricultural Policy (CAP) 26, 134
community xi, 77, 91, 92, 107, 108, 111, 122, 154, 169, 181, 184, 192, 194
competition/competitiveness ix, 66, 71, 78, 89, 94, 123, 153, 164, 165
complementary/informal economy xiii, 17, 27, 30, 46, 49, 59, 123, 126, 158-9, 164
consumption *see* household consumption
       conspicuous 31
cooperation 40, 93-4, 164, 165
cooperatives 86, 87
corporatism x, 65, 75, 85-102, 195, 203
contracts *see* labour contracts
craft 19, 25, 130, 187, 189

culture
    enterprise 153, 164
    urban 175-84
    youth - *see* youth culture
cultural change 34, 151, 202

D
daily life/lives *see* everday life
deindustrialisation 71, 73, 75-79, 99, 158, 163, 199
democracy *see* social democracy
Denmark 86
dependency 54, 56, 90, 119, 167
depression (for economic depression see recession) 105, 125
deregulation x, 4, 27, 84, 85, 96, 196, 204
deskilling 123
dignity 104, 118-20, 124, 198
discouraged workers 82
disembedded *see* embedded
disjunction *see* institutional disjunction
discourse 34
discrimination 30, 32, 62, 181
diversification 66, 73, 154
division of labour 49, 104, 107-112, 118, 126, 128, 131, 136, 137, 139, 144, 148, 168
divorce   42, 62, 117, 128, 204
domestic labour debate 32
double burden   120, 205
dugnad 92

E
economic activity rates *see* labour market participation
education 81, 107, 110, 122, 127, 167, 177, 191
efficiency 57-58, 92, 95
embedding/disembedding/reembedding 1, 4-8, 44, 52, 66, 77, 87, 140, 141, 143, 193, 197
emotions 21
employment *see* full employment
    part-time 54, 57, 61, 71, 78, 80, 96, 104, 174
    female 74, 78, 80, 95, 96
enabling 9, 111, 196
enterprise culture *see* culture
entrepreneur/ial 57, 129, 154, 158, 162, 163, 200
equality/equity/egalitarianism 56, 108, 143, 144
Erweben 18-20, 23, 30, 34, 163
European Union/Commission ix, 73, 76, 84, 91, 134
everyday life 47, 108

exclusion, social *see* social exclusion
exploitation 32, 165

F
family
    business/firms 18-19, 23, 133, 200
    economic unit 153, 164
    farms 26, 135, 147-156
    nuclear 41-42, 123
    succession 148-56
farming 88, 91, 105, 108, 133-4, 188, 200
feminism 2, 32
Finland x, 56
fishing 85, 86, 91, 95, 105, 108, 133, 139, 188
fission 94, 96, 100, 102, 122
flexibilty
    functional 122,159
    numerical 122, 159, 169
flexible
    firms 122-3
    household 87, 121, 127, 129, 136, 141, 158, 195-204
    labour market xi, 35, 66, 72, 75, 97, 103, 122-8, 202
    specialisation 24-5, 122
flourishing x, 44-6, 52, 104, 106, 204, 206
Fordism 24, 89, 105, 121, 131, 198
fragmentation 135, 170, 181
France 56, 59
full employment 54, 205-6

G
games 2-4, 171, 202, 203
GATT (General Agreement on Trade and Tarriffs) 26
gender
    coding 48, 135, 140, 143, 145, 200
    definitions 21, 41
    divisions 30, 48, 198
    identity 48, 104-5, 110-12, 119, 128, 137, 145, 167, 177, 188, 197, 202-3
    roles 6, 35, 106, 108, 111-2, 113-9, 135, 167, 183
geography 17,33
Germany 53, 55, 56, 59
gifts 45
global
    culture 34, 168, 184
    economy/market x, 90, 123, 203
globalisation/global restructuring 34, 65, 71, 167, 173

grandparents 47, 108, 141, 198

H
habits/habitus 2-4, 37, 129, 196, 197, 198, 202, 203
Haushalten 17-20, 23, 26, 30, 34, 163
hierarchy 22, 24, 94, 129
hobbies 117
household
    boundaries 42-3, 51, 52, 105, 167, 170
    consumption 31, 49
    farming 148-56
    flexibility *see* flexibility, household
    rural 139-45, 188-94
    teams 1, 21, 47, 104, 138-9, 144, 145
    work strategies/coping strategies/livelihood strategies 7, 50, 63, 103, 119, 134, 136, 158, 189
housing 57, 59, 63, 80, 109, 127, 128, 168, 177, 180, 187
human capital 27, 32, 38

I
identity *see* gender identity, youth identity
ideology 53, 119, 143, 144
IMF (International Monetary Fund) 66
incentives 56, 84, 104, 141, 154, 162
income
    basic / citizens 63, 206
    maintenance 55-57
    replacement ratio 53
individualism 104, 164, 187, 191
industrial districts 25, 77, 163
industrial /labour relations 71, 72, 73
inflation 72
informal economy *see* complementary economy
innovation 24, 25, 87, 164
insecurity 60, 63, 121, 122, 125, 164, 196, 199
institutional
    ambiguity 19
    differentiation 16-21, 201
    disjunction/stress 9, 21, 171, 197
    transformation xiii, 4, 29, 46, 196-7
integration *see* social integration
interdisciplinary xiii
investment, inward/foreign 66, 71, 73, 75, 76-7, 83, 95, 202
Italy 25, 56

K

Keynesian policy x, 66, 89-90, 205-6
kinship 6, 21, 41, 42, 124, 147

L

labour market flexibility *see* flexibility
labour market participation/activity rates 53, 59, 61, 62, 71, 81, 96
labour contract 96, 103, 105, 122, 129, 131, 171, 198
leisure 110, 112, 170, 179, 181, 183, 190, 192, 194
life cycle 31, 112, 148
lifestyle 48, 123, 134, 136, 151, 158, 167, 173-4
livelihood 31, 44
local authority *see* municipality
love 21, 40, 45, 112
low wages/pay 31, 60, 62, 83, 104, 184, 190, 199

M

macro-level 2, 4, 13, 14, 23, 24, 163, 197
market-led policy xi, 65, 74, 85, 90, 99-101, 195
masculinisation 140
mass consumption 26
mass production 24
meanings xii, 32, 38, 46-49, 136, 183
means test 53-63, 106, 134, 198, 204, 205
men's work 95, 103-4, 110, 138, 144
Methodenstreit 16, 17, 31
micro-level 2, 4, 5, 13, 14, 23, 24, 31, 163, 197
mining xi, 65, 78, 79, 95, 169, 174, 202
model 5, 43, 54, 118, 122, 158-9, 196, 197
modernisation/modernity 1, 19-20, 24, 50, 72, 73, 86, 87, 123, 154, 167, 173-4, 187, 191-3, 197, 201-2
moral economy/community 14, 27, 32-3, 46, 50, 104-5, 111, 170, 192
municipality 66, 74, 88, 89, 145

N

nationalisation 76, 89, 137, 145
needs 17, 18, 38, 50, 201
neighbouring/neighbours 29, 151
neo-classical economics 14, 17, 20
Netherlands 59, 64
networks 25, 27, 40, 51, 77, 105, 120, 130, 154, 159, 163
New Household Economics 5, 6, 16, 20, 22, 31, 33, 43, 45, 164
New Right 133, 153, 154, 162, 164, 196, 197, 204
norms 23, 24, 191, 196
nuclear family *see* family, nuclear

nurturing 40, 43, 198

O
omstilling i trygget (restructuring in safety) x, 90, 95, 96
opportunism 22-23
order *see* problem of
orthodoxy 3, 17, 203
overtime 57, 126

P
patriarchy 62, 116, 118, 170, 174
peasant 19, 25, 85, 86, 121
pensions 55, 56, 60, 61, 83
peripheral regions x, 66, 71, 83, 89, 113, 153, 163
political science/politics xii, 16, 20
post-Fordism 14, 24, 27
post-industrial 174, 177, 181-4
post-modern xi, 32, 154, 184
poverty trap 54, 57, 60, 64, 118
power 5, 41, 104, 179
privatisation 46, 72, 90, 92, 100, 120
problem of order 8, 201
psychology 6
public sector services 89, 95, 122, 145

Q
qualifications 105, 125, 130, 131, 192-3, 194

R
race 32, 184
rationality 18-20, 50, 118, 119, 164, 195
recession 54, 71, 135, 164, 168
reciprocity 5, 22-23, 43, 153, 164, 165
redundancy 103, 108, 117, 121, 162, 197
reflexivity 8, 32, 105, 122-3, 130-1, 196, 199, 201, 203, 204
regional policy 72, 74, 75
regulation 24, 87, 153, 156, 196, 203
reproduction *see* social reproduction
retirement 60, 61, 82, 83, 93, 104, 107, 108, 114, 204
rewards 45, 58, 117, 162, 163
risk 7, 22, 55, 56, 123, 129, 152, 154, 169, 174
ritual/rites 170, 181-3, 187
routines 3, 129, 130
rural households *see households*
    sociology xii, 26, 33

S

savings 54, 58, 128
Scandinavia 53, 59, 85, 88, 195, 203
self-employment 59, 80, 81, 130, 133, 157, 162, 164, 177
self-help 58, 59, 133, 164
self-respect 118
seniority, principle of 93-4, 102, 122, 124
service economy 26-27, 46
service sector 78-9, 84, 89, 95, 99, 104, 111
shipbuilding xi, 65, 72, 73, 76-7, 100, 169, 173, 202
Singapore 55
skill 74, 81, 100, 112, 126, 140
small business/firm 72, 74, 76, 94, 164, 200, 202, 205
social
    cohesion/integration ix, 3, 8, 201
    democracy x, 38, 85, 88, 93
    exclusion 72, 101, 111-2, 205
    policy xiv, 53-63
    reproduction 31, 38
    security 53-63, 123, 128
    stratification/divisions 53, 59, 62
socialisation 42, 196, 202
solidarity 5, 53, 54, 56, 93, 170, 183
standard of living 51, 141
state *see* welfare state
    benefits 53-63, 79, 94, 103, 105, 106, 113, 163, 170
    intervention 66, 72, 74, 168
status 38, 45, 50, 110, 149, 187
steel industry 65, 85, 91-97, 104, 121
subsidies 90, 92, 134
substantive institutional analysis 5, 7
succession *see* family
supply-side 71, 72, 114
Sweden x, 56, 61, 86
Switzerland 55
symbolic 46, 48, 133, 136, 137, 140, 183, 187, 189

T

tax/taxation 55, 63, 84, 101, 141, 204
teams *see* household teams
time 16, 18, 50, 51, 114, 125, 138
trade union 40, 66, 75, 77, 88, 92, 93, 122, 126, 203
training 125, 126, 128, 167, 177, 187, 188, 189
transaction costs 22, 130
transition *see* youth transition

U

uncertainty 103, 123, 125, 130
underclass 60
undeserving poor 58
unemployment
    trap 106, 118
    youth 82, 175, 190, 193, 199
United States/USA 5, 59, 84, 90
unpaid work 31, 159, 198
utility maximisation 14, 43, 51

V

voluntary work 29, 159, 193

W

wages *see* low wages
    minimum 61
welfare state x, 14, 19, 24, 30, 53-63, 111, 121, 129, 133, 141, 145, 188, 196
well-being 45
women's work 95, 103-4, 110, 138, 144, 175
work
    work hours 79, 89, 116, 162, 200, 205
    organisation 1, 34, 115
    strategies, see household work strategies
    unpaid *see* unpaid work
working-class 58, 62, 113, 202

Y

youth
    culture xi, 168, 169, 173-84
    identity xiv, 169, 171, 173-84
    transition 135, 173-84, 187-94, 199, 204